HOME HACKS

HOME HACKS

CLEANING   STORAGE & ORGANIZING   DECORATING
GARDENING   ENTERTAINING   CLOTHING CARE   FOOD & COOKING
HEALTH & SAFETY   APPLIANCES & GADGETS   EASY REPAIRS

Reader's
Digest
New York | Montreal

Contents

We are committed to both the quality of our products and the service we provide to our customers. We value your comments, so please feel free to contact us.

Trusted Media Brands, Inc.
Adult Trade Publishing
44 South Broadway
White Plains, NY 10601

For more Reader's Digest products and information, visit our website:
www.rd.com (in the United States)
www.readersdigest.ca (in Canada)

Printed in China.

1 3 5 7 9 10 8 6 4 2

WARNING
All do-it-yourself activities involve a degree of risk. Skills, materials, tools, and site conditions vary widely. Although the editors have made every effort to ensure accuracy, the reader remains responsible for the selection and use of tools, materials, and methods. Always obey local codes and laws, follow manufacturer's operating instructions, and observe safety precautions.

Introduction

Have you been looking for a comprehensive collection of ideas, inspiration and wisdom covering every corner of your house and home? Well, look no further! *Home Hacks* delivers a wealth of expert information on how to maintain your home and your belongings. Decorate your home so it is both safe and beautiful, buy and handle your appliances like a pro, and do minor repair jobs with confidence. You'll get your household chores done more easily, quickly and economically with the latest hacks from our experts, plus the wisdom of our grandmothers. And no matter how experienced you are at running your home, you'll find some insiders' hacks that will make you say, "Of course! Why didn't I think of that before?" You're bound to discover some exciting surprises.

Cleanliness Counts

The best way to clean

When it comes to cleaning our homes, most of us are self-taught. But there are people who specialize in this work; you can adopt their professional hacks to make cleaning tasks quicker and easier.

Which EQUIPMENT you need

Our homes never cease to get dirty, so we'll always need to clean. The right equipment can make the job much easier. You don't need a lot of stuff, just a few good-quality items and the right cleaning products for the job.

YOU DON'T NEED A LOT OF STUFF, JUST A FEW GOOD-QUALITY ITEMS.

✳ Plenty of soft cleaning cloths, preferably cotton, which you can also use for dusting. Choose cloths that can be machine-washed and reused.

✳ A supply of old towels you no longer use. Put towels down for jobs where dirty water may fall on the floor, such as cleaning doors. Towels are better for this job than newspaper.

✳ A bucket of warm water with a splash of dishwashing liquid or another all-purpose cleaning product is good for most jobs.

✳ A window-cleaning tool with a squeegee blade – also useful for mirrors and other glass surfaces.

✳ If you have pets that shed hair on your upholstered furniture, you will definitely need a lint roller (preferably the adhesive kind) and a brush attachment for your vacuum cleaner.

✳ A mop for wet or dry use on floors. Opt for a design that comes with a matching bucket to rinse and wring out the mop. Also check if the mophead can be removed, machine-washed, and replaced as needed. The handle should be comfortable to hold and adjustable to suit your height.

✳ An alternative for cleaning floors is a long-handled scrubbing brush with a cloth that wraps around the head. As with a mop, look for one that has an adjustable handle and replacement cloths that are readily available.

✳ A broom and a dustpan and brush for sweeping jobs. Choose a broom that is not too heavy. When choosing a dustpan, have a close look at its leading edge to be sure it will scoop up dust easily.

✳ There are two basic kinds of vacuum cleaners: those with bags and those without. Bagless cleaners generally cost more and are noisier, but they work out to be better value in the long run. Cleaners with bags lose suction as they fill up, and the cost of replacement bags does add up over time. In addition to your main vacuum cleaner, it's useful to have a powerful handheld vacuum (preferably bagless as well). Choose machines that are easy to empty and have additional filters for the outflowing air.

Easy fix When cleaning decorative features and carved surfaces, use a wooden skewer or toothpick to get into fine grooves.

Save money For removing dirt from hard-to-reach nooks and crannies, an old toothbrush does just as good a job as a special cleaning brush.

A little CLEANING PRODUCT goes a long way

There is a wide range of cleaning products on the market that are designed to take on all kinds of jobs. Normally, you only need to use a small amount.

✳ A good-quality all-purpose cleaning product is fine for most cleaning jobs. For day-to-day cleaning, use a small amount in a bucket of warm water. For tougher jobs, use hot water and add more product. Allow time for it to work on the surface before rinsing it off thoroughly. Putting the solution in a multipurpose spray bottle makes it easy to spray dirty surfaces with one hand and wipe off with a cleaning cloth in the other.

✳ A handy descaling agent, citric acid is available from supermarkets as an inexpensive white powder. Dissolve a few teaspoons in hot water and add a little all-purpose cleaner if desired. Place the item to be cleaned in the solution and let stand, then

A MULTIPURPOSE SPRAY BOTTLE MAKES IT EASY TO SPRAY DIRTY SURFACES.

rinse well to finish. Be careful not to inhale the citric acid powder or allow it to come into contact with your eyes.

✳ Denatured alcohol is a useful general solvent for removing various kinds of residue, especially adhesive substances. Use a mixture of one part denatured alcohol to two parts warm water and a dash of all-purpose cleaner for cleaning your windows. Take care when working with denatured alcohol as it is flammable!

✳ Washing soda (a common name for sodium carbonate) is good for tackling greasy messes. Dissolve a cup of washing soda in a quart of hot water and add a dash of all-purpose cleaner. You can use this solution on dirty dishes (such as soaking greasy pans), but it is also good for removing mold and as a drain cleaner. Wear rubber gloves when handling washing soda and take care to avoid contact with the eyes.

✳ For specific jobs, you may wish to round out your cleaning product collection with a scouring cleanser, a specific product for tiles and the bathroom, and furniture polish. Buy a selection of plastic spray bottles to make it easier to use cleaning products in appropriate quantities.

Insider's hack Use cleaning products sparingly – using a lot doesn't always give better results. Also protect your clothing, hands and face as many products contain harsh ingredients.

USE A SYSTEM OF FOUR COLORS FOR CLEANING CLOTHS, WITH A DIFFERENT COLOR FOR EACH AREA OF THE HOME.

GOOD PLANNING
is half the battle

Preventing a mess is better than cleaning it up afterwards. Avoid leaving windows open for too long to stop excessive dirt and dust from blowing in. Doormats outside and inside the front door will catch most of the dirt brought in from the street. Leave wet weather boots outside if possible.

✳ Devise a cleaning plan for your whole house, with daily, weekly and monthly tasks. Make cleaning more fun by putting on some music – time will go by more quickly and you will probably do a more thorough job.

✳ Start by clearing things away, and removing everything (if only temporarily) that might get in the way in the room you are about to clean. Keep a container handy to gather up things that are lying around so you can put them away later.

✳ It's annoying and a waste of time to always be looking for your cleaning gear or to go searching through other rooms to find things. Put all your regular cleaning items in a dedicated cleaning basket: cloths, dustpan and brush, squeegee for any glass, old toothbrush, rubber gloves, cleaning products and a plastic bag for any rubbish you pick up. When cleaning, take your broom, mop and vacuum cleaner with you as you move from one room to the next. If your home has more than one floor, it's a good idea to have a separate set of cleaning gear on each floor.

✳ No one likes the idea of the dining room table being wiped down with the same cloth you've just used to clean the bathroom. To prevent this, use

TAKE CARE

Don't mix different cleaning products together in an attempt to get better results. They are formulated to work best on their own. What's worse, mixing products can cause hazardous chemical reactions, such as producing toxic chlorine gas.

Expert advice

An all-purpose cleaning agent

Some professional cleaners prefer to use a cleaning agent made from combining the following simple ingredients:

★ 1 quart warm water
★ 1 teaspoon delicate laundry detergent
★ 1 teaspoon vinegar

Mix well to create plenty of suds and then use with a cleaning cloth.

a four-colored system for your cleaning cloths: reserve red for the toilet and surrounding floor and tiles; yellow for the rest of the bathroom including basin, bathtub, tiles and bathroom mirrors; keep green exclusively in the kitchen for the countertops, dishwasher and fridge; and blue for living areas, chairs, shelves, and so on.

Save time Get the job done faster by using both hands whenever you can. For example, spray on a cleaning product with your left hand and wipe it off with your right.

Best hacks for
REMOVING DUST

Dusting can be one of the least satisfying cleaning jobs – because dust has a way of coming back so quickly. Here are ways to make the task easier and get the upper hand over household dust.

An old sock lightly sprayed with furniture polish is good for wiping dust off wood furniture.

✳ Use clean, white cotton dusting cloths. Dampen them with soapy water or, for moisture-sensitive wood furniture, a small amount of furniture polish (a squirt from a spray bottle will do). Change to a fresh cloth frequently and wash in the machine. You can also buy single-use dust-attracting cloths. These are relatively expensive but are especially good for moisture-sensitive electronic devices. Take care with microfiber cloths as they can scratch delicate polished surfaces.

✳ An old sock, worn like a glove and dampened with water or furniture polish, is good for dusting.

✳ For baseboards and hard-to-reach areas, such as behind furniture, attach a cleaning cloth to your broom with elastic bands – no bending necessary!

BE SYSTEMATIC ABOUT CLEANING

1 Dress appropriately – wear an apron to help keep your clothes clean. Choose one with several pockets for cleaning cloths and other small items. Well-fitting rubber gloves will protect your skin from harsh cleaning products and grime. Put a little talcum powder or cornflour inside to make them easier to get on and off. Safety glasses will protect your eyes from stray squirts of cleaning product and knee pads will make it easier to tackle jobs down at floor level.

2 Clean up spills as soon as possible. Once mess starts to dry out, it takes longer and requires more effort to clean off. Always try gentle cleaning methods first, moving on to harsher products only when these don't work.

3 Work from top to bottom and start with dry cleaning methods (dusting and sweeping) before moving on to wet wiping or mopping.

4 Read the labels on your cleaning products before use. The label will tell you how to use the product correctly and how much to use, and will warn you about any potential problems. When in doubt, test the product on an inconspicuous area first.

USE YOUR VACUUM CLEANER'S SOFT BRUSH ATTACHMENT TO CLEAN A WHOLE SHELF OF BOOKS IN ONE GO.

✳ Finish dusting with the vacuum cleaner. Vacuum upholstered furniture first, then baseboards and other pieces of furniture, and finally the floor, starting from the furthest corner of the room and working towards the door. To get the best results, go over each area with a series of vertical strokes followed by a series of horizontal ones. Don't forget to use the crevice tool to get into edges and corners where dust and germs lurk.

Insider's hack   Never use a cloth to dust books as you will only push the dust in between the pages. It's better to blow the dust away (through an open window), then open the book and snap it shut to get rid of any dust inside. If this seems too laborious, use your vacuum cleaner's soft brush attachment to clean a whole shelf of books at one time.

Save time   It's extremely handy to have a powerful handheld vacuum cleaner sitting at the ready on its charging stand. Look for one with plenty of suction and don't go for the cheapest option. Bagless models are best.

✳ Wool dusters are good to avoid scratching delicate surfaces. They pick up dust and cobwebs in one go. A duster with a telescopic handle will save you from climbing on an unstable chair or ladder and risking an accident.

✳ Move around the room slowly so as not to stir up dust unnecessarily and work from top to bottom. Start with light fixtures, lamps, picture frames and the top surfaces of tall furniture, then move on to surfaces at eye level and below. End with window-sills and baseboards.

Expert advice

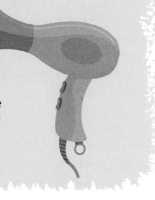

Hairdryer = dust buster   A hairdryer can do more than blow-dry your hair. In fact, there is a whole range of uses for this humble household appliance. Use the cool air setting to blow dust off books, ornaments and other surfaces, and small objects. To prevent the dust from just being blown somewhere else inside, it's best to use this technique at an open window or on a balcony.

LEMONS, an all-round defender

High in vitamin C (ascorbic acid), lemons are not only good for you, they have a number of practical uses, too. The high acid content in lemons makes them handy for cleaning jobs. It's with good reason that images of lemons are used to promote countless cleaning products.

NATURAL DESCALER

Use a cut lemon to rub accumulated dirt off bathtubs, mirrors and porcelain basins – the acid in the lemon breaks down the mineral scale that accumulates in hard-water areas. Where the build-up of scale is more severe, such as in a kettle or coffee machine, citric acid in powder form will do a better job – just be careful not to inhale this product or let it come into contact with your eyes! Dissolve the powder in warm water, leave to work for 30 minutes to an hour, then rinse thoroughly.

TOILET REFRESHER

Citric acid is also effective at removing scale deposits in the toilet caused by urine and hard water. Dissolve the powder in hot water and pour into the toilet bowl. Allow to work for a good length of time then flush clean.

COLOR STAIN REMOVER

The vitamin C content in lemons is able to remove certain kinds of colored stain. For instance, rubbing your hands with lemon juice can help remove stains from your fingers after peeling fruit or vegetables.

AIR FRESHENER

Adding a few drops of lemon juice to an air humidifier can improve the quality of the air in the room. Keeping a cut lemon in the fridge can also help reduce odors.

TAKE CARE

Under no circumstances should you use lemon on surfaces that are sensitive to acid. This includes marble and limestone tiles as well as some types of grout.

Sparkling floors and clean carpets

Take proper care of your flooring to ensure it stays in good condition for many years. Different surfaces – wood, synthetic materials, tiles or carpet – need to be handled appropriately. Some surfaces will not take kindly to being treated with the wrong cleaning product.

WOOD FLOORS need looking after

Traditional wood floors are among the most prized of flooring materials. Most of the time, a regular sweeping is all a wood floor needs. Use a good-quality broom with bristles that aren't too coarse. When vacuuming, use an attachment with bristles that won't leave scratches behind. It is important to sweep and vacuum to remove all the outside grit that gets walked in and can leave visible scratch marks on your floor.

✳ If your floor still looks dirty after sweeping or vacuuming, you will need to wash it as well. Avoid cleaning the floor with an excessive amount of water as this can leave marks or even cause the wood to swell. Wring out your mop thoroughly so it is only just damp.

✳ As there are so many different types of wood flooring, in terms of both wood varieties and floor finishes, it's a good idea to seek advice from your dealer or floor installer on the most appropriate way to care for your floor.

AS THERE ARE SO MANY TYPES OF WOOD FLOORING, SEEK ADVICE ON HOW TO CARE FOR YOUR FLOOR.

✳ Traditional floor wax can be used on unsealed wood flooring. If the natural charm of unsealed floor appeals to you, the effort involved in applying floor wax can be well worth it. The wax forms a protective layer but it needs to be re-applied frequently (about once a month). The next step is to polish the floor with a soft cotton mop. If this seems too laborious, you can opt for a modern wood floor-care product and simply follow the directions on the bottle or packet. If these products are too expensive, try adding a dash of linseed oil to your cleaning water, remembering to keep the mop only just damp to prevent water stains.

✳ Treating a floor with wax or oil reduces the build-up of the static charge that can give you a shock when you touch a metal object.

✳ Even with a sealed floor – where the wood is protected by a coating of varnish – keep in mind that, while the sealant reduces the risks associated with washing, it is not foolproof protection from moisture. If water finds its way into gaps between the boards, the wood can still swell up.

Treating a floor with wax or oil reduces the build-up of static charge.

✳ When children choose to express their artistic talents on the floor before we can intervene, the pencil or wax crayon marks they leave behind are a particular cleaning challenge. You can remove pencil marks with a kneadable artist's eraser that won't leave behind colored marks. For wax crayon marks, place an ice pack or cold compress from the freezer over the area and scratch the marks away carefully with a plastic spatula (the kind designed for non-stick pans) or your fingernail.

✳ For any other kind of spill, soak it up with an absorbent cloth or paper towel as quickly as possible, and don't let the spill dry out under any circumstances.

A COTTON SWAB CAN HELP YOU GET DIRT OUT OF THE GAPS BETWEEN FLOORBOARDS.

Save time Do you have a baby at home? Use a disposable diaper to soak up liquid spills fast. The absorbent material in diapers makes them much more effective than paper towels.

Easy fix Dirt can sometimes collect in narrow gaps between floorboards, where a conventional brush or even an old toothbrush can't reach. Try toothpicks or cotton swabs (for wider gaps) to help you get the dirt out of these tight spaces.

Insider's hack Stick felt pads to the bottom of chair legs and other movable furniture to prevent them from ruining your wood floor.

TAKE CARE

Don't use microfiber mops on unsealed wood flooring (such as wood treated with wax or oil). These materials will draw moisture out of your floor, drying the wood out and leaving it prone to cracking.

ADD A DASH OF OLIVE OIL TO YOUR CLEANING WATER.

Keep LAMINATE looking good

✳ Laminate flooring consists of wood fiberboard with an appliqué layer (a synthetic printed or photographic layer) covered by a layer of hard melamine resin. In most cases, laminate flooring consists of boards or tiles that click together. This means that there are gaps between the pieces where water can infiltrate and cause the fiberboard to swell. Sweep or vacuum laminate floors regularly as fine particles of grit carried in from outside will act like sandpaper on the protective resin layer. When you want to wash the floor, wring out your washcloth or mophead thoroughly to ensure it is only just damp. You can add a little neutral cleaning solution to your bucket but avoid alkaline or soap-based products.

Easy fix If you mop the floor in the same direction as the boards are laid you will reduce the appearance of streaks or lines.

Insider's hack Add a dash of olive oil to your cleaning water to prevent static building up.

TAKE CARE
Products designed for wood floors, such as floor wax, are not suitable for laminate surfaces and will leave streaks.

CARPETS, a source of stubborn stains

Vacuuming once a week (with the cleaner head on the carpet setting) is the best way to keep rugs and carpeted floors clean. High-traffic areas require more frequent vacuuming to prevent dirt from working its way in.

✳ As far as possible, run the vacuum in the same direction as the carpet's weave as this is more gentle on the carpet. Occasionally, you will need to vacuum against the weave to loosen dirt out of the deeper pile, but smooth the carpet down again after doing so.

✳ If you have somewhere you can hang a rug up outside, try taking to it with an old-fashioned carpet beater. You'll be amazed at just how much dirt and dust billows out!

Run the vacuum in the same direction as the carpet's weave as this is gentler on the carpet.

✳ You can clean a heavily soiled rug or carpet with a steam cleaner, which you can hire from most hardware stores. Be sure to follow the directions carefully. A carpet shampooing machine, also available for hire, is another option for a really dirty carpet. Fill the machine's tank with warm water and cleaning solution. Start in the furthest corner of the room and work your way towards the door to avoid treading on newly cleaned areas. Allow carpets to dry for several hours before walking on them. Empty the dirty water from the machine periodically and refill with fresh water.

✳ This kind of thorough cleaning will remove any stain-repellent sprays that the carpet has been treated with, so it's a good idea to reapply a stain protector to the carpet afterwards. These products are usually available at the same places that hire out carpet cleaners.

✳ You should entrust Persian carpets, especially ones made with plant-based dyes, to a professional carpet cleaner. After cleaning the carpet, these specialists will apply a conditioning substance that acts as a stain protector.

Save time Picking pet hairs out of carpet by hand is an onerous task and, while lint rollers work well on upholstered furniture, they are not suitable for larger carpeted areas. Buy a turbo brush attachment for your vacuum, which has a motorized roller brush to pick up pet hairs. This accessory is definitely a worthwhile investment if you own a cat or dog.

Insider's hack Before using organic solvents such as dry-cleaning fluid on carpet stains, test on an inconspicuous area first to ensure they won't damage your carpet.

Save money Instead of going to the expense of hiring a machine to shampoo a rug, people who live in colder regions can take advantage of a heavy fall of fresh snow. Leave your rug outside for a few hours to get cold. Then lay it face down on an area of clean snow and give it a thorough beating. You will be amazed by the amount of dust that comes out and turns the white snow grey. Turn the carpet over, cover it with clean snow, then sweep off the snow thoroughly. Bring the carpet back inside, allow the surface to dry completely and then vacuum to separate out the fibers again.

Entrust Persian carpets with plant-based dyes to a professional carpet cleaner.

Expert advice

Solving a problem carpet stain

Rule number one: Don't let the stain dry out.

★ If you don't know what the stain is, treat it with carpet shampoo. Spray it on, rub with a cloth, then vacuum to remove the shampoo.

★ For red wine spills, soak up as much as you can with paper towel, then rinse with lukewarm club soda or carbonated mineral water and continue to blot up with more paper towel. Using hydrogen peroxide or chlorine bleach runs the risk of leaving a lighter mark. The traditional salt treatment for red wine stains isn't effective. Salt simply dries the stain out – it draws in liquid but leaves the color behind.

★ For oily stains, sprinkle kaolin (white clay) powder, available from some pharmacies or online, over while still fresh. Leave the powder overnight then vacuum up the next day.

★ Soak up coffee spills with paper towel and apply soda club or carbonated mineral water.

★ Place blotting paper over waxy stains and apply an iron at a low temperature – just warm enough to melt the wax. Repeat the process several times with fresh blotting paper.

★ For chocolate or chewing gum on a carpet, apply a cold gel pack or ice pack to harden the offending substance, then scratch it away in small pieces.

Expert advice

Treat stained terracotta, marble and limestone

★ Untreated terracotta tiles are porous and therefore susceptible to staining. Try cleaning them with a solution of warm water plus a teaspoon of vinegar. For greasy stains, you'll require a specific product available from a specialist retailer.

★ You can usually wash off spills on marble and limestone with warm water. For greasy stains, add a little cleaning fluid – try white spirit (mineral turpentine) or denatured alcohol.

YOU WON'T GO WRONG USING JUST PLAIN OLD WATER ON A MARBLE OR GRANITE FLOOR.

Keep TILES AND STONE looking their best

Tiles made from marble, terracotta, slate and granite have long been used outdoors, and are increasingly popular indoors as well. These materials are attractive, hard-wearing and very easy to keep clean.

✳ Whether your tiles are glazed or not is key to determining how you should go about cleaning them. Glazed tiles will take just about any punishment – they won't stain, and water is all you need to keep them clean. Unglazed tiles, on the other hand, are a little trickier to maintain. Seek advice from the manufacturer or retailer about the best way to deal with the type of tiles in your home.

✳ All a marble or granite floor needs is to be swept or vacuumed and cleaned with a microfiber or sponge mop. You can use either a little water or a lot – the surface isn't sensitive to moisture. You won't go wrong using just plain old water and this will also prevent soap streaks. In hard-water areas, to avoid mineral deposits from appearing, dry the floor thoroughly with a cloth or use deionized water available from hardware stores.

✳ While granite is fairly resistant to most cleaning products, you need to take care with travertine, marble or other forms of limestone. For these porous surfaces, it's best to simply sweep or vacuum and wash with plain water.

✳ Untreated terracotta tiling is beautiful and lends a Mediterranean touch to any home. To improve its

TAKE CARE

Never use acidic substances (such as vinegar or citric acid) on marble or limestone. Acid will attack the surface, leaving it dull and blotchy. Some people recommend polishing marble with linseed oil, but this is not a good idea either as it can leave spots on the surface.

TAKE CARE
Avoid using abrasive cleansers on linoleum, whether powders or creams. These can dull the surface and it will get dirty again more quickly.

MODERN LINOLEUM CAN GENERALLY BE CLEANED WITH WATER AND A DASH OF DISHWASHING LIQUID.

stain resistance, wipe over terracotta with a waxy emulsion available from tile retailers. This will allow you to remove stains with soapy water. A terracotta floor's charm will increase over time, as it develops a patina with age.

Insider's hack Sweeping or vacuuming is not the most reliable way to pick up tiny fragments of broken glass. It's better to use an adhesive lint roller, the same kind for removing pet hairs. In a pinch, a slice of fresh bread will also do the job. Obviously, throw it in the trash when you're done!

Save money Expensive stone-floor cleaning products sold in hardware stores are not always necessary to get the job done. Try wetting the floor with a well-wrung mop, sprinkle it with sawdust (try your local hardware store), then give it a good scrub with a stiff brush. When you're done, sweep up the sawdust then vacuum to catch the rest.

LINOLEUM, what works and what doesn't

Modern linoleum flooring bears little resemblance to the linoleum of old. This hard-wearing surface feels warm underfoot and is easy to keep clean, generally needing only water and a dash of detergent or all-purpose cleaner.

✳ It will benefit from regular sweeping or vacuuming. Like wood and laminate floors, linoleum is prone to scratches by fine particles brought into the house. Floor polish, applied with a wool mop, will help cover small scratches.

Save money You don't have to use an expensive cleaning product specifically made for linoleum. Use a mixture of equal parts water and milk to give a linoleum floor a fresh shine.

PVC AND VINYL for easy care

PVC has been used as a flooring material for several decades. This inexpensive, hard-wearing material is available in a wide range of colors and patterns. You can install it yourself readily, with little prior expertise required.

✳ More expensive but even more durable, modern vinyl flooring comes in the form of boards or tiles. It's available in a wide variety of styles, from wood boards to cork and stone tiles, with many designs almost indistinguishable from the genuine article. Vinyl is also extremely tough, resistant not only to water but also to physical impacts.

✳ The smooth surface of a vinyl floor is easy to keep clean. Sweeping or vacuuming is usually all it takes. When necessary, wash the floor with water and a dash of all-purpose cleaner. When the floor gets really dirty, you can use heavy-duty cleaning products without hesitation. There is almost nothing that will harm a vinyl floor.

Beautiful and easy-to-clean CORK

Cork is obtained from the bark of the cork oak tree. It is warm underfoot, sound-absorbing and durable. Cork floors are sealed, making them relatively easy to keep clean. Simply sweeping or vacuuming a cork floor is usually enough.

✳ When you wash a cork floor, wring out the mop or washcloth thoroughly first. It isn't good to use too much water as it will cause the cork to swell. For best results, add a specific cork care product to the cleaning water.

MAKE YOUR OWN FURNITURE MOVERS BY CUTTING OFF THE BOTTOM OF WATER JUGS.

> Simply sweeping or vacuuming a cork floor is usually enough.

✳ Avoid using products designed for wood floors as these tend to damage the sealant used on cork.

Insider's hack   Clean up spills as quickly as possible to prevent liquid from soaking in, which will cause the cork to swell and leave a permanent stain. You can remove old stains on cork floors but it will take some effort. The gentlest way is to use warm water and a mild cleaning product. If this doesn't work, try using a stain remover specifically designed for cork floors.

How to move HEAVY FURNITURE

If you want to clean a room properly, you really need to clean behind and underneath the furniture. This usually requires temporarily moving the furniture out of the way. There are a few tricks to make this easier, but always try and get one or two people to help you – especially for heavy items of furniture – and take proper care of your back. Don't take on more than you can do safely!

✳ Buy a set of furniture rollers and a furniture lifter from a hardware store or online. You will need one or two helpers for this task, depending on the size of your furniture.

✳ Make bookcases and sets of shelves as light as possible by emptying them out. Check whether the item has been secured to the wall to prevent it from tipping over. If so, undo the fastenings. Have your helpers at the ready.

✳ Use the furniture lifter to lift up one corner of the furniture and slide a roller underneath. Your helpers will need to make sure tall items don't tip over. Then slide a roller under each of the remaining corners or legs. You are now ready to roll the item out of the way.

If these walls could talk

The dust that collects on walls, doors, windows and radiators is something we are more likely to overlook than dirt on the floor or dust on furniture, so it's worth paying particular attention to these areas of the home.

Painted WALLS AND WALLPAPER

Airborne dust particles can land on the tiniest imperfections in painted or wallpapered surfaces. If you run your hand over a wall that appears to be clean and find that your fingers are picking up dust, it's time to take action.

✳ Start by running a dry microfiber dusting mop over the wall. Leave it at that for delicate surfaces such as fabric wallpapers. For painted walls, if it's absolutely necessary you can wipe them down with a damp cloth. Just add a dash of dishwashing liquid to the cleaning water. Never use harsh chemicals or abrasive products, and avoid rubbing excessively. All of these can cause discoloration and leave ugly marks on the wall.

Always clean an entire wall surface in one go. Otherwise you can end up with unsightly edge marks.

✳ As an exception to the usual top-down rule, when cleaning walls you should work from the bottom up, because any water drips will be easier to remove from a clean wall surface. Nevertheless, be sure to wipe these drips away as soon as they occur so they don't become permanent fixtures.

✳ Always clean the entire surface of a wall in one go without taking a break. Otherwise you can end up with unsightly edge marks.

USE A DRY MICROFIBER MOP TO REMOVE DUST GENTLY FROM DELICATE WALLPAPERS.

A SOFT MAKEUP BRUSH IS IDEAL FOR REMOVING DUST FROM DECORATIVE PICTURE FRAMES.

✳ Moisten spots and stains with a solution of water and dishwashing liquid. Wait for the mark to dissolve, then blot it up with a microfiber cloth. Do not rub!

✳ Stair balustrades, whether made of wood, wrought iron or stainless steel, can be wiped down with a damp cloth.

✳ Wood baseboards, whether painted or not, are always a problem area. They get dirty easily, they are difficult to clean – especially those with a profiled design – and, as time passes, they inevitably start to look worse for wear. Try cleaning with soapy water first. Allow the baseboards to dry, then run a fabric-softening dryer sheet over them, which will slow down the build-up of more dust. If this doesn't restore their appearance, the only thing to do is give them a fresh coat of paint or varnish.

Save time Don't attempt to scrub a small mark off a pure white wall. You may cause it to smear, making the problem worse and creating more work to clean it off. Instead, cover the mark with a dab of correction fluid – it's quick and it really works!

Easy fix Cobwebs in hard-to-reach ceiling corners can be tough to reach with a vacuum cleaner. Try throwing a piece of scrunched up newspaper into the corner to remove them.

Insider's hack A soft makeup brush is an ideal tool for removing dust from decorative picture or mirror frames. Use a really soft brush designed for applying blush.

Expert advice

Caring for oil paintings

Leave oil paintings be as much as you possibly can. At most, a light touch with a feather duster is the only contact you should ever make. While a hairdryer is a useful weapon in other areas, don't use it on an oil painting as the warm air will damage the paint. If the paint colors have darkened with age, entrust it to an art restorer for professional cleaning and your painting will once again shine with vibrant color.

TAKE CARE

Be especially careful with water around electrical switches and power points. The plastic covers over switches and outlets can be wiped down with a well wrung-out cloth but make sure water doesn't penetrate inside.

DOORS AND HARDWARE need
a good wipe down

Doors with smooth, painted surfaces just need to be wiped down with a dry dusting cloth or a damp washcloth plus a little dishwashing liquid. Always work from the top down and regularly rinse your cloth to avoid wiping dirt back onto the door. For stained wood doors, wring out the cloth thoroughly so it's only just damp. If you like, follow up with furniture polish for a beautiful finish.

✳ It's easy to forget about the dust that settles along the top edge of a door. It's worth climbing up to cast your eye over them every now and then, or just to give them a wipe from where you are standing.

Clean stained wood doors with a thoroughly wrung-out cloth, then apply furniture polish for a beautiful finish.

✳ Never use vinegar to clean tarnished brass hardware as the acid will attack the metal.
✳ Decorative features on a door can be tricky as they often have tight corners that are hard to access with a cloth. An old toothbrush dampened with your cleaning water is a handy tool – or even a toothpick for really tight spaces.

THE ART OF CLEANING WINDOWS

How often you need to clean your windows will depend mainly on their location. If a window receives a lot of sunshine, for example, dirt will be more noticeable. Hot days are not the best for cleaning windows as the water will dry too quickly, leaving marks behind.

1 Add detergent to a bucket of warm water and wipe down the window frame using a soft cloth. Use fresh water and dishwashing liquid to clean the glass itself, adding some denatured alcohol – up to 2/3 cup per 5 quart of water.

2 Use a rubber window squeegee to remove the water from the glass. Start with a horizontal stroke from the top left corner to the top right and work downwards, using a cloth to catch the drips.

3 Continue with overlapping vertical strokes, again working from the top left to bottom right. Wipe off the rubber blade of the squeegee after each stroke.

tube attached to the nozzle. The oil will run back out of the lock bringing most of the grime with it. Press a scrunched-up ball of paper towel against the lock to soak up the oil as it runs out.

Save money Clean brass with toothpaste instead of a specialty brass cleaner. Apply toothpaste with an old toothbrush, allow to dry, wipe off with a wet cloth and then polish to finish.

WOOD HEATERS and open fireplaces

Fireplaces and wood heaters provide both pleasant warmth and the visual appeal of a burning fire, but it is essential to keep them clean to ensure your ongoing enjoyment.

Warm water with a few drops of dishwashing liquid is all you need for stainless steel or chrome hardware

✳ The best way to clean handles, hinges and other metal hardware will depend on the material from which they are made. Warm water with a few drops of dishwashing liquid is all you need for stainless steel or chrome hardware. Polish with a soft, dry cloth to finish.

✳ Brass hardware that is not protected with a clear sealant requires special treatment. Apply a brass cleaning product to a soft cloth and spread it over the surface with a rubbing action. Then wipe the product away with lukewarm water and polish up with a soft, dry cloth.

✳ Door locks don't usually get all that dirty. If your doors are made from untreated wood, wipe over the outside of keyholes with a piece of paper towel and use a cotton swab to clean inside. If your doors are painted or protected with a synthetic sealant, you can use a stronger product to tackle a dirty lock. Put some newspaper down to protect the floor beneath the door, then carefully spray a penetrating oil (such as WD-40) into the lock using the fine applicator

✳ Empty ash pans regularly. A good time to do this is the morning after a cozy night by the fire, as the ash will have had time to cool down. Always take care with glowing embers and never place ashes in a plastic trash can – this mistake is a known cause of house fires. Don't forget to clean out the area underneath the ash pan.

✳ Use a dustpan and brush to clean out inside a fireplace. You only need to do this when a significant amount of unburnt material has accumulated, or at the end of winter, which is also when you should give a fireplace a thorough cleaning inside and out. Take care when removing ash pans and cleaning open fireplaces with a dustpan and brush to avoid stirring up the ash and spreading it around the room.

✳ Hire a chimney sweep to clean your chimney regularly to remove built-up soot. This is important because soot can catch afire and cause a chimney fire. Make sure that any flue piping running between your fireplace and the masonry part of the chimney also gets checked and cleaned regularly – a chimney sweep may not normally reach into these areas.

✳ Check the extent of any creosote build-up in the chimney. Creosote is a black or brown, highly flammable and foul-smelling residue, which can vary from a dripping tar-like substance to a shiny hardened mass. It mostly occurs in the top third of the chimney, and is a major cause of chimney fires.

TAKE CARE

Don't use your regular vacuum cleaner to suck up ash. You risk ruining the filters and motor, and the machine will get so dirty you'll barely be able to get it clean again. If you really want to vacuum out a fireplace, look for attachments for regular vacuum cleaners that collect ash separately.

A quick way to tell if your chimney needs cleaning is to run the point of your fireplace poker along the inside of your chimney liner. If you find a layer of build-up 1/8 in. or more, call a chimney sweep.

✳ To reduce creosote build-up, burn wood that's been dried for six months to a year, burn hardwoods instead of softwoods and never burn painted or chemically treated wood.

Creosote, a dripping tar-like substance, is a major cause of chimney fires.

Save money There's no need to buy expensive products to clean the glass door of your wood heater. When the door is cool, simply dampen a sheet of paper towel, dab it in some pale-colored wood ash then rub it over the glass to remove the layer of soot and brown-colored deposits. You will be amazed by how easily this works. The secret is that potash (potassium carbonate) contained in the ash acts as a natural cleaning product.

THE FLUE PIPE BETWEEN THE FIREPLACE AND THE MASONRY CHIMNEY ALSO NEEDS REGULAR CLEANING.

A home filled with furniture

The way we furnish and decorate the rooms in our home is an expression of ourselves and our personal taste. What really counts is that we feel at home, and to achieve this it's important for our furniture to be clean and well maintained.

DARK-COLORED WOOD LOOKS ESPECIALLY GOOD WHEN TREATED WITH WAX POLISH.

✳ If you have inherited items of old furniture with sentimental value, or if you have valuable antique pieces, get expert advice on how best to look after them as there is a wide variety of delicate materials, each with their own specific requirements. Shellac, for instance, is a finish that is very easy to ruin.

✳ With modern wood furniture, on the other hand, you'll virtually never go wrong with an appropriately colored furniture polish. Dark-colored wood looks especially good if you apply a thin layer of wax polish, although wax polish is more expensive than the regular kind.

✳ You don't need to use an expensive furniture-care product all the time. A few drops of fabric softener on a damp cloth will help to keep freshly cleaned surfaces free from dust for longer. The secret lies in fabric softener's anti-static properties.

✳ High-gloss surfaces (painted or treated with a synthetic sealant) need only to be wiped down with a soft, damp cloth. Avoid microfiber cloths as they can leave fine scratches.

Easy fix A packet of disposable wet wipes for babies is good for cleaning furniture, too. Simply take one out of the pack and away you go. Test on an inconspicuous area first.

Maintain the beauty of WOOD FURNITURE

To ensure your wood furniture lasts a long time, you need to care for it regularly using the right techniques. In addition to proper surface care, other things to consider include avoiding excessive exposure to sunlight as this can change how the wood appears over time. It's also important not to place furniture too close to sources of heat, as this can cause the wood to warp and may lead to surface finishes cracking, glued joints loosening or veneers splitting away.

Insider's hack Caused by condensation on cups or glasses, you can remove those white rings left on a wood surface with toothpaste. Squeeze a little onto a damp cloth and wipe over the stain. If that doesn't work, try adding a little baking soda to the toothpaste. Allow to dry and then clean the table with furniture polish as you normally would.

TAKE CARE

Never use furniture polish, wax or oil on a natural wood surface that is untreated. These surfaces should be allowed to age without the use of such products. They can be wiped down with a thoroughly wrung-out cloth and sanded down every now and then.

THE RIGHT WAY TO DUST

1 Ideally, dusting should be done once a week. Arm yourself with a soft, lint-free dusting cloth, a feather duster, a soft dusting brush and your vacuum cleaner with the crevice tool and dusting brush attachment. Dust won't stand a chance.

2 Work from the top down. If you like, put a small amount of appropriately colored furniture polish on your dusting cloth.

3 Don't perform dangerous stunts by climbing all over the house. Use your feather duster to reach the places you can't reach ordinarily. Get a duster with a long handle or a telescopic handle.

4 Don't use a dusting cloth on decorative features or carved surfaces as you will only end up chasing the dust deeper into the grooves. Use a dusting brush or your vacuum cleaner's brush attachment for these areas.

5 Try one of the modern "dust magnet" styles of duster made with dust-attracting fibers. They are noticeably more effective than a traditional dusting cloth but they do need to be replaced periodically.

DON'T CLIMB ALL OVER THE HOUSE. USE A LONG-HANDLED FEATHER DUSTER FOR THE PLACES YOU CAN'T REACH.

Handle LEATHER FURNITURE with care

There is a classic elegance to living room furniture upholstered in uncoated leather, such as leather that is left in its natural, open-pored state. Unfortunately, however, natural leather does stain easily. Spots and oily marks can be extremely difficult if not impossible to remove. If you have small children or pets, it's worth considering whether an easier-to-care-for material is a better option.

✳ Take regular, gentle care of natural leather by wiping down with a thoroughly wrung-out cloth and vacuuming with a soft brush attachment to remove dirt and dust. Even microfiber cloths can be too harsh for natural leather surfaces. Try rubbing spots and oily marks gently with a kneedable artist's eraser or putty rubber. Sunlight and heat exposure can also damage leather, drying it out and making it prone to cracking. Avoid placing leather furniture too close to heat sources or windows.

✳ Coated leather is easier to keep clean. Most of the time, dust and dirt can be easily wiped off with a damp cloth. Once or twice a year, rub in a leather care product recommended by the manufacturer to remove dirt and return the coated surface to its best.

ARTIFICIAL LEATHER is stain-resistant

Modern kinds of artificial leather no longer have the unappealing plastic feel they once did. From an aesthetic point of view, they are certainly a feasible alternative to genuine leather. And they are much easier to look after, too.

✳ Apply a suitable artificial leather-care product two or three times a year. Remove dust with a damp cloth too. If the surface gets really dirty, you can add a little liquid laundry detergent to your cleaning water or use a specific cleaning product for artificial leather. It is essential to remove colored stains as quickly as possible to prevent any discoloration of the material.

DUST AND DIRT CAN BE EASILY WIPED OFF COATED LEATHER FURNITURE WITH A DAMP CLOTH.

Keep UPHOLSTERED FURNITURE looking good

Regular vacuuming, using a brush attachment on plush fabrics or a smooth upholstery attachment on flat woven fabrics, will prevent dirt from being driven into furniture by repeated sitting. Don't beat upholstered furniture as this can have a negative impact on the layers of cushioning material between the outer covering and the core.

✳ As far as possible, avoid sitting on upholstered furniture in your raw denim jeans as it will wear away at the fabric over time and dark denim can also bleed color onto light-colored fabrics. If you wear jeans often, place a blanket or throw over your upholstered furniture.

Denim will wear away at fabric over time so protect your upholstered furniture with a blanket or throw.

DON'T FORGET TO VACUUM THE FLOOR UNDERNEATH YOUR UPHOLSTERED FURNITURE.

✳ Most modern upholstery fabrics are treated with a stain protector. To help maintain its effectiveness, try to just clean the fabric with a damp cloth for as long as possible – it's better still if you can use deionized water.

✳ Microfiber fabrics, such as microsuede, look good initially but when subjected to mechanical wear and tear they are susceptible to pilling – small balls of fibers on the fabric's surface. For this reason, avoid rubbing excessively when dusting or vacuuming.

✳ Natural fibers, such as cotton and linen, are also susceptible to mechanical wear and tear. If you have premium cotton or linen fabrics, they require careful cleaning using a soft brush attachment on a vacuum cleaner.

✳ When you have finished vacuuming all the little nooks and crannies in your upholstered furniture, don't forget the floor underneath. Use your vacuum cleaner's crevice tool, which is narrow enough to slide under the couch. Then every couple of months,

engage a helper to help you turn your furniture on its side and vacuum the underside with your cleaner's brush attachment.

✳ Do you have a cat or dog? Use a lint roller to pick up stray hairs on furniture or their favorite spots on the rug or carpet. With their anti-static properties, fabric softener sheets – the kind you place in the dryer instead of liquid fabric softener – are another good option.

Easy fix The same rules apply for stains on fabric upholstery as for carpets. Never use harsh cleaning products! Try water first – deionized water is best – or sparkling mineral water or club soda.

Insider's hack Re-arrange your furniture from time to time, or at least switch around the loose cushions. Most of us have a favorite place to sit and the upholstery in these spots gets dirtier more quickly. Switching things around reduces the degree of uneven soiling.

SILVER WILL TARNISH OVER TIME. THERE ARE MANY WAYS TO REMOVE THE BUILD-UP OF OXIDATION.

ORNAMENTS and knick-knacks

If you go travelling a lot, you may have amassed a collection of colorful souvenirs that just keeps growing by the year. Then there are all the other ornaments we like to display in our living rooms to give our homes a personal touch. Before long, we face the challenge of keeping all these things clean, not least because they tend to be first-class dust collectors.

✳ Objects made of glass, porcelain or smooth plastic are the easiest to keep clean. If a simple dusting isn't enough, they can be wiped clean with a soft, damp, lint-free cloth with a dash of all-purpose cleaner added if necessary. You can even wash these items the same way you would do the dishes.

✳ Wooden objects are best cleaned with a dry dusting cloth. If they are painted or varnished, they will also tolerate a damp cloth.

✳ For delicate items made of copper and brass, you should purchase a corresponding metal-cleaning product. Using any other product runs the risk of leaving spots on the surface. If the metal has been protected with a sealant, on the

other hand, it should be reasonably resilient. Simply clean it with a soft cloth dipped in warm water with a little dishwashing liquid added.

✳ For really dirty silverware, use a silver-cleaning cloth. Or leave the item overnight in warm water with a dash of dishwashing liquid added. If the silver is so tarnished it's black, dissolve a teaspoonful of baking soda in a bucket of warm water and place a sheet of aluminium foil in the bottom of the bucket. Place the silver item in the bucket in contact with the foil. Leave for several hours and the silver becomes shiny again thanks to an electrochemical process that reverses the oxidation. Take care with using this technique, however, as it will also restore the shine to any deliberately darkened decorative features (such as on antiqued silver pieces), causing them to disappear.

Easy fix Dolls and other decorative items made of fabric are not easy to clean. You can try dabbing at the fabric laboriously with a damp cloth, but a simpler, more effective method is to place the dolls in a plastic bag with a teaspoon of baking soda. Give the bag a good shake and then brush the powder off the fabric. The cleaning properties of baking soda enable it to remove surface dirt. You

FRESHEN UP PLAYING CARDS THAT HAVE STARTED TO STICK TOGETHER WITH BAKING SODA.

can also use the same technique to freshen up playing cards that have started to stick together after prolonged use.

Insider's hack Your precious, fragile items are best kept in a glassed display cabinet to protect them from dust.

Save money If you don't have a suitable space for a display cabinet, you can simply place a transparent cover over individual pieces that are particularly susceptible to gathering dust, such as model ships. An inexpensive plastic fish tank works well.

Let the light of LAMPS shine on

Lamps not only gather dust, they also attract insects that fly towards the light source, become trapped in the lamp and die. For these reasons, lamps need regular cleaning.

✳ Rule number one: always switch a lamp off and allow it to cool down before cleaning. Always take care cleaning with water as it can cause electrical appliances to short.

✳ For lampshades that need to be unscrewed, set the screws aside carefully and remember exactly where they should go. Take a photo if necessary.

✳ Give all glass and plastic components a careful wipe down with a damp cloth. Remove dead insects by tipping the lamp to one side or by vacuuming. Any removable glass parts that are really dirty can also be washed in the kitchen sink using warm water and dishwashing liquid. First place a thick hand towel in the bottom of the sink to prevent breakage.

✳ Use the brush attachment on a vacuum cleaner or a damp microfiber cloth to remove dust from plastic or metal lampshades.

✳ Ideally, lampshades made of delicate fabric or paper should be cleaned with a fine brush. Stitched fabric shades can also be soaked carefully in the bathtub with warm water and a little dishwashing liquid. Rinse with clean water and then dry the shade carefully – start by soaking up water with

WORK QUICKLY AND DRY THE SHADE COMPLETELY TO PREVENT THE METAL FRAME FROM RUSTING.

paper towel and finish with a hairdryer. Work quickly and ensure the shade is dried completely to prevent the metal frame from rusting.

✳ Anyone with a chandelier in their home will take great pleasure in the magnificent light it produces, but they will also have their work cut out keeping it clean. At the installation stage, you should ensure the chandelier can be lowered for easier cleaning. A feather duster is the best tool for the job; use it regularly to keep the crystals sparkling. If the cut glass pieces become dull over time, you will need to remove them individually and wash them in the sink as you would any other glassware. The same applies to acrylic chandeliers.

Save money When cleaning your lamps, take the opportunity to replace the light bulb with an economical LED bulb. LED bulbs are easier to keep clean and will save you a lot on electricity.

Fresh household fabrics

From curtains and tablecloths to towels and sheets, the fabrics in our home create a sense of comfort when they are clean, crisp and fresh-smelling. Modern fabric-care products make this easy to achieve.

CURTAINS with drapes and sheer inners

Any time you clean your windows is also the ideal moment to pay some attention to your curtains. While it is not absolutely necessary to take the curtains down to clean the windows, dirty curtains on a clean window is not a good look.

✳ Sheer curtains, which are usually made from synthetic fabrics, should be washed on your machine's delicate cycle with a gentle spin. Hang them back up while they are still damp and the sheer fabric will dry crease-free without the need for ironing. If the weather permits, leave the window open to allow the moisture to escape the room.

✳ If your curtains have heavy drapes, it may be either impossible or inadvisable to wash them yourself and you will need to get them cleaned professionally. Between cleanings, vacuum these curtains occasionally using the upholstery attachment and reduced suction. Fabrics you shouldn't try to wash yourself include brocades, velvet and chintz.

VACUUM YOUR CURTAINS OCCASIONALLY, USING THE UPHOLSTERY ATTACHMENT AND REDUCED SUCTION.

✳ You can machine-wash cotton fabric curtains on the delicate cycle but be aware they tend to shrink the first time they are washed. One solution is to make your curtains with a double-folded hem so that you can let out fabric if the curtains become shorter after washing. The drawback with this technique is that it may not be possible to iron away the unwanted crease completely. Another solution is to wash the fabric first, before hemming.

Insider's hack Buy or make curtains that are liable to shrink longer than needed so that they reach the floor. This creates a decorative puddling effect, and even fabrics that are unlikely to shrink are sometimes deliberately cut to a generous length to achieve this.

Easy-care curtains

Wash all the curtains in a room at the same time. If you have a lot to do, aim to wash them all within two or three days at the most so they are all equally clean. This is especially important if you have a smoker in the house or for kitchen curtains, as your curtains will get musty and develop yellow or grey discoloration quickly in these situations. Open fires, wood heaters and candles are also major culprits when it comes to dirtying curtains.

✳ Take curtains down only when you are ready to wash them, as leaving them lying around for any length of time can cause unsightly creases that can be difficult to remove.

TAKE CARE

Curtains of any kind – whether heavy fabrics or sheer – should not go in the clothes dryer. They should be hung out to dry, unless they are dry cleaned.

✳ Remove any metal accessories (pins, rings or weights) from the curtains before washing as they can damage the fabric or the washing machine's drum when spinning around inside.

✳ You can leave plastic rollers in place, but put the whole curtain in a large washing bag for delicates. This will reduce the chance of the rollers getting caught up in the curtain tape.

✳ A washing bag is also a good idea for curtains made from delicate fabrics as it will protect them from mechanical abrasion caused by the drum of the washing machine.

✳ When you're washing white sheer curtains, use a whitening laundry detergent to get rid of any grey discoloration, and add a fabric softener to ensure the curtains come out of the machine wrinkle-free and help them stay clean for longer.

✳ Modern washing machines, and front loaders in particular, use very little water. This is not ideal for curtains as they need to be able to move about freely in the wash to avoid creasing. Select the extra water option if your machine has one.

✳ Curtains made from especially delicate fabrics can be handwashed in the bathtub. First rinse them then gently immerse them in lukewarm soapy water. Rinse out thoroughly several times. Do not wring out, simply hang them up over the bathtub. Once they have stopped dripping, hang the curtains back in their usual position.

Insider's hack Instead of just hoping that stains will disappear in the wash, pre-treat them with liquid gall soap (available from online retailers), or a prewash treatment suitable for delicates.

Tables look better with a TABLECLOTH

Tablecloths can be made from many different materials. Consult the washing instructions for each item to find the answers to the following questions: Can you machine-wash the fabric and, if so, at what temperature? Is it dry-clean only? Can the item go in the clothes dryer and, if so, at what temperature? (See page 132, "What do those care labels mean?").

✳ For tablecloths made of cotton or linen, try pre-soaking them overnight in cold water before washing them for the first time to help minimize shrinkage. The item can then be washed at 140°F, using a full-strength laundry detergent for white fabrics or a color-care laundry detergent for colored fabrics. Use a hot iron while the tablecloth is still slightly damp.

USE A HOT IRON ON COTTON TABLECLOTHS WHILE THEY ARE STILL SLIGHTLY DAMP.

✳ Polyester fabrics are the easiest to look after. They do not crease easily and they are resistant to staining. You can wash them between 100°F and 140°F using a full-strength laundry detergent (whites) or a color-care laundry detergent (colored fabrics). Use a washing bag for tablecloths that have lace or embroidery and don't overfill the machine. Use a warm iron, applying gentle pressure, while the fabric is still slightly damp.

Easy fix Removing oily stains is easier if you act quickly and treat the stain while it is still fresh – it will be more effort if you allow the stain to dry. Most fats will dissolve at temperatures of 100°F and above so first head to the sink and hold the stain under hot running water. Then apply your preferred pre-wash stain remover, liquid laundry detergent or a paste made from powdered detergent mixed with water directly onto the stain. Wash immediately after pre-treatment at an appropriate temperature for the fabric.

DON'T IRON TOWELS; SIMPLY FLATTEN THEM OUT AND FOLD CAREFULLY.

Insider's hack It can be especially difficult to iron all the creases out of a damask tablecloth made of linen or a linen blend, even with the iron on the hottest possible setting and using starch ironing spray. The solution: fabrics like this need to be put through a mangle or wringer. Drop them off at the dry cleaner's to get them professionally pressed.

Change TOWELS regularly

Your hand towels, bath towels, washcloths and tea towels are all breeding grounds for germs so change them frequently and always wash them at the highest possible temperature.

✳ Don't put wet towels in the laundry basket. If you are not ready to wash them immediately, hang them up to dry first. Leaving towels wet will encourage the growth of bacteria, leading to bad smells.

Towels can tolerate fast spin speeds, which will also dry them more quickly.

✳ Sort towels into white, dark and other colors before washing. You don't want to end up with pink towels instead of white ones.

✳ Wash colored towels at 140°F, which is normally hot enough to ensure that towels are hygienically clean. Don't use a temperature any lower than this for towels. White towels will withstand temperatures of up to 200°F.

✳ Towels can tolerate fast spin speeds, which will also dry them more quickly. If you don't have a clothes dryer, hang your towels up outside to dry, as this will have a softening effect. Towels hung-dried inside, especially near a heater, will end up stiff and hard.

✳ Don't iron towels even if you think they look better that way. The pressure of the iron will flatten out the loops of the towelling, reducing its capacity to absorb water. Simply spread towels out and fold them carefully.

TAKE CARE

If you hang colored towels outside to dry, don't be surprised if their color starts to fade. Ultraviolet light has the effect of turning water into a bleaching agent.

Insider's hack For energy-saving reasons, you may prefer not to set your washing machine to 210°F, but the high temperature not only kills bacteria and fungi in the fabric, it also gives your machine a thorough clean.

Save money Wash several towels in one load to make the most of your washing machine's capacity. Towels get heavy when they are full of water so washing several at the same time can prevent the machine from getting out of balance. Doing a large load also saves on water and laundry detergent.

How to look after BED LINENS

Stacks of neatly pressed white linen bed sheets were once the pride of many a homemaker – and created no end of work. Today's easy-care fabrics are quick to wash, dry and put back on the bed so it's no longer necessary to keep extensive supplies of bed linens.

✳ Jersey, seersucker, terrycloth, microfiber and brushed fabrics such as flannelette are all iron-free. These materials should be washed at 140°F.

✳ Woven cotton and linen sheets will generally withstand near-boiling water temperatures but they do require ironing.

✳ Whites and colored fabrics should be washed separately. Ensure zippers are closed, especially with low-cost knit fabrics as this will help covers retain their shape. Premium fabrics are less likely to lose their shape.

Save time If you have a small load of washing, select a quick cycle. Even with a reduced wash time, your sheets will still come out perfectly clean.

Expert advice

Fabric softener: pros and cons

There are two schools of thought on fabric softener. Here are a few of the arguments for and against and a suggested alternative.

Pros

★ The washing comes out softer. Fabrics feel nicer on the skin and have a pleasant smell.

★ Fabric softeners reduce the build-up of static electricity in clothing, especially synthetics, which means you're less likely to get a shock when you touch a metal surface.

★ Using fabric softener makes the laundry easier to iron as the fabric is less crumpled.

Cons

★ Some fabric softener ingredients can cause problems for people with allergies.

★ Towels feel softer but they are less absorbent.

Alternative to fabric softener

Invest in a clothes dryer. Your laundry will come out soft and fluffy (especially your towels). Even delicate items that you prefer to hang out to dry can, once dry, be placed in the dryer for a short time (on a low heat or cool setting). This will make them soft and in many cases remove wrinkles, too. If you must, place a fabric softener sheet in the drum to give your clothes a fresh smell.

Keep it clean in the bedroom

We spend a third of our lives in our bedroom, most of that time asleep. When we sleep, we are largely immobile, we breathe deeply and we may sweat to some degree – all good reasons to keep our mattresses and bedding clean.

The bedroom needs
REGULAR CLEANING

Making the bed, changing our clothes, and ordinary everyday activity all generate a significant amount of dust, which is why our bedrooms need frequent dusting and vacuuming or sweeping.

✳ Don't forget about bedside tables, drawers and anywhere else you keep things. From time to time, these all need to be cleared out, cleaned and packed away again. Wipe out your closet with a damp cloth twice a year – a good time to do it is when you're going through your clothes at the start of a new season.

CHOOSE THE RIGHT LINENS TO SUIT YOUR INDIVIDUAL SLEEPING HABITS.

A WELL-KEPT BED
for a good night's sleep

It is well worth investing in good-quality sheets, comfortable pillows, an orthopaedic mattress and a sturdy base. Keep in mind that everyone has different needs – some break out in a sweat at night, while others feel a chill. Choose the right linens to suit your individual sleeping habits.

✳ When it comes to mattresses, some like a firm surface while others prefer something softer. And then there is the height of the bed to consider and whether you want to adjust the angle of the head or foot of the bed. Whatever you end up with, it's essential to take good care of your bed and keep it clean to ensure many years of enjoyment.

BEDDING, a close comfort

For the sake of good hygiene, refrain from making the bed as soon as you get up. Allow the bedding to cool down and air out for a little while – with the window open if possible. This will allow much of the moisture the bedding has absorbed during your night's sleep to dissipate.

✳ Change the sheets every two weeks and wash them at 140°F. If you have been sick or have been sweating a lot, change the sheets more often – daily if necessary.

✳ Down or feather-filled comforters should be shaken out daily to plump it up and keep it free of wrinkles.

Give your bed time to cool down and air out every morning – with the window open if possible.

✳ These days, most down and feather comforters or duvets can be machine-washed at 140°F. But while this may be theoretically possible, whether it will actually fit in your washing machine depends on its size and amount of filling. Many household washing machines are simply not large enough so you may need to head to your local laundromat, which has large-capacity machines.

✳ Alternatively, send your duvet or comforter to a professional cleaning service – these services specialize in bedding and can also check the cover material of the quilt and make any necessary repairs. You can also use this as an opportunity to increase the filling. It's up to you to decide whether this will be financially worthwhile or if you would prefer to put the money towards a new comforter or duvet.

✳ You should gently handwash wool comforters or duvets – pure or blended – in an approved wool detergent. Squeeze it gently to release the dirt. Do not spin. Line dry, but don't tumble dry. You should be able to dry-clean pure wool comforters, but this is not recommended for wool blends.

KEEP YOUR BED HYGIENICALLY CLEAN

DAILY	Air out the bed linens with the window open.
EVERY TWO WEEKS	Change the sheets. If you have a futon mattress, roll up and turn over at the same time. Turning futon mattresses regularly keeps the filling evenly distributed and prevents mold.
MONTHLY	Lift up the mattress – no matter if it's a feather, latex or foam mattress – and wipe down the supporting base.
EVERY THREE MONTHS	Wash your pillows.
TWICE A YEAR	Switch between summer and winter linens and turn the mattress over. If your mattress has areas of varying firmness, be sure that these are placed the right way around.
EVERY THREE YEARS	Wash down comforters or have them professionally cleaned.
EVERY EIGHT YEARS	Buy a new mattress.

✳ Synthetic comforters, which are filled with various types of manufactured fiber, are easier to wash than down or feather ones and are ideal for people who suffer from allergies. But it's important

YOU SHOULD GENTLY HANDWASH WOOL BLANKETS AND LINE DRY, BUT DON'T TUMBLE DRY.

to read the care instructions for these comforters, too, to find out what temperature to wash them at and how best to dry them. Another advantage of synthetic comforters is that they generally will fit into a domestic washing machine.

✳ Eiderdown comforters made with the soft down of the eider duck are the lightest and softest quilts available and represent the absolute pinnacle in sleeping comfort. As a pure eiderdown comforter can cost several thousand dollars, it's worth getting a professional to clean it, top up the down and recondition the cover.

✳ You should wash your pillows more frequently than comforters – about once every three months. This is easy enough as pillows will fit readily into the washing machine.

Save time Use a machine-washable mattress protector or, in colder regions, a lightly padded, quilted synthetic cover. It's far easier to wash covers

of this kind than to remove stains directly from the mattress.

Insider's hack No matter where you live, it's a good idea to have different bedding for summer and winter. After you have washed one season's bedding, put it away in an inexpensive vacuum storage bag. Simply stuff the bag full, suck the air out with a vacuum cleaner, and close off the seal. These storage bags save space and provide reliable protection against dust mites.

TAKE CARE

Don't add fabric softener to the machine when washing a down comforter as it will cause the feathers to clump together.

The right way to DRY A COMFORTER

After they have been washed, take care to dry both down and synthetic comforters so that the filling doesn't clump. A clothes dryer is best, but most household dryers are too small to fit a comforter – there's no room for the feathers to spread out. Take your comforter to the laundromat and put a white tennis ball or a special dryer ball in the machine with it.

✳ If you want to dry your quilt out in the fresh air, avoid direct sunlight because it will make the feathers or down dry and brittle.

THE FEATHERS IN YOUR COMFORTER NEED ROOM TO SPREAD OUT.

Kitchens and bathrooms

The common feature of kitchens and bathrooms is that they have faucets and drains. In architects' jargon, they are known as the home's "wet areas." Some special attention will keep them hygienically clean.

Keep the KITCHEN under control

When you walk into a clean, tidy kitchen first thing in the morning, you feel like the day is already off to a good start. Keeping your kitchen clean involves a few regular tasks, but these smart techniques can help you take care of them pretty quickly.

✳ Put dirty dishes and cutlery in the dishwasher. Scrape food scraps into the trash can and rinse dishes off as necessary. It's better to wash large pots and pans quickly by hand to prevent them taking up unnecessary space in the dishwasher. If you let pans soak for a few minutes in hot water and a little dishwashing liquid, the greasy residue scrubs off easily with a dish brush. Dry with a dish towel and put away.

✳ Use separate bins for rubbish and recycling. If you have room, compost vegetable scraps and other biodegradable waste such as used coffee filters.

✳ Empty out the tea kettle after use to prevent mineral deposits from building up too quickly.

✳ Wipe down cooktops and work surfaces with your normal dishwashing liquid. If you do this every day, fresh spills will wipe away easily. If food scraps become stuck to a glass-ceramic cooktop, soak with water first to soften. The material will then be easy to remove with a razor-blade scraper (available from hardware stores). If you have kids or grandchildren who like sticking things up on the windows, the same tool is great for removing remnants of sticky tape without scratching the glass.

✳ Scrub the inside of the sink every day as this is an area that tends to get quite dirty. Remove mineral scale on stainless steel, enamel or ceramic sinks with a descaling product or a cut lemon. A cream cleanser will take care of greasy marks. Rinse well and buff to a shine with a dry cloth.

✳ Kitchen cloths are among the dirtiest objects in the home, typically harboring more bacteria than even the toilet seat. Cloths should be changed daily. Depending on the material, either throw them out or wash them at 140°F or 200°F.

Save time If you need a cloth or sponge in a hurry but don't have a clean one on hand, dampen the one you do have and microwave on maximum power for a few minutes. Very few microbes will withstand this treatment.

THE KITCHEN SINK TENDS TO GET QUITE DIRTY SO SCRUB IT DAILY.

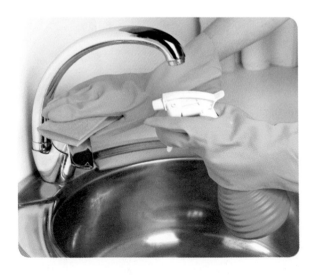

Easy fix Clean your ceramic cooktop in no time by rubbing it over with a dishwasher tablet.

Insider's hack There's no need to use a special cleaning product on a stainless steel sink. A mix of powdered garden lime and an inexpensive liquid soap is an environmentally friendly alternative. Apply with a sponge scourer.

Save money A cut raw potato is a surprisingly effective way to clean surface film from stainless steel. Potato peelings work well, too.

Spotless KITCHEN CUPBOARDS

Cupboards above and below the countertop should be cleared out and wiped with a damp cloth once every six months. Drawers especially benefit from a regular clean-out because they tend to collect crumbs – it's a bit of a mystery how this happens, since we only put clean cutlery and utensils in our drawers. It's best to suck out crumbs with a vacuum

NEVER USE ABRASIVE CLEANING PRODUCTS ON KITCHEN CABINETS AS THEY WILL ROUGHEN UP THE SURFACE.

cleaner as it can be difficult to get them out of the corners using a cloth.

✳ The outsides of kitchen cabinets get significantly dirtier than the insides as cooking vapors tend to collect there. Using an exhaust fan reduces the problem but will not eliminate it entirely. The film that accumulates, a mixture of grease and dust, is not that easy to wipe off. Try using hot water and a grease-dissolving dishwashing liquid or laundry detergent – both these substances are tolerated by all types of cabinet surfaces. A neutral cleaning solution is another good option and one that is suitable for use on wood surfaces.

Washing soda is an effective and inexpensive cleaning product.

✳ Never use cleaning products containing abrasive particles – such as a scouring stick or abrasive powders or creams – even if these are the quickest way to get the job done. Such products roughen up the surface causing it to get dirty again sooner.
✳ Clean kitchen cabinet handles with hot water and a healthy dash of all-purpose cleaner.
✳ Greasy dirt on the tops of kitchen cabinets also needs a strong cleaning solution, where it tends to build up in an especially thick layer.

Easy fix Run sheets of old newspaper on the tops of kitchen cabinets and stick it down with adhesive tape so that it can't be seen from below (note that paper towel won't work as well as newspaper). Now you can simply change the paper as needed and save yourself a lot of scrubbing.

Save money As far as cleaning products go, washing soda (sodium carbonate) is as effective as it is inexpensive. Simply dissolve in warm water or, for tough grime, sprinkle a little powder directly onto a damp cloth.

A sparkling and hygienically clean BATHROOM

As with the rest of the house, cleaning the bathroom is easiest if you do it regularly. Bathroom grime can be tough to remove if you allow it to accumulate over a long time.

✳ Clean the basin every day. Dirt from washing our hands accumulates constantly, as does hair, soap and toothpaste. An all-purpose cleaner is sufficient for everyday cleaning and you can also clean faucets and other hardware with it. When ceramic or enamel sinks get really dirty, give them a scrub with a cream cleanser. Use a bathroom cleaning spray and an old toothbrush to deal with dirt and scale deposits in hard-to-reach areas. Rinse well with clean water and dry the sink to finish.

✳ Solid surface basins can be cleaned with a cream cleanser. Always clean the entire basin including the countertop to ensure a consistent appearance. These materials are susceptible to staining by deeply colored substances such as hair dye so take care to wipe away any spills immediately. Follow the manufacturer's cleaning instructions carefully to deal with any residual marks.

✳ Bath products can leave an oily residue on the surface of the tub. If your bathtub has either an enamel or acrylic surface, spray with a degreasing cleaning product, rub with an old pair of pantyhose and rinse clean.

✳ Clean tiled walls with a cloth and an all-purpose cleaner. Avoid acidic cleaning products as they can attack the grout between the tiles. You can clean heavily soiled grout with a paste made up of washing soda (sodium carbonate) and a little water. Leave

CLEAN TILED WALLS WITH A CLOTH AND AN ALL-PURPOSE CLEANER.

for about an hour, then scrub clean with a brush and rinse well. Use an acidic descaling agent such as citric acid to remove mineral scale, but rinse the grout thoroughly with clean water before and after to prevent damage.

✳ Don't forget to give the doorhandles both inside and outside the bathroom a wipe-over – they are handled constantly.

Insider's hack You can get your bathroom faucet and handles to really shine by using a little dishwasher rinse aid to rub away at the scale deposits. Rinse well with water and polish up with a dry cloth.

Save money You don't need to use a specific glass cleaning product on mirrors. Try a mix of one part denatured alcohol to two parts deionized water (available from hardware stores). This solution will remove even sticky hairspray residue. Spray on and rub thoroughly to dry the mirror off.

TAKE CARE

Don't use concentrated vinegar to remove scale from chrome hardware as it will damage the thin layer of chrome plating and attack the brass underneath.

Keeping the SHOWER clean

As far as possible, clean your shower, including the floor, walls, shower screen and fixtures, immediately after showering. Otherwise, a build-up of mineral scale, and shampoo and soap scum will form on the walls and shower screen, and especially on the grout between the tiles.

✳ To clean the entire shower, spray on a bathroom cleaning product and let it work for a few minutes. Then wipe down with a damp cleaning cloth. If necessary, use a brush to scrub off any remaining dirt – use an old toothbrush for hard-to-reach areas. Rinse well with clean water and dry off with a towel to prevent scale deposits from forming.

✳ Really dirty areas of grout can be rubbed with a paste made up of washing soda (sodium carbonate) and a little water. Apply, leave to work for about an hour then scrub clean with an old toothbrush. Rinse well to finish.

✳ You can use the same paste of washing soda and water to scrub off mold stains that have formed on silicone chalk provided they are not too old. If this doesn't do the job, try a mold-removing product from a hardware store; if this is still not enough, the sealant will need to be replaced.

✳ Shower doors made of glass or acrylic get dirty quickly, and spots on shower screens are particularly noticeable. Bathroom cleaner or all-purpose cleaner

DESCALE A SHOWERHEAD OR FAUCET AERATOR

You could buy special descaling solution, but white vinegar is ideal for attacking mineral deposits.

FOR A SHOWERHEAD

1 Unscrew the showerhead and soak overnight in a bowl of white vinegar (if it has several parts, unscrew these if possible and soak separately).

2 Remove any remaining scale or mineral deposits with an old toothbrush.

If the showerhead can't be unscrewed, pour the vinegar into a plastic bag and pull it up around the head to immerse it. Secure firmly in place with twist ties or string and leave overnight before finishing off with the toothbrush the following day.

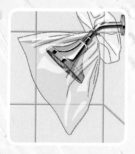

FOR A FAUCET AERATOR

An aerator is a piece of hardware that screws onto the end of a faucet. It is a fine sieve that introduces air into the water stream to reduce splashing. When mineral deposits are visible even on the outer ring that holds the sieve in place, it's high time to give the aerator a thorough cleaning.

1 With a thin cloth wrapped around the ring to prevent damage, unscrew the aerator with a pair of tongue and groove pliers.

2 Place the outer ring and the sieve in a bowl of white vinegar or descaling solution and leave for several hours. Then rinse both components thoroughly and screw back onto the faucet.

and a cloth are sufficient for everyday cleaning. Tackle stubborn mineral deposits with a descaling product containing citric acid. Rinse off with clean water and dry the door with a soft towel. If the surface is smooth and flat, you can use a rubber squeegee to remove the excess water, similarly to cleaning a window.

✳ Attack mold and mildew on shower curtains with a paste of washing soda and a little water. Rub on thoroughly, then rinse off. Finish by washing the shower curtain in your washing machine at 90°F. Do not spin!

An immaculate TOILET

Start by cleaning inside the toilet. Allow the cleaning product to work for half an hour, then scrub with a brush and flush away. Meanwhile, spray the rim, toilet seat and lid with bathroom cleaner and wipe down with a cloth that you will then wash in the machine on the hottest possible setting.

✳ Don't forget the tank, the toilet roll holder and other fixtures. And every time you clean the toilet, you should also clean the toilet brush and its holder. These items get dirty quickly and should be replaced periodically.

✳ There are a few ways clean your toilet brush. One is to add 2 cups of bleach to a bucket of hot water, and soak the brush and holder in it for about an hour. Another is to use the same technique with 3 cups of washing soda and a bucket of cold water, leaving to soak for a few hours.

IF YOU DON'T HAVE CLEANER ON HAND, SCRUB A TOILET CLEAN WITH SOME MOUTHWASH OR A CAN OF COLA.

Easy fix If you don't have toilet cleaner on hand or you prefer not to use it (it's quite a harsh chemical product), pour a capful of mouthwash or the contents of a can of cola into the toilet. Leave for half an hour, scrub with a toilet brush, then flush clean.

Save money If you are looking for an alternative to toilet cleaner for a less resilient surface, you can use a dishwasher tablet or a denture cleaning tablet, leaving it to work for a few hours. To finish, scrub the bowl well and flush clean. Or make your own tablets: mix ½ cup citric acid with 1 cup bicarbonate of soda, 2–3 drops tea tree essential oil and a little water, press into silicone molds and leave to dry.

Tidy Home, Tidy Mind

Everything in its place

Someone in the first world has an average number of possessions running into the thousands – and some own well above that average. Getting our homes organized and keeping them that way is a real challenge; there are a few strategies that work really well.

A PLACE for everything

Given how much clothing, household objects, books, CDs, DVDs, bedding, tools, mementos and other stuff we own, it is hardly surprising that our homes are not always tidy. We often spend ages searching for something, or may even forget that we own it. But if we designate a set place for everything, it makes it easier to put things away after use. If we don't know where to put things, it becomes impossible to really tidy up – we find ourselves moving mess from one place to another.

✳ Sure it can be tedious, and tiring, but tidying up the house feels good when you see the end result. Tidying can involve a lot of going back and forth, dragging baskets and boxes around, and emptying and repacking drawers and cupboards. It often makes sense to clean at the same time.

✳ Almost as demanding as the physical exertion is the constant decision making. Where should that object go? How do we put things away so we can remember where they are? Do we want to keep a particular item at all? Maybe we should get rid of it? Or will we need it one day?

✳ Before you embark on a major tidying-up project, first consider what's lying around the room – toys, magazines, clothing, DVDs, other odds and ends. Then think about how and where you can best organize these things. Next, gather together any containers you may need, ensuring they are of an adequate size and you have enough of them. Make the most of the overwhelming array of storage systems and organizational products available – cardboard boxes, plastic containers of all shapes and sizes (including some that fit into chests of drawers), magazine racks, drawer organizers, folders, baskets ... the list is endless.

TIDYING UP THE HOUSE CAN BE TIRING, BUT IT FEELS GOOD WHEN YOU SEE THE END RESULT.

Save time Always consider how much time you might spend organizing your possessions against how much time your efforts will actually save you when you need to find something. For instance, it would probably be faster to find a particular book on a shelf of 200 randomly arranged titles than it would to painstakingly organize and catalogue your entire book collection.

Tidying is BETTER AND QUICKER than searching

The key for keeping a tidy house is for everything to have a place where it belongs – somewhere it can be put when it's not being used. Objects that don't have a place of their own end up being schlepped around from one spot to another and they always seem to be in the way. Decide upon a set place for each and every thing you own and, when you have finished using it, put it back where it belongs as soon as possible.

✳ Make a habit of quickly putting the most important things away before you go to bed at night.

✳ Encourage your family members to be organized by making it as easy as possible for them to be so. Why not put a laundry basket in your child's room where they can throw their dirty clothes themselves? Or put a little basket for mail near the front door so it doesn't end up on the kitchen table or a chair? How about keeping a magazine rack in the living room so your magazines don't get left lying around on the coffee table, couch or kitchen counter?

TAKE CARE

Don't insist on doing a perfect job when tidying up; you will be bound to fail if you do. At the end of the day, it's normal for there to be a bit of clutter in a house where people live, especially if there are children or pets in the family.

STRATEGIES FOR ORGANIZING

DON'T OVERDO IT	Don't take on too much at once. Each day, choose a small area to organize. It can be as little as a single drawer.
ENJOY YOUR SUCCESSES	Start tidying up in areas where you can achieve the most in the shortest time (or areas that need it most). The results will motivate you.
DON'T HESITATE TO TOSS IT	When you are tidying, keep a box at the ready for things you want to throw in the trash, give away to friends or relatives, donate to charity, or sell.

✳ Organize things according to how often you use them – all the time, less often, seldom if ever. Put the things you use all the time in readily accessible places. Things you use less often can live at the back of your cupboards, and things you seldom use can go to the attic or basement, or be disposed of.

Put those important items away quickly before going to bed at night.

Easy fix Make a space in the hallway or kitchen where you can put things that you don't have time to put away immediately – it could be a drawer or a basket. Then check through this drawer or basket regularly to ensure nothing important gets misplaced there.

LIVING, DINING AND MEDIA ROOMS need plenty of storage

It's impossible to keep a room tidy without an adequate amount of storage. Living and dining rooms typically need cupboards, cabinets or drawers for tableware and linens, and shelves for books, CDs and DVDs. Put kitchenware back in the cupboard as soon as they're washed. Place your "go to" pieces towards the front (unless you normally keep them in the kitchen) and your "good china" towards the back.

✳ As soon as you've finished using CDs, DVDs, books, albums and magazines, put them away – if you leave them lying around on the table, you will soon have piles of clutter to deal with. And piles of things have a tendency to grow – the longer you leave them, the more work you're giving yourself to put everything away.

PUT BOOKS AND CDs AWAY AS SOON AS YOU HAVE FINISHED WITH THEM.

TAKE CARE

Avoid putting things in piles. It might look tidy but it is hard to access things when they're stacked on top of each other.

✳ Do you have four different remote controls? Before going to bed at night, put them away in a basket or drawer so they don't lie around creating clutter, or fall down the back of the couch.

✳ If there is a tangle of cables behind your TV, stereo or computer, you can bundle them together with plastic cable ties (available in black, white or bold colors). You can also install cable ducting or use cable wraps to conceal a bundle of cables.

✳ Tour the living room a few times a day to pick up things that don't belong there, such as empty bottles and glasses or used plates. It's quick to do and the room looks tidier immediately.

✳ Work out the best spot for small and frequently used items – your wallet, cell phone, glasses, car keys and house keys – so you can find them when you need them. Always return these items to their designated place.

Save time If you have several electronic devices connected to a power board (such as the television, DVD player and stereo system), put labels on the power cords. If ever there is a problem, you'll know which cord to unplug.

An inviting FRONT HALL

The front hall is the ideal place for hooks, baskets or a small cabinet with drawers to keep your house keys, car keys, bus and train tickets, incoming and outgoing mail, dog leashes, sunglasses, and so on. This will ensure these frequently used items stay within easy reach. It's not, however, the best place to store reusable supermarket bags, as the pile of bags will stop the space from looking neat and tidy.

DIVIDE UP YOUR CUPBOARDS AND DRAWERS TO MAKE THE MOST OF THE AVAILABLE SPACE.

✳ A shoe rack at the entrance helps to prevent wet or dirty shoes from being brought into the house. The floor in the front entrance is usually a surface that is easy to keep clean.

✳ Keep a flashlight in the front hall so you don't have to go searching for it in the event of a blackout. Make sure all the members of your household know where the flashlight is kept.

✳ Each change of season, have a purge of seasonal or sports-specific clothing – there's no need to keep your winter coat out in summer or have your beach gear floating around in winter.

Save time Setting up a coat rack with a name tag over every hook for each member of the family makes it easier to hang coats up neatly and find them quickly. Children should have their own rack, installed at a lower level.

Easy fix If you have a lot of individual keys, a single key rack or key cabinet may not be enough. Install a peg board in your front hall with as many hooks as you have keys.

Insider's hack Seldom-used keys should have a tag to tell you what and where they're for.

TAKE CARE

Don't place key hooks or the basket or drawer where you keep your car keys, wallet and cell phone within reach of someone standing at or just inside the front door; otherwise, you will run the risk of these items being stolen.

Making KITCHEN storage easy

Make the effort to keep your kitchen counters well organized. If you don't have a lot of counter space, leave out only those appliances you use most often, such as the electric kettle, coffee machine and toaster. Divide up your cupboards and drawers to make the most of the available space – cupboards should have enough shelves, and drawers should have internal dividers or baskets.

✳ Keep countertops tidy to prevent cleaning products and food from coming into contact with one another. When unpacking your grocery shopping, keep these two groups separate. A scouring cleaner for the sink has no place alongside the apples.

✳ Paper towel, tea towels, an apron, a bottle opener, cling wrap, aluminium foil and a pair of kitchen scissors should all be within easy reach. The same goes for a fire blanket or extinguisher.

Easy fix The top shelves in kitchen cabinets are hard to reach so use them for objects you don't need very often. Replacing a top shelf with a sheet of toughened glass, which is relatively inexpensive and can be cut to size by the supplier, will allow you to see what's up there from below.

Insider's hack Don't leave dirty dishes lying around, not even in the sink. If you don't have space for a standard dishwasher, where you can put dishes immediately, you could buy a small countertop model.

Calm the chaos in KIDS' BEDROOMS

Train your children to be tidy from an early age – if you wait until they're teenagers, you'll face a tough battle. Most children don't have an innate sense of tidiness and many will sit happily in the midst of their creative chaos. Instill a rule that toys get put away when your child has finished playing with them – you can make an exception for building toys that the child wants to come back to and continue working on. Explain that the benefit of tidying up is that, when everything is back in its proper place,

HELP YOUR CHILDREN TO TIDY UP, AS THEY MAY NOT GET THE HANG OF IT ON THEIR OWN DESPITE THEIR BEST INTENTIONS.

their favorite toys will be quick and easy to find. Support your child's efforts with plenty of storage options in their room.

✳ Help children to tidy, as they may not get the hang of it on their own despite their best intentions. Working with them will get the job done sooner.

✳ If possible, organize the child's bedroom into different areas for different activities. For example: an area for sleeping (must be clear at night), an area for craft (painting and messy activities can only be done here), a cozy corner (with cushions for reading or listening to music), a construction zone (where Lego creations may remain in place for a few days), and a study zone (for homework). Depending on your child's interests, you might also designate an area for a doll's house or model train set.

✳ Sit with your child and organize their toys into different colored boxes. For instance, you might have a box for Legos, soft toys, computer games and coloring books. But don't be too rigid – if teddy really needs to keep his ball with him, then both can live in the soft toy box.

✳ Another solution is to sort toys and storybooks into three or four play baskets, and only bring out one basket at a time. Then everything goes back in the play basket at the end of playtime. Rotate the baskets every few days, putting one away and bringing a fresh one out.

Save time Don't spend too long thinking about where to put an item for which there is no obvious place. Simply have a box for odds and ends.

Insider's hack When children share a room, provide a way for them to keep their possessions separate. This will help prevent arguments.

BEDROOM storage strategies

To make your bedroom a haven of tidy calm, it is essential that your closet and dresser are adequately sized and that they have well-designed hardware. There are shelving and hanging systems for just about every type of clothing and accessory. Give some thought to what specific storage options you may need.

✳ Compartments of various sizes that fit into drawers are especially useful for storing small items such as handkerchiefs, belts, ties and socks. Compartments should be see-through so you can see what's inside at a glance.

✳ For the same reason, drawers within closets should have clear or transparent fronts. If you can't find these, wire baskets are another option.

Save time If you share a dresser or closet, each person should have their own section to make it quicker and easier to find their things.

Insider's hack Instead of tossing your clothes just anywhere in the evening, have a chair on which you can lay things neatly to keep them from getting crumpled. This also lets your clothes air out before they go back into the closet or laundry basket.

Save money If an elaborate interior set-up for your closet seems too expensive – anything involving drawers does tend to add up – try using colorful plastic storage bins, which are stackable. Attractive containers, such as decorative boxes or cookie tins, can also work well.

AVOID A FIGHT WITH YOUR DUVET COVER

With the right technique, inserting a comforter into a duvet cover is a simple process, involving a second or two of preparation, a straightforward flick of the wrists and a few moments more to complete the job.

1 Lay the comforter flat on the bed. Turn the cover inside out then reach inside to grasp the two corners furthest from the opening.

2 With your hands inside the cover, take hold of the top corners of the comforter and lift both of them at the same time.

3 Flick your wrists and shake the two top corners so that the cover unfurls over the comforter the right way out.

4 Hold the corners in the air, and carry on shaking. Smooth out the duvet and close the fasteners or buttons.

Find extra storage space

There is space to be found even in the smallest home. And with a few tips and tricks, even a humble corner that you might have previously overlooked can provide useful storage space.

Most furniture is designed for rooms with straight walls of a certain height. If you have sloping ceilings in your home, you often have to leave the space underneath the ceiling unused, or go to the trouble of designing and building (or employing someone else to build) custom furniture. There is, however, a variety of flexible shelving systems available with adjustable shelves that you can adapt to suit sloping ceilings, letting you make better use of upstairs living areas and attics.

✳ Knee walls in attics – short vertical walls below the sloping ceiling – can be furnished with shelves or low cupboards. This is also an ideal place to put plastic boxes with lids and rollers. These simple containers provide lots of storage space and are easy to pull out when needed.

✳ Check out low-cost furniture stores as they often have storage solutions for top-floor living spaces with sloping ceilings that are well designed and look surprisingly good.

✳ Don't try and build something into every sloping space as this will make the room feel cramped. Avoid dark colors on the walls and ceilings as they will make the room seem smaller than it really is.

Don't overlook STAIRCASES

In most houses, the potential to store things under staircases is generally wasted. But there is a wealth of possibilities in this area. Whether you want to make use of this potential will of course depend on the location and design of the stairs in your home – are they close to the front door, in the basement, or a feature in a duplex apartment?

✳ Stackable drawer systems that follow the sloping line of a staircase can be stylish.

SHORT ON CLOSET SPACE? UNDER THE STAIRS IS A GREAT SPOT FOR A DRAWER FOR STORAGE.

✳ Wood staircases can be built to be like a set of drawers, with a drawer sliding out from under practically every step. The drawers provide an enormous amount of storage space without taking up floor space.

✳ There is also a lot you can do underneath a flight of stairs – often considered a dead space – depending on what you want to store there. If you have an open-style staircase, bear in mind that a considerable amount of dirt and dust will fall through the stairs to the area below.

✳ To convert the area beneath a closed staircase into a closet, enclose it with shutter doors you can buy from a hardware store. Hang long coats at the tall end, jackets in the middle, and leave the really short space for children's clothes, or for bags, purses and umbrellas.

✳ Book lovers seldom have enough library space. Under the stairs is a great spot for bookshelves. If your staircase is wide enough, you can also install shelving along the wall going up the stairs. The stairs themselves will provide easy access to your books – no library ladder required!

Easy fix   No room to keep your bike safe indoors? With some hooks from a hardware store you can hang up your bike underneath the stairs.

The great ROOM DIVIDE

If you have a large room or open plan area, you may want to erect a partition wall with drywall and wood studs to divide some of the available space. The new room could be a walk-in closet or set it up as a study or guest room. Depending on how you plan on using the space, you can leave the entrance open or fit it with a door. If space is tight, a sliding door that recedes into the partition wall may be a good option.

Insider's hack   Have you considered using free-standing shelving as a room divider? Accessible from both sides, a room-height shelving unit that's

WHEN USED AS A ROOM DIVIDER, FREE-STANDING SHELVING IS ACCESSIBLE FROM BOTH SIDES.

just 6 feet wide can provide almost 100 feet of shelf space.

CAUTION For safety, you must anchor free-standing shelving to the ceiling with sturdy brackets.

Think outside the box for MAXIMUM STORAGE

With a little imagination, you can find plenty of extra space even in rooms that appear full. Most people only think horizontally, overlooking the vertical dimension. Take a look further up the wall, above your head. It's often possible to put shelving up high to keep things out of eyesight and out of the way – especially in the front hall.

✳ If your cabinets have limited internal shelving, you can install additional shelves to make the most of the unused space inside.

FLEXIBLE SHELVING SYSTEMS ARE GOOD IN ATTICS, AS THEY FIT IN WITH THE SLOPING ROOFLINE.

* It's a good idea to sort clothes in your closet by length. By hanging all the shorter items, such as jackets and blouses, at one end you will create space below for a box or two. There are storage boxes and drawers designed to slot straight into existing closet spaces, but measure carefully before you buy to ensure you will still be able to close the closet door!

* Another space in the bedroom that is often ignored is under the bed. Plastic containers designed specifically to slide underneath beds can hold large amounts of linens, clothing or cushions. Make sure the containers have tight-fitting lids as this is a particularly dusty area.

* If you have deep kitchen cupboards, the space at the back can be wasted. Create stepped-up shelves using shelving boards supported on bricks. This will allow you to see and access what's at the back of the cupboard.

* In many kitchens, there is space available on top of the wall cabinets. You can place jugs, bowls and tureens up here that are too bulky to fit inside the cupboards themselves. Be sure to wash these items

well before using, as dust and grease accumulates in these areas.

* Install cupboards or shelves above the washing machine and dryer, as well as under the sink, for additional laundry space.

Make the most of the ATTIC

Don't let your attic or basement degenerate into a junk room you can't even wade through. An attic is a suitable space for items that won't be affected by fluctuating temperatures, such as seasonal clothing, toys, unused sporting equipment or magazine back issues you want to keep. Ensure that everything is well packed to protect it from dust, moisture, rodents and other pests.

* Flexible shelving systems are a good option for attic spaces, especially ones that fit in with the sloping roofline. Check your hardware store for stable, value-for-money shelving.

Save time Make a list of what's been put in the attic – even if it's only a rough one – noting which container each item is in and where that container is located. Keep the list somewhere handy. Of course, it's also a good idea to label each container with its contents. Put a label on each side so it won't matter which way the container is facing.

Don't underestimate the BASEMENT

Basements are a storage haven. Basement ceilings are usually the same height as those in a normal room, meaning you can put old cupboards or shelves down there and create a huge amount of storage space. Remember that the air in a basement can often be a bit cool and damp. That might be all right for potatoes but most things will need to be packed carefully. There is a wide variety of containers on the market that seal tightly.

Basement ceilings are usually the same height as a normal room, meaning you can fit standard-sized cupboards and shelves down there.

Easy fix Label storage containers to save yourself spending too much time looking for things in what might be a confined and seldom visited space. Ideally, keep a list near the stairs of what's in your basement and where it's located. This will enable you to send other members of the family down to the basement to get whatever you need, even if they don't know their way around as well as you do.

Insider's hack Squeeze storage into every last corner of the available space in a basement. To this end, square storage containers are more effective than round ones.

WE ALL NEED DRAWERS

1 To keep things from rolling around, use drawer dividers or partitions, available in many shapes and sizes. It's best to keep really little bits and pieces in clear plastic containers that let you see what's inside.

2 For small objects, boxes can be a better option than drawers. Plastic, cardboard and wood boxes come in a variety of decorative styles.

3 In the study or spare room, it's useful to put labels on drawers to identify the contents; in the living room, however, labels on drawers are a bit over the top.

4 When you purchase a cupboard, it's worth choosing one with drawers in different sizes and depths, although items of furniture with built-in drawers are more expensive than those with just shelves.

IT'S A GOOD IDEA TO LABEL EACH CONTAINER WITH ITS CONTENTS.

To keep or not to keep?

It's not always easy to part with possessions but it can feel liberating and make your life simpler when you do. It comes down to drawing a line between what's important and what you can do without.

SORTING STUFF OUT
takes willpower

Have you ever had a conversation with someone who had to sort out their parents' place after their mother or father had passed away? It's likely that the person found the task challenging, but for sheer lack of space they simply had to deal with it – by throwing out or giving away most of contents of the house. They might have sold off some items and, in the end, kept only a very few treasured keepsakes

themselves. So, depressing though it may be, there's sense in starting this process ourselves, to avoid leaving our loved ones with a lifetime's worth of accumulated stuff to sort out.

✳ It's not always easy to part with things. We all have well-loved possessions that have been much enjoyed over the years, or that we scrimped and saved to buy. Some have strong memories associated with them and we can feel attached to seemingly insignificant items. It can also be hard to know if we might need something again after we've thrown it out – this is a common cause of hesitation when trying to do a clear-out.

✳ It can be a good idea to hang on to something we don't use ourselves anymore because we know it will come in handy for someone else.

✳ If you are running out of space despite having a number of storage areas, it's time to think about getting rid of a few things. This isn't an easy task, because it involves constant decisions about what's important and what isn't. But you'll also experience how therapeutic it can be to part with possessions that, when you really think about it, are little more than dead weight.

✳ Tidying up and getting rid of all that stuff takes willpower. Give yourself a little shove and just get started. But don't take on too much at once – start

IF SPACE IS TIGHT, IT'S TIME TO THINK ABOUT GETTING RID OF A FEW THINGS.

with one set of shelves or a cupboard rather than an entire room. Just don't fall trap to the siren-song of an empty shelf and go on a spending spree!

Easy fix Start by clearing out completely and cleaning the area you want to sort out. You'll find the task of deciding what to get rid of and what to put back easier that way.

The THREE-PART SECRET to success

Find three big containers and have them at the ready. Label the first one "Definitely Keep." If you are unsure about a particular item, ask yourself two questions: Have I used it in the last year or two? If someone stole it, would I buy a new one? If you still need the item, it still works well and/or there are memories associated with it, put in the first container. If you own several of the same item, keep the one that is in the best condition.

✳ Label the second container "Throw Away." Toss away those broken, unnecessary or outdated items,

GIVE YOURSELF A LITTLE SHOVE AND GET STARTED WITH JUST ONE SET OF SHELVES.

or things that perhaps you have never liked. You may find it hard to decide whether you really want to get rid of some things or whether you would rather keep them after all. Don't spend too much time thinking about it – put these "maybe" objects into the third container.

✳ Put the objects in the first container back where they were or in a new place. Then label the "Maybe" container with the contents and date, then set aside in your storeroom, garage or a similar location. Go through this container again in another 6–12 months – don't forget they are there! – and you'll probably find you can get rid of most of it. Put the rest away – if you still want them at this point, they belong in your house.

Toss away those broken, unnecessary or outdated items, or things that perhaps you have never liked.

✳ As you go through this process, think carefully about whether you really want to keep heirlooms from long-departed family members but never use, or impulse purchases that you equally have no use for. Don't go by what an item might have cost when you bought it, but by what it's actually worth to you now. And don't labor under the delusion that you need to have a stockpile in your home to be ready for every possible twist of fate. For most of us, there really isn't a time of great need waiting around the corner.

Don't labor under the delusion that you need to have a stockpile in your home to be ready for every possible twist of fate.

✳ Now, what to do with the contents of that second container? It all depends what's in there – sort it again to work out what you can give away and what should go in the trash can. Then sort the rubbish according to the recycling and waste recovery facilities available in your area.

BOOK A HARD WASTE PICK-UP TO GET RID OF BULKY ITEMS.

PAST ITS PRIME? Give it the flick

If you have furniture or other bulky items to get rid of, you may need to book a pick-up in your area or check where you need to place items for collection. In some locations, it may be easier to take your junk to a waste disposal facility yourself.

✳ Depending on what you have and what condition it's in, you may be able to sell clothes and fabrics on eBay or through a second-hand store, give them to a charity, or put them in a clothing collection bin. There are online second-hand clothes stores that will take your old clothing after you have registered with them. Some fashion labels and clothing stores will also take back old clothing to donate to people in need.

✳ Books, interesting magazines in good condition, working electronic appliances, digital media, toys, tools, art and decorative pieces (clocks, ornaments, vases) and various other items can be offered for sale at a flea market, or given away through online ventures such as Freecycle – search "give things away for free" in your area and see what appears.

✳ Your local preschool might be happy to accept toys or children's books in good condition.

✳ Old, potentially defective electronic appliances should be disposed of at an e-waste drop-off center.

✳ Antique dealers or second-hand bookshops might take works of art, jewelry or old books in good condition. Ask a jeweler to value your jewelry for you – they may also be interested in purchasing some pieces. If you think your jewelry includes precious stones, it's better to get it valued by a registered professional.

✳ The online auction site eBay is a place where you can sell all kinds of things to the highest bidder. Make sure you read the terms and conditions carefully, and look at other items being offered on the site to gauge demand, starting prices and success rate.

Easy fix Garage sales can still be a good way to get rid of unwanted items. It's as easy as putting up flyers around your neighborhood to let people know when and where.

Insider's hack Facebook groups are growing more popular for buying and selling second-hand goods, particularly fashion labels and children's equipment. Search "buy sell swap" with your region and area of interest to see what's around.

DON'T BE TOO KEEN to chuck everything out

Don't be too quick to give away that scuffed old wood dining table that's come from an old great aunt! Find out whether you can restore it – many an ugly duckling has been transformed into a beautiful swan. Old chests of drawers can definitely be worth keeping as they provide valuable storage space.

✳ The work involved in restoring an old piece of furniture depends on its condition and the paint or varnish that was applied previously. In general, you'll need to clean the piece thoroughly, unscrew any hardware, and then remove the paint or varnish.

✳ Depending on the surface, use a heat gun and scrape the finish off with a paint scraper, or rub it off with sandpaper or steel wool. If the layers of paint are especially thick, it may be better to hand the job over to a specialist to treat with a chemical paint stripper.

A BIT OF RESTORATION WORK CAN TURN AN UGLY DUCKLING INTO A BEAUTIFUL SWAN.

✳ To finish the piece, apply a primer and a coat of your choice of stain, oil, varnish or acrylic paint.

✳ Clean the handles and screw them back on, or you may want to purchase new hardware in an appropriate or alternative style.

✳ If you like, after painting you can roughen up the edges with fine sandpaper to give the piece a fashionable shabby chic look.

✳ If the piece needs to be repaired, see page 296, "Marks on furniture."

Easy fix Old drawers tend to jam easily. If you encounter this problem, rub the contact surfaces with a candle. The wax will act as a lubricant.

TAKE CARE

Antique furniture may have been painted with lead-based paint, which is toxic if handled incorrectly. Testing kits are available from hardware stores. When handling lead paint, wear protective clothing, eye protection and a respirator. Do not sand or heat the surface.

Preserve and organize collectibles

Most of us have belongings collected over time that we would hate to part with. Keeping treasured collectibles well organized and in good condition is not always easy, but help is readily at hand.

ENDLESS POSSIBILITIES
for collecting

Most of us keep family photos, especially of our children and grandchildren. Many households have a stockpile of CDs, DVDs and books as well. Beyond that lies an endless variety of paraphernalia that people deliberately set out to collect – autographs, beer coasters, model cars, minerals, baseball cards, military equipment, embroidery patterns, shells, buttons, metal toys, records, original manuscripts by famous writers or composers, and even old typewriters. Many people's collections relate to what they do for a living. Collectors of miniature books, for instance, often work in the printing trade, while vintage fashion magazines are often favored by dressmakers or costume designers.

✳ No matter what a person collects, you need to ask yourself a few basic questions: How am I going to store my collectibles in a way that preserves them and does not take up too much space? Do I want them out on display? What's the best way to keep searchable records about my collection, including where they are kept?

✳ If your collection consists of 20 model sailing ships or 10 vintage cars, space may be a problem, but record-keeping may not. A simple set of index cards will do the job.

✳ If, on the other hand, you collect smaller objects, which number into the hundreds or even thousands, you will face issues with both storage space and information management. For an elegant, modern-day solution to the latter problem, see page 67, "Your laptop personal assistant."

Save money   If you are someone who was born to collect and love the idea of amassing a huge number of items, try to find a less expensive option – think bottle caps or stamps rather than vintage cars!

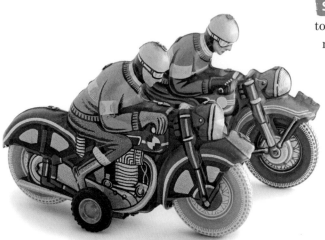

PEOPLE COLLECT AN ENDLESS VARIETY OF PARAPHERNALIA, INCLUDING TIN TOYS.

MAKING ROOM for collectibles

✳ For dustproof storage, you can't go wrong with clear plastic containers in different sizes. These are often stackable and larger ones often have wheels.

✳ Albums are suitable for keeping and displaying stamps, coins, photos, postcards, stickers and other conveniently flat objects. They are neatly and easily stored on a bookshelf.

If you want to display model cars, metal soldiers or shells out in the open, use a hairdryer to blow the dust off them.

✳ For three-dimensional objects, use a display cabinet or a cupboard with a glass door. This will keep dust off collectibles such as dolls, teddy bears, figurines, silver pitchers and fine porcelain dinnerware. If you have a particularly attractive item, you may want to put it on more prominent display in the open, but be prepared to dust it more frequently.

✳ Model cars, minerals, watches, toy soldiers, fossils or shells can be preserved in a cardboard or plastic box with a lid but the downside is you won't

IF YOU HAVE AN ATTRACTIVE COLLECTION, YOU MAY WANT TO DISPLAY IT PROMINENTLY.

be able to see them. If you prefer to display them in the open, you can use a hairdryer to blow the dust off (see page 14, "Hairdryer = dust buster").

✳ A bookcase is, of course, the best place to keep books. Don't get into the habit of putting two rows of books on a shelf as it is extremely awkward to get at the books behind, not to mention the fact that you are likely to forget what's even back there. If you have more books than space to put them, place some books horizontally on top of the others. You will be able to read the spines and it will give your bookcase a nice informal look.

✳ When we go travelling, we often bring back maps, brochures from museums and other attractions, postcards and mementos that we want to keep together in one place. Document boxes made from decorative colored cardboard work well. Or you could cover a plain box with copies of photos from the trip. Label them (for example, Vermont, Autumn 2018) and store them on a bookshelf.

EGG CARTONS ARE A GOOD WAY TO STORE VERY SMALL KEEPSAKES.

✳ It's best to store your magazines vertically on a bookshelf – if you allow them to pile up too high horizontally, it becomes hard to find the issue you want. Sort them by year and, to stop them bending in the middle, keep them in magazine files, available from an office supplies store. Look for magazine files that have a low front side as these let you read the spines easily and select the one you want.

✳ Celebrity autographs or postcards are best kept saved in plastic sleeves inside a ring binder. Use index cards and tabbed dividers to help organize your collection.

✳ Ordinary egg cartons are a good way to store very small keepsakes. For the smallest of your tiny treasures, try using the plastic insert from a box of assorted chocolates.

Easy fix Don't have a display cabinet but want to protect a treasured object from dust and still be able to see it? Try using a plastic fish tank. They're available in plenty of shapes and sizes, and the transparent plastic will keep your item on show.

Save money It's not absolutely necessary to buy CDs and DVDs these days. For a reasonable fee, you can legally download a lot of music and movies from the internet and store them on your computer. The same goes for e-books, which you can simply read onscreen.

KEEP TRACK of what you have

Finding space to put everything in your collection is only half the battle. The other challenge is keeping track of it all. For instance, what is the best way to organize your photo albums so you can quickly and easily find the vacation photos from your trip to the Grand Canyon five years ago? For coin collectors, what's the quickest way to find the purchase details of that Roman sestertius, what year it dates from, and where exactly you filed it away?

✳ Organizing your books, CDs and DVDs is only worthwhile when the collection exceeds a certain size. Americans love books, in 2017 spending more than $396 billion on book purchases, an increase of almost 30 percent from 2007. Before embarking on a project to organize your books, it's worth sorting through what you have and deciding on what you do and definitely don't want anymore. A second-hand shop might take some of your unwanted books, but exercise caution when it comes to parting ways. In years to come, you may want to revisit books you were reading in your

TAKE CARE

Don't under any circumstances keep books in the basement. Down there, they will inevitably develop a musty smell, not to mention the potential damage caused by moisture, insects and rodents.

youth. Once books are gone, they can be very hard to find again.

✳ If you are moving in with your partner and you each own a lot of books, it's a good idea to keep them on separate shelves – not in anticipation of a possible break-up but simply because each of you knows your own books well and will best be able to find a sought-after title in your own collection.

You could do worse than organize books by size, especially when you don't have any space to waste.

✳ If you have a lot of books, the physical space on the shelves may lead you to organize your collection partly by size. In simple terms, you can save a lot of space by placing all your large-sized books on a tall shelf and all your smaller books and paperbacks on a shorter shelf. This approach may let you fit another row of books in a bookcase with adjustable height shelving. We also generally know the size of the book we are looking for and, in many cases, the color of the cover or spine. Often these details are all we need to pinpoint the book we want.

✳ If you have a really large collection, consider using additional criteria to organize your books, such as separating fiction and non-fiction. You can further sort non-fiction books by subject area, and fiction books by the author's surname.

Expert advice

When you have a lot of books

If your book or music collection runs into the thousands – and collections truly can build up to this size over time, especially if you inherit books – you should do what any librarian would do and create an inventory of what you own.

★ As this is only worth doing when you have a significant number of books, it will by definition be a laborious task – one that can take several weeks to accomplish.

★ The best approach is to divide the work between two of you, with one of you reading out the titles and the other keying them into a computer spreadsheet.

Save time It can be difficult to read the small print on the spines of CD covers, especially if your shelving is poorly lit. Compartmentalizing and then sticking labels on the outer edges of shelves will let you quickly and easily identify broad categories within your music collection.

Insider's hack As CDs and DVDs all tend to be a standard height, it's a good idea to adjust your shelves to fit these exact heights. This will save a lot of shelving space.

PLACE YOUR SMALLER BOOKS AND PAPERBACKS ON A NARROW SHELF TO HELP SAVE SPACE.

Order the chaos of your OLD PHOTOS

Some families have a set of photo albums in which someone once upon a time neatly inserted and labeled all the photos. But a more common scenario is a shoebox or several filled with a chaotic jumble of photos from years gone by. Many people give up when faced with the daunting task of sorting out photos and putting them into albums. But someone in the family needs to bite the bullet because if it's left for too long, younger generations may never know who the people in the photos are, much as they might like to.

If you don't know anything about a particular photo, ask an older relative.

✳ Avoid mixing your photos up any more than they already are. They are probably in some degree of

SCAN YOUR BEST AND MOST IMPORTANT PHOTOS TO PRESERVE THEM IN DIGITAL FORM.

chronological order and that's not a bad place to start when organizing them. Arrange your photos by decade as much as possible. On the back of the most important ones, write the names of the people and, if you can remember, where and roughly when the photo was taken as well as any other interesting details (such as "circa 1970 on the way to school in Richmond"). If you don't know anything about a particular photo, ask older relatives or friends if they can help.

✳ Look for photos that relate to a particular event, such as a baptism, a wedding or a holiday. There will often be several photos, if not a whole album full, relating to such events. These are usually easy to label and it makes sense to keep them together in one place.

✳ With any luck, you may find a set of negatives alongside your photos – photos and negatives often do get left together in the original envelope from the photo lab. Negatives often include the date the photos were taken.

✳ It was once common for amateur photographers to use slide film and many households still have a few boxes of old slides. Special boxes were once made to store slides and these can still be found on the second-hand market.

Insider's hack   If your photos are really important to you, it might be a good idea to scan them so as to preserve them digitally.

Your LAPTOP personal assistant

Computers are enormously powerful tools for organizing immeasurable quantities of all kinds of things. A tablet can be just as useful as a laptop or desktop for this task. You can also keep your favorite files close at hand by saving them to your smartphone.

A HOME CURATOR

There are apps (small computer applications, or programs) specially designed to manage collections. No matter whether your passion is for beer coasters, photographs or fine porcelain dolls, you enter data about each item, including its physical location, into the app. Then you can sort and search through your collection using any of the keywords entered.

MEMORY FOR MUSIC AND MOVIES

Computers are fabulous for organizing photos and music. With the right software, you can digitally archive your old record collection and all your CDs. You should also be able to store copies of films you have purchased for private use, provided there is no copy protection to prevent this. And, of course, there is no restriction on copying over videos you have shot yourself. If you have home movies shot on video tape or even old Super 8 film, there are businesses that can digitize these for you.

A PHOTO ALBUM ON YOUR HARD DRIVE

A scanner will let you scan slides, prints and negatives. Once digitized, you can retouch your photos and organize them any way you like, using either filenames or, better still, keywords called "tags." In many cases, modern photo management software can even recognize faces, allowing you to bring up all your old photos of grandpa with the click of a mouse.

KEEP PRECIOUS MEMORIES SAFE

Consider making copies of your photos, music, movies and data about your collectibles on a DVD or external hard drive and keeping this in a safe location outside your home. In a worst-case scenario, this sort of precaution can help you provide detailed information to your insurance company.

A well-organized study

Even our home life seems to involve an abundance of paperwork – some in hard copy, some in digital form. Having an effective filing system will help you stay on top of the important documents that come across your desk

MAKE CLEVER USE OF A CLOSET IN A HALLWAY OR GUEST BEDROOM INSTEAD OF A SEPARATE STUDY OR OFFICE.

All kinds of bits of paper come fluttering into our homes, almost daily. Hiding in among the reams of junk mail, there are bills to be paid, contracts to be renewed and bank statements to be sorted and filed away so we can find them again. There are personal letters and emails that we hope to reply to, and then there are the interesting articles we find online or in magazines that we want to keep – and, ideally, be able to find when we think of them again several months down the line.

✳ Staying on top of all this requires a well-thought-out, consistent approach. Unfortunately, no one can opt out of paperwork completely. Unpaid bills, incomplete tax records or misplaced insurance policies can be a real headache at best, and incur financial penalties at worst.

Set up that HOME OFFICE

Managing the household paperwork is much easier when you have a dedicated, well-equipped work area. If you can devote an entire room to be a study, you're in luck. But a cleverly recommissioned corner in the front hall can do the job, too. The main thing is that you have a workspace dedicated solely to managing household paperwork.

✳ It goes without saying that a desk and chair are essential equipment. Ideally, you will also have a computer, printer and scanner at your disposal. It's also handy to have a set of shelves close by, on which to keep file folders and any manuals you need for your computer or software.

✳ Label your desk drawers with their contents and label document trays according to their purpose, for example "Incoming mail," "Outgoing mail," "To do." If your desk has few drawers or none at all – modern minimalist designs often overlook storage – buy a set of hanging files and a filing cabinet on wheels. A small filing cabinet typically takes up no more space than a side table and can slot underneath the desk. Use different colored files with snap-on tabs and labels to identify the contents.

✳ Reserve one drawer in the desk for your office supplies such as a hole punch, pens, tape and paper-clips. If you don't have a spare drawer for this purpose, you can place these items in a container on top of the desk, although this will create more

Managing household paperwork is much easier when you have a well-equipped work area.

TAKE CARE

Even though it may sound harsh, don't let other people use your desk. If you do, it won't take long before your workspace is constantly occupied.

CREATE DISTINCTIVE HOOKS

Wall hooks or coat racks come in handy for more than just hanging up your coats. Add them to your office to hang bags, sweaters, scarves, and more. While there are many options in home and furniture stores, they can be pricey. Making your own keeps the cost down while allowing you to create a one of a kind piece. Not only are these racks useful, they're so attractive they double as art.

1 Using a piece of window trim approximately 5 in. wide and 3 ft. long, paint the trim to give it an aged look. Insert antique door knobs or drawer pulls.

2 Starting with a pre-made shelf, paint it with chalk or latex paint and allow to dry completely. Add knobs such as faucet handles.

USE COLORFUL CLOTHES PEGS TO CLIP LOOSE DOCUMENTS TOGETHER.

work when dusting. Use document trays, available in different colors, as a temporary holding place for your paperwork "To do" list.

Save money To prevent documents you haven't dealt with yet from flying everywhere, clip them together with an ordinary clothes pin. Use pretty colored ones to brighten up your desk.

FILE FOLDERS and plenty of them

A crucial step in getting your home office up and running smoothly are folders. Reserve one folder for important documents that should be kept long term. Since many of these documents will be things you won't want to punch holes in, insert them into three-hole punched clear plastic sleeves before filing them in the folder.

✳ Use each of your folders for a specific category of documents, such as personal documents (birth certificate, marriage certificate, educational qualifications, living will, employment contracts); children (birth certificates, school reports); house (lease, title deed, floor plans, extract from the land title register); health (health insurance documents, medical certificates, doctor's notes); car (lease agreements, registration papers, mechanic's invoices relating to warranty claims); insurance policies; contracts (loan agreements, cell phone contracts, powers of attorney, sales contracts, subscriptions); and valuables (valuation certificates, invoices, inventory lists and photos of valuables).

✳ You will only need to open up these folders occasionally – when you need to update something (such as taking out a new insurance policy) or when you need to refer to a specific document. Put your important documents back where they belong as soon as you have finished with them. You should go through your folders at least once a year to check for things like subscriptions that are about to expire, insurance policies that need to be renewed or cell phone contracts that are out of date.

✳ Use another folder for documents that only need keeping for a certain period of time. This will mainly be invoices and receipts. Once you have dealt with

FOLDERS ARE A CRUCIAL STEP IN GETTING YOUR HOME OFFICE UP AND RUNNING SMOOTHLY.

them, file them away in chronological order. The same goes for bank and credit card statements. When the tax time come around, take out this folder and work out which invoices you can claim as tax deductions. File the rest away and work out how long you need to keep them – for example, 7 years for tax returns.

✳ Go through your mail every day and place any bills in your in-tray. As soon as you have paid or set up a transfer for a bill, file it away in your invoices folder. Use the same folder to keep receipts for any purchases that are either tax deductible or covered by a warranty.

✳ You may also want to keep another folder for private correspondence – such as birthday wishes, post cards from travelling friends and family, or letters from your children. You could also keep copies of the letters you write in the same folder.

Save time If you have ever had to search high and low to find the user manual for a particular household appliance, try keeping all your user manuals together in a magazine file or documents box on your bookshelf. Keep receipts and warranty information in the same place.

Insider's hack Take the time to photocopy the contents of your important documents folder. Place these in a folder of their own and keep it somewhere safe outside your home, such as at a relative's house or a bank safety deposit box. You will be glad you did if ever there is a fire or a break-in.

TAKE CARE

Don't be too quick to throw away receipts for things you buy. A receipt is your proof of purchase if ever you need to make a warranty claim. Scan, photograph or photocopy receipts on thermal paper as the ink can fade rapidly.

THE ROAD TO A PAPERLESS OFFICE

COMPUTER	Make the most of your computer! You can fit more documents on your hard drive than would fill an entire home.
SCANNER	Purchase a reasonably priced scanner. Scan your documents (such as contracts, certificates, letters and bills) and save them as PDF files.
NAMING DOCUMENTS	It's important to name your saved documents in a way that will make it easy to find them again. Put the date at the front, using the format YYYY-MM-DD – i.e. January 8, 2018 becomes 2018-01-08. Then add an underscore followed by a descriptive name. You might like to use a standard set of abbreviations to identify the type of document, e.g. "Inv" for invoices, "Cert" for certificates, "Contr" for contracts, "Mail" for correspondence. Add to this list as you like – all that matters is that you remain consistent in the abbreviations you use.
FINDING DOCUMENTS	If you have named your documents consistently, you can use search to pull up all your invoices from 2018 or all the letters from your Uncle Fred. Your filenames might look something like this: 2018-12-03_Inv_Water or 2018-04-05_Mail_Uncle_Fred.

Organize yourself

Many people say they find everyday life hectic. They never seem to have enough time and it gets harder and harder to stay on top of everything. There is a lot we can do to make life easier for ourselves. It starts with making better use of our time and employing a few clever strategies to become more organized.

TELEVISION IS A MAJOR TIME WASTER, ESPECIALLY IF YOU JUST SIT AND SOAK UP WHATEVER IS ON.

Don't give TIME WASTERS a chance

There are only a certain number of hours in the day and there is nothing we can do to increase the amount of our available time. But what we can do is make decisions about how we are going to use our time. It's important to be clear in our own minds about what we want to do with our time, what is really important to us and what is less so, and to what extent we will allow external influences and time-wasting activities to dictate how we spend our time. This implies that we need to consciously plan what we do with our day, rather than simply being carried along, and that we need to stick to our plan, even if only roughly.

* Imagine for a moment you just find out you only had six months left to live. What would you do? What would you leave aside? Even though this exercise may seem morbid, it will help to clarify your own priorities.

* For a few days in a row, write down exactly what you spend your time doing each day. Ask yourself if these were things you really wanted to do. Then try to avoid these common time-wasting activities. Television is a major culprit, especially if you just flop down on the couch and soak up whatever is on. Sitting at the computer is another great time waster, especially if you use social networking sites ("I'll just have a quick look at what's happening on Facebook/Twitter") and click on the links to all the articles and videos people post there. Stop and ask yourself which articles you are really interested in and want to spend time reading – you wouldn't read a newspaper from cover to cover.

✳ Try to avoid wasting time when doing everyday activities. Make a list of everything you need from the shops for the coming few days, then blitz it all in one shopping trip. This will take much less time than if you forget something and have to make a separate trip with all the inevitable time that gets lost – waiting for a bus, driving halfway across town, getting stuck at every red light, looking for a parking spot, and so on.

✳ Make use of unavoidable waiting periods or time spent on public transport. Hand-held crafts such as knitting or crochet fit easily into a bag. If you get stuck in traffic, listen to an audio book. Your car's CD player, or a well-stocked e-reader, smartphone, tablet or MP3 player are your best allies.

Always carry something interesting to read or listen to with you.

Easy fix Share certain tasks out between other members of your household to take some of the load off you. Make sure you all stick to the agreed plan. If necessary, remind people of their tasks at the appropriate time – try not to do it reproachfully when it's already too late!

Insider's hack Try to fill up no more than 50 percent of your free time with planned activities. You'll have time in reserve for unforeseen events and the leisure time you need to replenish your energy and reflect on the day.

A CUSTOM-MADE PINBOARD

A pinboard is a great place to keep shopping lists, cleaning rosters and notes of all kinds. Sure you could just buy one from a store, but you can make a new or existing bulletin board more attractive by covering it with felt and attaching ribbons to hold your stuff.

1 Start by choosing felt in the color of your choice. Then cut it 4 inches larger than the board on all four sides, pull it taut over the board and staple the overhang to the back.

2 Use upholstery tacks to secure ribbons to the board, pulling them as taut as possible so that the papers slipped behind the ribbons won't fall through.

3 You could criss-cross the ribbons to create a latticework or diamond-shaped pattern over the whole board; both will work well.

Learn the skill of SAYING "NO"

If someone wants you to do something that is going to take a lot of your time, take a moment to think about it and consider what will actually be involved. Do you really want to take on the time commitment and, in many cases, the stress and aggravation that come with it? Also think about whether there will be any benefit to you in taking on the task.

✳ Examine the reasons why you might say yes to the request. Is it really something you would do without question, such as helping a friend in need or standing in for someone on a task that only you can do? You should say yes when, and only when, your heart is in it. Ask yourself if you are worried that if you say no it won't look good or you might lose a friend. Or are you perhaps craving the feeling of being needed?

✳ Learn to say "no" diplomatically. Don't forget it's your time that people are asking of you and you will never get it back again. Give a plausible reason, show empathy and thank people for thinking of you. You might also suggest someone else.

You can outsmart PROCRASTINATION

"Never do today what you can put off until tomorrow" has been the motto of sluggards throughout history. But procrastination is often not so much laziness as the difficulty that many of us experience making a start on certain tasks. The problem can be serious enough for some people to seek professional help from a psychologist. As the saying goes, the first step is always the hardest.

✳ There are a few tricks to help you overcome your inner procrastinator. One especially useful technique is to write a to-do list at the start of each day or week and refer to it throughout the day. A list will keep you from forgetting (or subconsciously ignoring) important tasks and gives you a sense of accomplishment when you check off the things you have completed.

An old writer's trick: never try to start a writing task by sitting down in front of a sheet of blank paper.

✳ A task that involves writing, such as writing a letter, can pose a problem for many of us. Here's an old writer's trick: never try to start a writing task by sitting down in front of a sheet of blank paper. There is virtually no better way to stop your thoughts dead and make your mind go blank. Start by making some notes – collect your thoughts and jot down words as they cross your mind. When you have done that, you will find yourself in the midst of the exercise and should have so many ideas on hand that writing will come easily.

Save time Another useful strategy is to make small lists – for instance, the tools you need to do a job such as hanging a picture that has been lying around for ages. Bring the tools together one by one and cross them off the list. Once you build up the momentum, you will have everything ready and you will get the job done in no time.

JUST SAY NO

LEARN TO SAY "NO" DIPLOMATICALLY.

THE SUREST WAY TO PREVENT FORGETTING IMPORTANT EVENTS IS TO KEEP A PLANNER.

Keep a diary to FIGHT FORGETFULNESS

We all have appointments to keep track of and tasks to do – household chores such as cleaning, shopping and cooking, doctor's appointments, hairdresser's appointments, dates of events happening at our kids' schools, birthdays, parties, getting the car serviced and inspected, filing a tax return, going to the bank – the list goes on. With so much going on, it can be easy to forget something important. The surest way to prevent this is to keep a planner.

✳ If you prefer to have things written down on paper and you want other members of your household to see what's coming up, a good solution is to hang a large year planner up on the kitchen wall. Onto it, write down events that are specific to the current year, such as the dates on which trips start and end, as well as recurring events, such as birthdays and wedding anniversaries.

STRESS-FREE APPOINTMENT TRACKING

1 Every time you make an appointment, write it in your diary immediately. You run the risk of forgetting it otherwise.

2 Make a firm habit of checking your diary every morning. Cast an eye over the next few days, too, since many appointments require some preparation, such as gathering together necessary documents.

3 Write in all the information you need for each appointment – a contact phone number is essential, plus any important details, such as what you need to prepare for the appointment, anything you need to bring along, and other important dates or addresses. This will save you the trouble of trying to pull this all together when you are in a hurry.

4 Keep your diary with you at all times, including when you go travelling. That way you won't forget to wish Uncle Harry a happy birthday while you are on vacation in Bali.

✳ Another option for keeping track of appointments, especially over a long period of time, is to use an index card system. This consists of a box filled with appointment cards separated by 13 divider cards – one divider for each month of the current year and one for the following year. If you're a stickler for being organized, this system has some appealing advantages. This is how it works: every appointment (both individual and recurring appointments) gets written on a card with all the necessary details – date and time, nature of the appointment, contact number, address if required, plus any additional notes. At the start of every month, you take the cards for that month out of the box and place them neatly on a central bulletin board. If you have a large household, using a different card color for each person will help everyone see which appointments are specific to them.

ELECTRONIC CALENDARS
make life easier

If computers and smartphones are already part of your everyday life, keep your calendar and contact list electronically and synchronize all your devices through a cloud-based service. This means that when you make a note of an appointment in one

device it will automatically appear on the calendars of all your other devices. If it suits you, share your calendar with the rest of your household.

Easy fix Use your electronic calendar to remind you of your appointments automatically. This can be set to an hour, a day or even a week before.

Save stress by BEING ON TIME

Some people find it so hard to be punctual they'd probably be late to their own funeral. If this sounds like you, you should try to overcome your tendency to run late because it's likely to mean you are stressed, in a rush a lot of the time and putting other people out. Here are a few tips that can help get into the habit of being on time.

✳ When you have an appointment, don't try to "quickly" get something else done beforehand. The same goes for checking emails or voicemail. This is a guaranteed way to make yourself late.

✳ Give yourself plenty of time to gather together everything you want to take with you so you don't have to start doing this at the last minute. In a rush, you are likely to forget half the things you need.

✳ Plan your travel times to include a buffer for late-running public transport or traffic jams. If your trip usually takes 30 minutes, for example, allow 40. You can virtually always count on some sort of delay.

Save money If you are running late and can't find a parking spot, don't be tempted to park illegally. You will only end up wearing the cost of a parking fine. Keep looking until you find a spot, accept that you are going to be late, and leave yourself more time next time.

SHARE YOUR CLOUD-BASED APPOINTMENT CALENDAR WITH YOUR HOUSEHOLD.

Get your FINANCES IN ORDER

To stick to the basic principle of not spending more money than you earn, you need to know the exact details of your financial situation – and this is an area where many people lack clear information. Here are a few tips that can help you stay on top of your finances.

~~~~~~~~~~~~~~~~~~~~~~

You need to know the exact details of your financial situation.

~~~~~~~~~~~~~~~~~~~~~~

✳ The first step is to work out your exact household income, which is usually easy to determine.

✳ Next, gather together all the details of your fixed costs: rent or mortgage, electricity, gas, insurance, taxes, cell phone, subscriptions, installment payment plans, interest payments, daycare fees, and so on. An easy way to get these figures is to look through your bank statements.

✳ The third element is your variable or discretionary expenses – the money you spend on things such as food, clothing and gas. Make a rough estimate of several months' worth of these expenses. If you always use your credit card at the supermarket or gas station, it will be easy to pull the figures out of your credit card statement. If not, make a note of every purchase you make over a few months.

✳ Now add your fixed and average variable expenses together and estimate how much money you have left over each month. If there is nothing left over and you consistently end up in the red, it's time to ask yourself a few questions: Are you paying too much for where you are living? Are your hobbies costing you too much money? Do you have a tendency to buy things you don't need?

Save money To get out of debt, ask your bank about a personal loan. The interest rate on a loan could much be less than the fees and interest you might be paying on an overdrawn account.

PLANNING A TRIP

MAKE A LIST	Make a list of what you need: clothes, shoes, toiletries bag, reading material, electronic devices (and chargers), travel adapters for power points.
AIRPLANE LUGGAGE	Before flying, find out your carry-on luggage allowance. Be aware that with some discount airlines, the ticket price includes carry-on luggage only. If you want to check your bags, extra fees may apply. In some cases, these fees can be more than the price of the ticket itself.
LABEL YOUR BAGS	Black is a popular color for suitcases so it's a good idea to make yours stand out with a brightly colored tag, sticker or strap. Write both your home and destination addresses on your luggage tags.
KEEP A COPY OF YOUR TRAVEL DOCUMENTS	Before you leave, scan your travel documents (passport and airline tickets) and send copies to your personal email address. If you lose the originals in transit, head to an internet cafe and print out copies. This will make the process of getting replacement documents easier.

chapter 3

A House to Call Home

Which place is right for me?

You know you're in the right home when you feel at ease as soon as you walk through the front door. If that doesn't happen in your current home, think about what it is that you don't like about the place. If you then decide it's time to move, consider these things to help you avoid repeating past mistakes.

Be clear about YOUR NEEDS

If you are not happy with where you are living or if you need to upsize, downsize or move for another reason, it's time to work out what type of housing will best meet your needs.

✳ The size of a home depends mainly on how many people will be living in it. If you are just one or two, you won't necessarily need a large place; families need much more room.

✳ If you're considering moving into a multi-storey building, you should take into account what floor you'll be living on, especially if it's an older building

without an elevator. The view from three floors up might be spectacular, especially if there aren't many other tall buildings in the neighborhood. If you are young and fit, climbing all those stairs won't be a problem. But even if you are in top shape, you'll have your work cut out lugging a heavy load of groceries or a water cooler bottle upstairs.

✳ Older people should think carefully about moving into this type of apartment, as should families with small children or a baby who would need carrying up and down those stairs several times a day. If that's you, don't underestimate the difficulties that come with living in an upper-floor apartment without an elevator. It really is worth looking for something else on a lower floor or in a building with an elevator.

LOCATION, location, location

Another important consideration in determining how satisfied you'll feel with where you live is the location. What makes an ideal location varies depending on your needs. Age is a factor here, too –

THE VIEW FROM THREE FLOORS UP MIGHT BE SPECTACULAR – BUT IT'S NO GOOD IF THE BUILDING DOESN'T HAVE AN ELEVATOR.

young people need and want different things from their neighborhood than people in their 60s or 70s. Your family situation also plays a role. Young families typically prefer to live in greener areas, ideally with their own garden. Playgrounds, daycare centers and schools need to be close by.

✳ Singles and young people generally prefer to live closer to the hustle and bustle of the city as opposed to the quiet of the outer suburbs or the countryside. Whatever your demographic, convenient access to public transport is a huge plus.

✳ For older people, they like to have a supermarket, hospital and pharmacy all close by. Especially appealing is an indoor shopping center, where you can shop regardless of the weather. Modern shopping centers typically have elevators, ATMs, open-space cafés where you can meet up with friends, and taxi and bus or shuttle services right outside the door – everything you need in one place.

Handy HOUSE-HUNTING hints

If you want to move and are about to start looking for a new place, try to avoid the usual weekend inspection times and make an appointment for early one weekday evening instead. At this hour, streets and apartment buildings will be filled with activity as people arrive home from work. Visiting at this time will give you an indication of how noisy the elevator is when it is busy, and whether you can

Expert advice

How big should my house be?

Your financial situation and personal requirements will both impact on the size of your new home. Usually, this calculation is based on how many people are in your household. With an average floor space of 2,700 sq. ft. in 2013, North America's new homes are among the world's largest. Yet the number of people living in them has been declining steadily over the years – it now hovers at around

2.6 people per household. A home for two or three people does not need to be double or triple the size needed by a single occupant, because shared spaces (kitchen, bathroom, hallways) don't need to be much larger to be used by more people. In contrast, the average home size in Germany is 1,170 sq. ft. and in the UK is just 818 sq. ft. Before thinking that bigger is better, so it's worth bearing these figures in mind.

A LARGE OPEN-PLAN KITCHEN AND LIVING AREA IS IDEAL FOR FAMILIES.

* A large open-plan space where the kitchen flows into the living area is ideal for families. In large families, a lot of time is spent preparing meals. An open-plan design means the person working in the kitchen can keep an eye on what the rest of the family is doing. The downsides are that if the kitchen is untidy it will be on full display when you have visitors, and cooking smells will tend to spread into the living area.

* Older couples may prefer a home that is divided into traditional rooms. Their priorities may include having a presentable separate living room and a large bedroom in which they will feel comfortable in case of illness – health concerns do become more of an issue as we age.

Insider's hack   To avoid territorial disputes and disagreements after moving to a new place, you should work out beforehand how much space each household member needs and who wants a room of their own. It's essential that everyone has their say and expresses their needs clearly.

hear the whirring of a neighbor's washing machine or the elementary-school children upstairs practicing their musical instruments with gusto.

Insider's hack   If you are interested enough after an inspection to consider buying or renting a property, try and speak with one of the next-door neighbors to see what they can tell you about the building, other residents and the neighborhood.

Getting the FLOORPLAN right

How a residence is divided into rooms makes a big difference to how you live in it. In older homes, the rooms are quite separate from one another: living room, dining room, kitchen, bathroom and bedrooms. In other cases, the living area, kitchen and sometimes even the front hall are combined into one multipurpose space.

Think about the FRONT ENTRANCE

It's not just inside the house that bears thinking about with regards to your needs, but the front entrance as well.

* If you use a shopping cart, child's stroller, mobility aid or wheelchair, a smooth path or ramp to the front door, rather than stairs, will make life a lot easier. You can replace steps in the backyard with ramps quite easily, too.

* Proper lighting will make a front entrance safer and make the front of the home more attractive, too.

* It's not mandatory, but it's a good idea to have your house number illuminated so that it's visible at night. At the very least, having a clear number visible makes it easier for the people who deliver your mail, packages, newspapers, and so on.

* Check that the button for the front doorbell is mounted low enough for a child or a person in a wheelchair to reach.

INSTALL A SLIDING DOOR FOR A SEAMLESS TRANSITION BETWEEN YOUR INDOOR AND OUTDOOR SPACES.

✳ Does your mailbox date back several decades? If so, you have probably noticed it is too small for the kind of mail we now typically receive. Instead of grumbling about your letters getting bent out of shape from being jammed into your old mailbox, invest in a new one of a decent size.

Save money A small light over your front door is the only one you should leave on all night. Install motion detectors on all your other external lighting. This will help deter unwanted visitors and save electricity at the same time.

BALCONIES and decks

In the warmer months, a balcony or deck is like a second living room. To gain maximum enjoyment from your outdoor oasis, it's worth putting some thought into how you set it up.

✳ If you have an older home, the balcony or deck may be accessible only through French windows with a high threshold. If you find this awkward, a low step or wooden ramp placed up against the threshold is a relatively simple solution. You could always raise the height of the entire balcony or

deck to match the threshold, but seek professional advice first about which material you might use. Options include sustainable hardwood, composite materials and tiles. Keep in mind that if you raise the height of a balcony, you'll probably have to adjust the height of the railing as well.

✳ Another solution is to do away with the threshold altogether by installing a sliding door between your indoor and outdoor spaces. Newer homes often have sliding doors already built in. If you live in an older building, talk to an architect to find out what would be involved in replacing existing French doors with sliding doors.

✳ It is essential for pavers on balconies and patios to have a non-slip surface.

✳ If you're planning a new balcony railing, ensure that the gaps between the vertical balusters are less than 4 in. – small enough to prevent a child's head from fitting through. The space between the deck and the bottom of the balusters must be no more than 4 in. as well.

TAKE CARE
A tiled floor weighs an enormous amount so it's essential to consult a structural engineer before deciding to lay tiles or pavers on your balcony. If you are renting, you must also gain the landlord's approval before you begin.

Interior decorating

Your home is a place to retreat from the world and unwind, especially at the end of a workday. You should make your home as appealing as possible so that you feel at ease and enjoy spending time there.

PLAYFUL, CREATIVE PEOPLE LIKE TO HAVE A BRIGHT, COLORFUL HOME.

WHICH STYLE suits me best?

To make your home a place you love, and to keep it that way, you need to find your own style of decor and mix it up a bit every now and then – whether it's a splash of color on a feature wall, a new piece of furniture or a revamp of a favorite nook that's been looking tired.

✳ The decor you choose for your rooms is the key for turning your house into a home. Some people like a classic look with antique furniture, some love modern design, and others like to mix different

styles to express their individual taste. Creating an environment to suit your own preferences is not too difficult. You just need to think a little bit about what your preferences are.

✳ A person's character and personal interests will influence their style preferences with decor. Playful, creative people like to have a bright, colorful home. Rational, practical types feel more comfortable in cool, elegant surroundings. They should opt for a minimalist style with a few, high-quality pieces, clean lines and a uniform color scheme.

✳ If a rustic touch appeals to you, farmhouse- or cabin-style decor might be the way to go. If you travel a lot or like to dream about faraway places, you could furnish your home with objects from your travels, together with antique maps and exotic fabrics. If you are good with your hands, you can jazz up your existing furniture and create your own eclectic mix of styles.

MANY WAYS to achieve results

There is, of course, a difference between decorating a room from scratch and updating the existing decor. But there is one rule that applies to every situation: give yourself time. If you are working on an empty room, you first have to get a feel for the space. Go into the room at different times of day to gain a sense of how the light changes. If you are dealing with an already furnished room, try to see the entire space with fresh eyes to work out where things need to be changed. Often, it will take just one or two ideas or adjustments to create a sense of harmony in the room.

✳ If you're ordering new furniture, or reupholstering existing pieces, gather swatches of the fabrics you like so you can test them in place in bright daylight, shade and at night-time. Hold them against other elements in the room, such as rugs, curtains and artwork, to see how the colors and patterns work together. You can buy an inexpensive pinboard and pin your sample fabrics, paint swatches and photos of the new furniture or other ideas for the room to it to create a mood wall. This will help keep your vision on track. Websites such as Pinterest are excellent tools to curate your ideas online.

✳ If you find yourself unable to envision what your empty room is going to look like, it's a good idea to invest in a few neutral basics. Start with a few initial items of furniture, such as a couch, a table and a bookcase, in restrained colors such as white, grey, beige or black, which will combine well with any other colors you choose later on. Eye-popping

RATIONAL, PRACTICAL TYPES FEEL MORE COMFORTABLE IN COOL, ELEGANT SURROUNDINGS.

fashion colors, such as purples, pinks and oranges, right through to various shades of blue and green will all go well with these neutral tones.

Save money   Don't make the mistake of buying a set of new furniture or completely redecorating a room on impulse or in a limited space of time. All too often, we buy things we later regret and then have to put up with the sight of them until we can afford to get something new … which will probably cost even more!

DIFFERENT STROKES
for different folks

There are some practical considerations to take into account when decorating your home. If you live alone, you can focus entirely on what you like. But if you have a family, it pays to be pragmatic and take other people's likes and dislikes into account. If you move often, it's probably not a good idea to lash out

Expert advice

Rooms with high ceilings

Older houses and apartments have wonderful high ceilings and decorative plaster features. But it can be awkward to create a cozy atmosphere in rooms with ceilings 9 ft. high.

★ Draw attention to the lower half of the room by adding a decorative pendant lamp that casts light downwards, or by placing several floor lamps around the room.

★ Another option is to apply wallpaper to a height of about 4 ft. from the floor, and install a picture rail above to offset the wallpaper from the bare wall.

★ To make the most of a room's generous high ceilings, decorate the windows with floor-length curtains – or even curtains that puddle on the floor – and hang large pictures on the walls.

FOR A NEW ATMOSPHERE IN NEXT TO NO TIME, FOCUS ON SOFT FURNISHINGS IN FASHIONABLE COLORS AND PATTERNS.

on that enormous baroque cabinet that looked so good in the antiques shop; opt instead for light-weight multipurpose furniture.

Easy fix Instead of wearing yourself out trudging around to all your local furniture shops, stay at home, put your feet up and flip through a few home decorating magazines and books to get inspired. Or browse the websites of furniture makers and shops that sell soft furnishings and decorative objects. These sites will help you develop your own ideas.

Old house, NEW LOOK

Fashions in interior design are no different from those on the runway – what's on-trend one day will be passé the next. Eventually, we reach a point where we're tired of looking at our old things and are ready to give our home a new look. This doesn't mean replacing absolutely everything – after all, who has the time, money or inclination to redecorate their house completely every couple of years? You can make a big difference around the house with just a few small, inexpensive touches.

✳ Just because we liked something a few years ago doesn't mean we'll still be partial to it today. The first step is to recognize when it's time to let something go. When we move on from certain styles or items, it can be a sign of our own personal development or a change in our living situation. Take action and don't hang on to something you really don't like any more.

The first step is to recognize when it's time to let something go.

✳ For maximum effect with minimum effort, focus on soft furnishings such as cushions, curtains and throws. Choose fabrics in fashionable colors and patterns for a new atmosphere in next to no time.

ACHIEVE A DRAMATIC EFFECT WITH NEW WALLPAPER – IT'S COME BACK FROM THE FASHION WILDERNESS.

✳ Be brave. If you are redecorating a room, choose some unique pieces to give the space its individual character. Possible suggestions include: a handwoven fabric throw for your couch, a distinctive vintage vase or bowl from a flea market, or an exquisite chair left to you by your grandmother. You should have some sort of emotional connection with the items you choose. Unusual objects need to be something that you enjoy looking at, otherwise they will seem really out of place in your home. Don't be afraid to be adventurous – if your idea doesn't work, there are ways to reverse the change without great expense.

✳ Inject color with a bold painting or print with a striking motif or colors. Some galleries let you take home a painting and live with it in place before you commit to buying, so you've nothing to lose.

✳ You can achieve a dramatic effect with wallpaper. Wallpaper has been in the fashion wilderness for a couple of decades but it's been making a comeback more recently. Whether you are applying wallpaper to a bare wall or papering over an existing wall covering, new wallpaper will change the appearance of a room enormously, creating new accents and giving the space a different feel.

Save money Applying wallpaper yourself is easy to do and will cost less than hiring a tradesperson. Ask for advice at your local hardware store.

SHIFTING FURNITURE around

Merely changing the position of your furniture can also create a completely different feel in a room.

✳ In a room that serves multiple purposes, such as a living room, you can rearrange the furniture to create separate spaces. A good way to do this is with a visual room divider, such as an open bookcase or generously proportioned sofa.

✳ Use rearranging the living room furniture as an opportunity to correct a commonly made mistake – that of lining up all the furniture against the walls. It's an incorrect belief that pushing furniture against the walls makes a room seem larger. Try moving the sofa into the middle of the room or placing a bookcase at right angles to add dimension and depth.

Insider's hack Use grid paper to play around with different ideas for arranging your room, by cutting out pieces to scale to represent the various items of furniture. You may find you come up with ideas you would not have thought of otherwise. You can also use your computer to help you design your room. Look for videos online about creating floorplans with programs such as Excel.

The effect of color

Whatever your design style, colors are a key in setting the mood and creating a sense of comfort. To ensure the colors you choose have a positive effect in your home, it's important to understand a few things about them and how they work.

CHOOSING COLORS IS HIGHLY SATISFYING, BUT YOU NEED TO HAVE GOOD INTUITION.

A quick lesson in COLOR THEORY

There is a lot of satisfaction in achieving the perfect harmony between materials, light and colors when decorating your home, but you need to have good intuition and understand a few basic principles to create the right effect. This is particularly true when it comes to choosing colors.

✳ A basic way of classifying colors is into warm and cool, and light and dark. Within these broad categories there are, of course, various degrees and permutations. Each of the four color groups has a distinct effect on our mood.

✳ Warm colors, such as bright reds and yellows, are stimulating to the senses – they're usually avoided in rooms where we want to relax. As these colors simulate the effect of sunlight, they are especially good for rooms that don't receive direct sun. In rooms that have a red or yellow color scheme, we perceive the temperature to be higher than it actually is.

We perceive the temperature to be higher in rooms that have a red or yellow color scheme.

✳ Cool colors – namely blues and greens – have a calming effect, making them especially suitable for bedrooms. The cooling sensation created by shimmering blue, mint and turquoise shades is ideal for bathrooms or sunny rooms that tend to get overheated in the summertime.

✳ Light colors – with a high proportion of white in the mix – include pale greens and blues as well as subtle yellows and oranges. These colors are friendly, bright and airy and they lighten the mood of the room.

TAKE CARE

Some think the color red stimulates aggression so it's probably not a good idea to decorate a bedroom or child's room in an overpowering shade of red.

✳ Dark colors – browns, charcoal shades, strong purples and deep blues, all with a high proportion of black in the mix – can have a gloomy, constricting effect. But when used judiciously, they create a sense of being tucked away and cozy.

Use color to overcome
STRUCTURAL LIMITS

Colors can help you make the most of a room's structural parameters. The right choice of color can make a room seem larger, smaller, higher or lower.

The basic rule of thumb is that darker colors have a diminishing, shrinking effect, while lighter colors create a sense of greater space and height. Utilize these properties to make the most out of your home's rooms.

✳ Small rooms will feel larger and more airy if you keep colors as light as possible.

✳ You can make large rooms seem more cozy and inviting by choosing warm, darker colors such as rich shades of red.

✳ Rooms with low ceilings will feel higher if you paint the ceiling a lighter color than the walls. A narrow cornice between the wall and ceiling will make the color transition a smooth one.

✳ You can visually lower a high ceiling when you paint it a darker color, but take care with really dark colors as they can visually bring the ceiling right down and feel oppressive.

✳ Bright, vibrant colors will make a narrow hallway feel longer and wider.

Expert advice

Demystifying the color wheel

Color wheels show the relationships between colors. German painter and art teacher Johannes Itten developed his version of the color wheel in the 1920s. According to Itten's color theory, there are three primary colors – red, blue and yellow; the primary colors mix with each other to form three secondary colors – green (yellow + blue), violet (blue + red) and orange (red + yellow). The primary colors then mix with the secondary to produce six tertiary colors – blue-green, blue-violet, red-violet, red-orange, yellow-orange and yellow-green. Itten's wheel shows the relationships between each of these colors. When it comes to choosing colors for your home, the wheel can help you to achieve certain effects:

★ You may choose to stick to one color but use different tones (levels of brightness) of that color. This creates a sense of calm.

★ Or, you could use harmonious colors – those that lie adjacent to one another on the color wheel – to create a natural sense of coherence.

★ Another option is to combine complementary colors – those that lie on opposite sides of the wheel and therefore contrast most strongly with one another. Complementary colors create a dynamic, dramatic effect.

✳ Warm, luminous colors such as yellow can compensate for the lack of natural light in dark rooms with small, south-facing windows.

Save money Light-colored walls reflect light back into the room. This reduces the need to keep lamps or overhead lights on during the day, thus saving on electricity.

Choosing the RIGHT COLOR

When it comes to deciding on your home's color scheme, it pays to be systematic. Take a close look at the fixed color elements that are already in the room – for instance, the flooring and any furniture that is going to remain as is – then select your new colors with these in mind. It's important to work with the existing colors rather than against them.

✳ If you are changing the whole room's complete color scheme, take a different approach. In this situation, choose any colors you like but you still should take into account the size and how much natural light the room gets.

✳ If you are not sure which color, a safe bet is to use neutral tones – white, beige or pale grey – on large surfaces. Both lighter tints and darker shades of these colors are calming in the room. They're a good choice for walls and curtains. The different tones also coordinate well with each other, so you can create layers of neutrals in the one room.

✳ The next step is to line up the upholstery fabrics, curtains, cushions and accessories you are going to use in the room. If you limit yourself to a single color, you will create a tranquil ambience but it can look a bit boring. One way to counteract this is to utilize a variety of different materials, with items made of wood, fabric, ceramic, glass and metal. Your featured color will appear different next to or reflected in each of these surfaces.

~~~~~~

The same color will appear different next to or reflected in different materials.

~~~~~~

✳ Another way to liven up a uniform color scheme is to choose contrasting patterns in the same color for upholstery, curtains and cushions.

✳ To create an atmosphere that is both harmonious and dynamic, use accent colors that are adjacent on the color wheel to your base color – for example, grass green as the base color with yellow-green or blue-green accents.

RESTRICTING YOURSELF TO DIFFERENT TONES OF ONE COLOR WILL CREATE A SENSE OF CALM.

USING TWO COMPLEMENTARY COLORS, SUCH AS BLUE AND YELLOW, CAN CREATE A STRIKING EFFECT.

✳ Using two complementary colors, such as blue and yellow, can create a striking effect, even more so if the room has an otherwise restrained color scheme. A white, grey or beige background will allow contrasting colors to really pop, while also providing areas of visual repose. Complementary colors are best reserved as accent colors on soft furnishings such as cushions, curtains and other accessories, but also consider using them on larger surfaces such as a feature wall, a rug, or a throw.

✳ If you want to use strong accent colors, limit yourself to cushions and smaller accessories to begin with to judge the effect. Experiment with red, green, blue, orange, pink, purple and turquoise – there's no limit so long as it's a color you like.

Don't overlook
the PRACTICALITIES

To avoid unpleasant surprises after bringing a new item home from the store – "But those bright purple curtains looked so good in the window!" – arm yourself with as much information as possible before making a purchase. Pick up paint swatches or sample cans of paint from the hardware store, and ask for samples of any wallpaper or fabric you might be considering. If you are redoing your floors, request wood samples or a carpet sample book from a specialist retailer.

✳ Don't just look at sample swatches in the shop; bring them home so you can see what they look like in combination with the light and the existing furnishings in the room. Leave them in the room for a good week – even paint patches of different paint colors onto the wall – so you can get a feel for how they look, and make an informed decision.

Easy fix Buy some home decorating magazines. They often have articles devoted to color, with experts showing combinations that work well and are in tune with the latest trends.

Save money We all make bad purchasing decisions from time to time. Make sure the store has a returns policy when buying cushion covers and other accessories.

TAKE CARE

If you have a number of bookcases in your living room, don't overload the room with color. Book covers are usually quite colorful and add a lot of busyness and interest to the room already.

Building material basics

In addition to your choice of decor, accessories and colors, what materials you use on the walls, floors and soft furnishings play an important role in creating your home's style. Choosing the right materials helps to create an inviting living space.

WOOD IS A CLASSIC CHOICE AND REMAINS ONE OF THE MOST ELEGANT FLOORING MATERIALS AVAILABLE.

The BEST FLOORING for your home

Comfy soft-pile carpets, hard-wearing tiles, beautiful wood floors, or affordable laminate – there are many flooring options on the market so how do you decide what's best for you? Knowing a few things about each material, and its pros and cons, can help make your decision easier.

✳ A wood floor is a classic choice and wood remains one of the most elegant materials available. A parquet floor, for example, can have the individual woods laid in different patterns, such as straight, herringbone and basket weave. Floors may be solid hardwood or softwood with a hardwood veneer. There is an almost endless range of woods available: ash, bamboo, beech, cherry, hickory, maple, oak, teak and walnut just to name a few. The sheer variety lends itself to myriad design possibilities and there is a wood to suit just about every style of decor.

✳ Wood floors are both hard-wearing and long-lasting. When the surface starts to wear, just sand it back. There may be a limit on how many times a floor can be sanded, however, depending on the thickness of the wood or wood veneer. Cheaply made laminated floors might only stand up to being sanded back once, whereas floors with a thicker surface wood layer can be sanded back several times. After the floor has been sanded, you will need to reseal it so that it resists spills and water stains.

✳ Wood has humidity-regulating properties that improve a room's air quality. Its thermal insulating properties make it a warm surface to walk on; it is also suitable for underfloor heating. One of wood's disadvantages is that it readily conducts the sound of footsteps and other noises. It is not recommended to use wood in bathroom and other "wet area" floors. Depending on the species, quality and how it is laid, parquet flooring can be quite expensive.

✳ Laminate and vinyl floors are a popular choice. They consist of a base layer, usually MDF board, topped with a decorative appliqué layer (often printed to look like wood boards) and sealed with a hard layer of resin. The layers are pressed together under considerable heat and pressure, making laminate especially hard-wearing. It is also impact-resistant, easy to care for and simple to install yourself – you can lay it as a "floating floor" over the top of another flooring material. There is now a wide range of designs available and high-quality laminate has a stylish, natural appearance as opposed to looking like cheap imitation wood. Compared to wood, laminate is also relatively affordable.

CARPET FLOORS HAVE MANY ADVANTAGES – THEY ARE NON-SLIP, WARM AND SOUND-ABSORBING.

High-quality laminate and vinyl flooring has a stylish, natural appearance while also being relatively affordable.

✳ One of laminate's big disadvantages is that it is sensitive to moisture and you can only use it in bathrooms under certain conditions. It also readily conducts the sound of footsteps so it is essential to use a sound-absorbing underlay. Vinyl flooring, on the other hand, is more water resistant than laminate and good for kitchens, bathrooms, and basements.

✳ A carpet floor covering has a big impact on the look and feel of a room, so you need to consider your choice of material carefully. It's also important that the color and pattern complement the rest of your decor. Carpet is not something we change all that frequently so make sure you choose something you won't get tired of looking at very soon.

✳ Carpets are made of either wool or a synthetic material such as nylon or polyester. Blended fibers are also common. The two main types of carpet are loop pile and cut pile (also known as plush pile). The underside of carpet is typically made of woven jute or foam. An alternative to carpet are floor coverings made from natural fibers such as sisal, jute and coconut fiber – these are typically woven so they lie flat on the floor without a pile.

✳ Carpeted floors have many advantages: they are non-slip, warm, sound-absorbing, soft to walk on and offer a wide range of design possibilities. On the downside, carpets can harbor dust mites – an issue that people with allergies should definitely take into account. Carpet floors are also not easy to keep clean, especially in high-traffic areas. Because the carpet in these areas gets walked on much more than elsewhere in the house, it tends to wear out sooner. Your only solution in this situation may be to place an area rug over the top until the time comes to re-carpet the entire house.

TILES ARE HARD-WEARING, EASY TO LOOK AFTER AND WORK WELL IN ALL AREAS OF THE HOME.

✳ Tiles are great flooring options that work well in any area of the home, including the kitchen, bathroom, hallway and courtyard. Tiles are hard-wearing, easy to look after and versatile – there are heat-resistant varieties perfect for around a fireplace and slip-resistant materials that are ideal in external applications such as a balcony or courtyard.

✳ Modern manufacturing techniques can create a wide variety of surface finishes, including tiles that resemble sandstone, marble or granite in both appearance and texture, as well as glazes in many fashionable colors and patterns. Tiles can range in size from 1 in x 1 in mosaic style squares to 12 in x 24 in tiles – consider combining different sizes for a stylish result.

✳ An advantage of tiles is that you can create a uniform floor covering throughout the entire house, eliminating awkward steps or thresholds between different areas. Tiles are easy to clean, usually just needing a wipe-down with a damp cloth or wet mop, which is ideal for anyone allergic to household dust. Tough and durable, tiles are long-lasting, which is good for both the environment and your wallet. Generally, the only reason you'll need to replace a tile floor is for aesthetic considerations.

✳ Tile floors have some disadvantages: they are cold underfoot, especially in winter. If you are planning on installing a tile floor in a new home, consider installing underfloor heating at the same time.

Easy fix Hooked on the beauty of wood, but crave the easy maintenance of tiles – perhaps in the bathroom or kitchen? Ask your flooring specialist about tiles that look like wood. It's practically impossible to tell these tiles apart from real wood.

Insider's hack The pattern of a tile or parquet floor can change the way a room looks, for instance making a narrow room seem wider. But it's not easy to judge this effect as a layperson, so it's best to seek advice from a professional.

Save money If you have areas where the floor is subject to a lot of wear and tear but you still want to carpet them, you might consider needle felt carpet (a synthetic felted carpet tiles). This is extremely durable and good value for money. In the past, carpet tiles were mostly used in commercial offices, but are now available for residential use. Carpet tiles can be rotated to spread or minimize wearing.

TAKE CARE

Don't purchase parquet flooring from a potentially dubious source, such as an online dealer. Be especially wary with tropical woods, which may be subject to export bans. There is a global black market in illegally logged wood. Stick with reputable, local wood sellers and sustainably sourced wood.

Treat YOUR WALLS right

A new wall treatment can provide a room with a whole new atmosphere. Walls don't always have to be plain white paint. If you don't feel at ease in a room or are starting to find it boring, it's time for a change. There are many options to choose from: giving it a fresh coat of paint, applying a textured paint, covering the wall with wallpaper or fabric, or even wood panelling.

Low odor and quick-drying, acrylic paints are easy to apply.

✳ Painting is the most straightforward way to decorate a wall. The type of paint you choose will make a difference to the end result. Water-based acrylic (or latex paint), containing color pigments and binding agents, is the most common type of interior wall paint. If you are going to do the job yourself, pay close attention to the paint's coverage rate and scrub resistance properties. A standard, good-quality wall paint will usually get the job done with a minimal number of coats. Acrylic paints go on smoothly and evenly, are low odor and dry quickly, meaning that with adequate ventilation, you will be able to use the room again in a short space of time.

✳ Natural paints, free from chemical solvents, are an alternative to conventional latex paints. They are the best option for maintaining healthy indoor air quality and are well suited to allergy sufferers and families with young children.

✳ Drawing inspiration from the Mediterranean, textured treatments are highly fashionable and allow for a wide variety of finishes. There is a range of texturing materials to choose from depending on the result you wish to achieve. After cleaning the wall surface, you apply the textured material using one of several possible techniques. A textured roller or a trowel is the most straightforward way, with the tool creating a textured surface as the material is applied. More elaborate finishing techniques involve using brushes or sponges, which you rub over the surface to create attractive patterns with interesting effects of light and shade. Wood planks are also quite popular, placed either parallel or perpendicular to the floor.

✳ An old favorite, wallpaper is very much back in vogue. With countless colors, patterns and textures in every style imaginable, wallpaper can make your walls truly eye-catching. Most modern wallpapers use non-woven wallpaper stock – this is a mixture of synthetic and natural fibers that is durable and washable. Many are "paste-the-wall" papers, where the glue is applied to the wall and the paper is laid on top. Different printing techniques are used, from traditional offset to digital printing; each offers a different texture and finish. Pay attention to the thickness – if you choose a very thin wallpaper the smallest imperfection in the wall surface will show through so you'll probably need to apply a layer of lining paper first.

AN OLD FAVORITE, WALLPAPER IS VERY MUCH BACK IN VOGUE.

WOOD PANELLING IS SUITABLE IN AREAS WHERE WALLPAPER WOULD LIKELY BE TO GET DAMAGED.

✳ If your wall's surface has irregularities, thicker papers and textured wallpapers are better able to conceal them. Some wallpaper is designed to split so that when you want to apply new wallpaper, the top layer can be peeled off dry, leaving behind a lower layer that acts as lining paper.

✳ Really heavy textured or embossed wallpaper, however, is not easy to work with. The profiled surface is typically built up with sprayed on or expanded polymers.

✳ Synthetic wallpapers are a practical alternative to traditional paper. They are especially easy to put up as the adhesive is applied directly to the wall, eliminating the need to lay out the wallpaper on a pasting table. Synthetic wallpapers are good at concealing irregularities in the wall surface, and they are designed to be easy to remove, with the top layer simply peeling away.

✳ Fabric wallpapers, with a surface layer made from silk, linen, cotton, jute or synthetic fibers, look very elegant. Depending on the fabric used, the finish can be either smooth, rippled, fine or coarse. Fabric wallpapers last a long time.

✳ More unusual options include murals and magnetic wallpapers. Mural-style wallpapers have no pattern repeat. The highest-quality products are produced by wallpaper manufacturers who use the best digital printing technology to produce standard-size and custom printed murals. Magnetic wallpapers consist of fine iron particles on a substrate of vinyl, which make the paper receptive to magnets – which is ideal for a home office or children's bedroom.

✳ If you have a wall with a particularly rough, unattractive surface, or an area where wallpaper is likely to get damaged, wall panelling is a good option. To cover a wall in panelling, you'll need to first install a substructure upon which to mount the panelling. You can use a wide range of materials, among them traditional wood panelling, which range from inexpensive panels available from a hardware store to fine joinery crafted by a skilled carpenter. Other possible covering materials include fabric, painted particle board, colored acrylic sheets, stainless steel or pressed metal, and even glass.

TAKE CARE

External siding should be of durable materials, which are properly insulated and sealed. It should also be treated to resist destructive pests, decay or mold growth.

Getting the light right

Natural light is the most important kind of light to have in your home. But the layout of a house won't always allow enough natural light to reach every room. Used well, artificial light sources can compensate for this and produce a pleasing ambiance.

GOOD LIGHTING isn't accidental

Lighting your home takes careful planning to create an inviting atmosphere and get the most out of each room. Whether it's your living room, bedroom, child's bedroom or study, getting the lighting right has such a profound effect on the feel of a room that it really does deserve careful thought. A well-thought-out lighting concept will ensure you have light available precisely where you need it.

✳ Every room and every person has specific lighting needs. In the living room and bedrooms, indirect light is usually adequate and creates a pleasant atmosphere. More light is needed over the dining table – pendant lights that shine downwards are suitable here. Proper lighting over kitchen counters makes cutting, chopping and cooking tasks much easier and safer. Plenty of light is also important in the bathroom – a combination of ceiling lights and spotlights over the mirror can work well.

✳ The most appropriate lighting for your child's bedroom will depend on their age and activities. For older children who do homework in their room, direct lighting over the desk is essential. A night light can help small children get to sleep more easily. Remember that any light you choose for a child's bedroom must be child safe (see page 194, "Child-proof from top to bottom").

✳ If you are building or finalizing a new house, or are having renovation work done, plan on installing a few extra electrical outlets to give yourself more lighting options.

OFF-CENTERED LIGHTING CREATES POOLS OF LIGHT, LENDING PLENTY OF VARIATION TO YOUR LIVING ROOM.

✳ A room that is flooded with bright light and has no shadows can feel stark and uninviting, a bit like a hospital waiting room. Off-centered lighting creates pools of light, lending plenty of variation to your living room. Play around with light. Use spotlights to highlight pictures, books or other special features in

WHEN BUYING A LAMP, ENSURE THE LIGHT SOURCE IS COVERED.

the room. Don't be afraid to create a dramatic effect – lights can always be turned off. You don't need to have them all switched on at once.

✳ When buying a lamp, ensure the light source is adequately covered – you don't want to be staring at a naked light bulb. The spiral energy-saving bulbs in particular need to be under a shade – they don't look very attractive on their own and provide the best light only when properly shaded.

Save money Lights are often left on even when there's no one in the room. Save electricity by turning lights off when you leave a room. Lights over the kitchen counter are also often left on for no good reason, needlessly wasting money.

Do you have enough NATURAL LIGHT?

Houses and apartments are often designed so that the living and dining rooms receive as much natural light as possible. Another common design principle is to have bedrooms facing east as morning sunlight can boost our energy levels. But what do you do if these design ideals are simply not achievable in your home? There are various ways to make excessively dark or bright areas more comfortable.

✳ If none of the windows in a room gets direct sunlight, you can install a mirror or mirrored tiles on a wall near the windows to reflect more light into the room.

✳ Hallways are often long, dark and narrow. These areas need to be illuminated evenly to make them brighter and more cheerful. Well-considered hallway lighting generally consists of several light sources that give the space structure. Recessed or pot lights, that is lights recessed into the ceiling, are good for narrow or low-ceilinged hallways. They're best located so that they cast an arc of light onto

PLAY AROUND WITH SPOTLIGHTS TO HIGHLIGHT PAINTINGS, BOOKS OR IMPORTANT OBJECTS.

the hallway walls. Lights suspended on cables or tracks are a more flexible option, allowing the position of the lights to be changed easily.

✳ In many homes, central areas such as bathrooms, hallways and staircases that aren't on an external wall are windowless. Without good lighting, these spaces can be oppressively dark. Installing a skylight may be an option for these areas. There are different varieties – fixed skylights consist of a flat window that cannot be opened; ventilating skylights are similar but can be opened with a pole attachment or remote control; and tubular skylights or sky tubes consist of a small dome and reflective tube that directs the light inside the house. A skylight can be expensive to install but it will reduce your ongoing costs by saving electricity.

Protect rooms from SUNLIGHT AND GLARE

Most people appreciate sunshine but, as pleasant as a sun-drenched room can be, the sun can be glary and hard on the eyes, especially in the height of summer. Too much sunlight can also cause your upholstery, carpets and wood furniture to fade. There are several ways to protect the inside of our homes from strong sunlight.

✳ External shutters, roller blinds or awnings provide effective sun protection, as they deflect sunlight away from the building.

✳ Vertical and venetian blinds can also provide effective protection from sunlight and glare. Made from synthetic fabric, wood or metal, these blinds are hung inside the window much like curtains. You can adjust the angle of the blades to provide more or less shade depending on the time of day.

✳ Panel blinds, which slide along tracks, are an attractive option. The panels reduce the intensity of direct sunlight and eliminate glare while still allowing diffused light into the room.

✳ Roman and roller blinds offer similar advantages to panel blinds in that some kinds allow diffused light into a room, while other kinds are available as

VERTICAL BLINDS PROVIDE EFFECTIVE PROTECTION FROM SUNLIGHT AND GLARE.

Expert advice

A light to read by

If you enjoy reading in the evenings, you need to have a good light.

★ Adjust your reading lamp so the light falls directly upon the book in your hands. If not, the words will soon start to swim before your eyes. Angle the light to come in from the side to stop troublesome reflections caused by light shining down onto bright white pages.

★ Any of the commonly available types of light bulb are suitable for a reading lamp, including energy-saving compact fluorescents, LED bulbs and low-voltage halogens. Bear in mind that as we get older we need up to twice the level of brightness to see as comfortably as we did when younger.

blockout blinds. There's not much difference between roller and roman shades, except that roman shades consist of horizontal panels that accordion up when raised.

Options for OUTDOOR LIGHTING

Whether it's at the front entrance, on the deck or in the garden, exterior lighting not only increases safety but also should enhance the atmosphere outside the home.

✳ Lighting is essential around entrances such as the front door and driveway. Proper lighting helps you find the way in and ensures that steps and any other trip hazards are easy to see. Your lighting here should be bright but not so bright as to dazzle guests and passers-by.

✳ Don't forget walkways. Appropriate lighting on paths lets you see steps and other obstacles before you stumble over them. Install lights at regular intervals along longer walkways to ensure the entire area is adequately lit and there are no "black holes."

CREATE BEAUTIFUL HIGHLIGHTS WITH FAIRY LIGHTS, WHICH LEND A TOUCH OF MAGIC TO PATIOS.

✳ Judicious lighting throughout your backyard will prevent it from disappearing into the darkness at night. This will allow you to use your outdoor space in the evenings, especially in summer, when the balmy evenings are perfect for dining outside or simply enjoying the company of friends.

✳ Lighting can create beautiful highlights in the garden, too. Strings of fairy lights lend a touch of magic to garden parties, while in-ground lights produce pools of light in the lawn or garden beds. Consider uplights to highlight feature plants.

✳ Especially elegant in the garden are LED spheres and cubes, which either sit on the ground or hang as pendant lamps. As they are waterproof, you can even float them in the pool or pond. If you want something even more striking, you might like the idea of a few illuminated stools and side tables as furniture.

✳ Don't just think about decorative garden lighting in the summer months. With night falling earlier in winter, the right lighting can turn your garden into a fairy-tale landscape, especially if you live in an area where it snows.

Easy fix If you like the idea of keeping your garden lighting flexible so you can vary the effect from time to time, opt for spotlights or flood lights mounted on stakes driven into the ground rather than hardwired lighting. This will let you highlight different features at specific times, such as beautiful rose bush or a plant in full bloom.

Save money Create an enchanted garden at night using simple paper lanterns with tea lights inside – without using much effort or any electricity.

Add a touch of greenery

The sight of lush green leaves and beautiful flowers can really lift our spirits. With a little knowledge of plant care, you can nurture and appreciate thriving greenery not only out in the garden but also on decks and balconies as well as indoors.

INDOOR SPOTS for pots

Tropical and subtropical plants have a special appeal for those of us who live in temperate regions. You can construct a flourishing paradise in and around your home with beautiful exotic plants that thrive indoors, on balconies or in containers. For lasting enjoyment from your potted plants, you need to position them where conditions most resemble their native environment.

✳ As sun moves with the seasons, the amount of natural light entering a room changes throughout the year. For example, in a room with a south-facing window shaded by a large deciduous tree, it will be quite warm on the windowsill in summer but not necessarily bright and sunny. In winter, on the other hand, the sun will shine straight in through the bare branches of the tree outside. A north-facing window on an upper floor of an apartment building will get more sun than a north-facing one on the ground floor shaded by evergreen shrubs. Even lightweight curtains will reduce the light intensity in a room. The size of your windows and the changing length of the day at different times of the year also play a significant role in how much light a particular spot receives.

✳ Most indoor plants prefer a warm, bright position where the air is not too dry. Phalaenopsis orchids, one of the most varied, beautiful and hardy orchid species, will thrive under these conditions.

✳ Sunrooms and rooms with windows facing south, east or west will typically provide warm and sunny, although somewhat dry, conditions. These locations may receive several hours of direct sunlight a day and are suitable for plants native to tropical or subtropical regions, such as fiddle leaf fig tree, snake plants, rubber tree, and palms including kentia, bamboo, majestic, dracaena, ponytail and sago.

PHALAENOPSIS ORCHIDS THRIVE IN A WARM, BRIGHT POSITION WHERE THE AIR IS NOT TOO DRY.

✳ Tropical and subtropical rainforest species will flourish in warm, humid, semi-shaded locations. A warm, moist bathroom window is a good place for plants such as Chinese evergreens, alocasia, rhipsalis, streptocarpus, philodendron, anthurium, miltonia orchids, bird's-nest ferns and African violets. Ferns, spider plants and peach lily will also do well in bathrooms that get plenty of light. If you have enough space, a small-growing variety of bamboo can look good.

✳ There are not a lot of options for those cool, shady corners in north-facing rooms. The few species that will do well in such locations are mainly

DECORATIVE PALMS WILL DO PARTICULARLY WELL IN A SUNNY BATHROOM.

TAKE CARE
Don't buy the biggest plants on offer at a nursery. Smaller, younger plants will usually adapt to a new position more quickly and easily.

those that originate in cool, highland forests in tropical and subtropical regions. These include baby's tears, fuchsia, maidenhair fern, aspidistra, peace lilies, rhapis palms and Zanzibar Gem.

✳ Front halls and stairways that are cool but get plenty of light are a good environment for plants from temperate high-mountain areas as well as Mediterranean species. These plants will tolerate a certain amount of direct sunlight and may also do well outdoors on a sheltered balcony or deck. They include cyclamens, azaleas, bellflowers (campanula), Chinese lanterns, gardenias, Japanese Aralia, daphne and citrus varieties.

✳ An outdoor location that is well protected from the wind – such as an atrium, a sheltered balcony, or a deck with a pergola or wall down one side – will make a good home for begonias, plumbago, dahlias, bougainvillea, angel's trumpet, bromeliads, hibiscus, cigar plants, trumpet vines and Abyssinian banana.

✳ Plants from dry regions need protection from too much rain, as do plants with flowers that are easily damaged by rain. The following appreciate having a roof over their heads in wet climate: plumbago, gazanias, buzzy lizzie, impatiens, heliotrope, hibiscus, oleander, lady's slipper, petunias, Chinese lanterns, yuccas and fan palms.

PROPER CARE of potted plants

Plants grown in containers need more tender care than those grown out in the garden. With the right kind of regular attention, you'll be rewarded with healthy growth and a profusion of blooms. First, you need to compensate for the disadvantages that

A SHELTERED BALCONY OR ATRIUM WILL MAKE A GOOD HOME FOR A BROMELIAD.

PLANT-BUYING CHECKLIST

DECIDE ON THE LOCATION FIRST	Before you buy plants for indoors or a balcony, think about the conditions they will be exposed to. When putting plants in large tubs, you need to consider if they'll need extra protection in winter.
THE BEST PLACE TO BUY PLANTS	You may find a decent range of plants of reasonable quality at some hardware or home improvement stores or online, but if you are investing in something more expensive, it's worth going to a nursery, where you can be sure the plants are healthy and well cared for.
WHAT TO WATCH OUT FOR	The overall appearance of the plant is important: look for even growth, clean fresh-looking leaves, visible new shoots and moderately moist soil. Flowering plants should have a good number of buds. Yellow, spotty leaves are a sign of poor health. Check the under-sides of leaves, too, as pests often hide there.

come with your plants' roots growing in a restricted space. Begin by potting the plant correctly and continue with suitable watering and fertilizing, as well as taking steps to help plants survive winter.

✳ No matter what sort of container you are going to use, it must have at least one drainage hole in the base. The potting mix you use is important. Only use a good-quality potting mix, as it has been designed to provide good drainage and all the nutrients the plant needs. Never use soil dug from your garden.

✳ Potted plants will only develop to their full potential when planted in the right-sized pot. If the pot is too large, the plant may not flower. If planted too deeply, the roots may rot; if not deeply enough, leaving the root ball exposed, the plant may dry out.

✳ A good-quality potting mix will usually do the job. Look for standard or premium potting mixes, to which you can then add some compost. There are also special potting mixes for specific kinds of plants – rhododendrons, camellias and azaleas, for example, prefer acidic soil, while succulents and cacti require a mix that is extremely well drained.

IF YOU ARE INVESTING IN EXPENSIVE PLANTS, IT'S WORTH SHOPPING AT A NURSERY.

TAKE CARE

Don't let potted plants get "wet feet" as waterlogged roots will rot. If you must use a saucer beneath the pot, empty excess water out of it immediately.

✳ All potted plants need water to survive. How often and how much plants need watering will depend on several factors, including the location, the current weather conditions, the soil and, of course, the plant's particular requirements. To determine if a plant needs water or not, push your finger about 1 in. down into the soil to check if it is slightly damp. You should water the plant only when the soil at this depth feels really dry.

✳ The limited amount of soil in a pot means there is only a limited supply of nutrients available for the plant. What's more, nutrients are flushed from the soil every time you water your plants. This is why it's important to fertilize potted plants: to keep their growing conditions consistent. There are many kinds of fertilizer:

✳ Artificial, or mineral, fertilizers are made up of various mineral ingredients. Typically, they are complete fertilizers, meaning that they contain the key plant nutrients nitrogen, phosphorus and

PLANT A HANGING BASKET

Choose drought-tolerant plants for a hanging basket and add water-retaining gel and slow-release plant food granules to the compost to reduce watering. Do this and you can enjoy months of color with minimal maintenance. You will need: hanging basket, bucket, moss (optional), liner, utility knife, trailing plants and some bushy varieties for the top, newspaper, soil-less potting mix, filled watering can, hairpins (optional).

1 Remove the detachable hanging chains if possible and stand the basket on top of the bucket. Line the basket with moss, if using, then the liner. Some baskets come with liner already fitted; otherwise you can buy rigid cardboard or cellulose liners, flexible ones made of felt, jute or other fibers.

2 Starting from the bottom, use the knife to make holes in the lining. If plants are delicate, wrap them in newspaper to protect the stems. Push the plants in roots first from the outside, filling in with compost as you go. Space plants evenly, staggering them in rows.

3 Put the tallest plants in the center at the top, making a depression in the soil around them to help retain the moisture. Plant more trailing plants around the rim, using hairpins if necessary, to attach stems to the frame, encouraging them to hang down.

4 Drench the basket with water and allow excess water to drain through. Attach the chains, then hang the basket, taking care not to squash any stems with the chains.

potassium, along with other nutrients and trace elements. Artificial fertilizers will take effect in the soil immediately.

✳ Organic fertilizers take longer to work because the nutrients contained cannot be taken up by plants directly. They must first be broken down by micro-organisms in the soil. Organic fertilizers include products of animal origin (such as feather meal, bone meal, blood meal) and products of plant origin (such as coco peat, compost, seaweed). Fertilizers come in a variety of forms – liquids, powders, sticks and pellets.

Easy fix It's not practical to repot plants in larger tubs every year. But to ensure these plants continue to thrive, it's a good idea to add a layer of fresh soil in the spring. To do this, carefully remove the top layer of the existing soil and replace it with fresh potting mix. Press down and water thoroughly.

Insider's hack Allow tap water to stand for a while before using it to water plants. This will allow the water to reach room temperature and chlorine to dissipate. In hard-water areas, this will also give minerals a chance to precipitate out.

A LIGHT BOOST for indoor plants

No plant can live without light. If one of your plants is not getting enough light in its current location, a plant light can help. They provide the kind of light plants need, spanning a range of wavelengths comparable to natural daylight. Leafy plants that have low light requirements require a minimum illumination of 400 watts, while flowering plants need between 75 and 100 watts.

✳ Old-fashioned incandescent bulbs are not suitable for plants. They produce too much heat and a large proportion of the light they emit is at the red end of the spectrum, which causes plants to produce pale, elongated shoots. The relatively low light output and high energy consumption of these bulbs also makes them uneconomical.

✳ Metal halide lamps (generally used for large-scale overhead lighting) make good plant lights but they are relatively expensive and too large to use at home.

✳ Fluorescent lamps are a good alternative, which include the modern compact fluorescents (CFLs) that insert into ordinary light fixtures. Fluorescents emit a minimal amount of red light. In fact, their spectral range is very similar to that of sunlight, with a high proportion of UV light that promotes compact growth in plants. This means that they're ideal for providing artificial light to small groups of houseplants.

THE RIGHT WAY TO FERTILIZE

1 Err on the side of too little fertilizer rather than too much. Plants do better when they receive regular, small doses of fertilizer rather than big doses less often.

2 Never sprinkle fertilizer onto dry soil as it can burn a plant's fine hair roots. It's best to apply fertilizer at the same time as watering.

3 Only apply fertilizer during a plant's growing periods, never when it is dormant. When a plant starts to emerge from winter, slowly increase the amount of fertilizer you give it. In late summer, slowly reduce the amount as the dormant period approaches again.

4 If you are pressed for time or tend to be forgetful, use controlled-release fertilizers that release nutrients over an extended period of time.

CONSIDER INVESTING IN AN AUTOMATIC WATERING SYSTEM TO ENSURE YOUR PLANTS SURVIVE VACATION PERIODS.

✳ LED lighting is a modern, energy-saving option with many advantages. You can use LED plant lights, or grow lights, in place of or as a complement to traditional plant lights. They have a long lifespan of between six and eight years, and they produce hardly any heat. As they are also free of toxic and environmentally harmful substances such as mercury, LED lights pose no risk in the event of accidental breakage.

WATERING while on vacation

If you have a reliable neighbor or friend who can water your plants while you are on vacation, you have nothing to worry about. But sometimes the people we would normally ask just aren't available. There are a few ways you can help plants survive your absence and remain in good condition.

✳ If you get into the habit of watering a potted plant sparingly, its root system and growth will adapt to having limited moisture. This will enable the plant to survive for longer periods without water and to get through the times when you are not there.

✳ An ordinary bottle can provide a plant with several days of self-watering. Simply fill a 2 liter plastic soft drink bottle with water and insert

three rolled-up paper towels into the neck. Stick the bottle upside down into the soil. The water will slowly trickle through the paper towels and into the soil for about a week.

✳ Watering spikes, available from garden centers and online, are another practical solution. They are designed to be filled with water, sealed and stuck into the soil. The spike is connected to a container of water with a small tube. Some models have a threaded part allowing a plastic soft drink bottle to be screwed on.

✳ If you have a lot of plants, you should consider investing in an automatic watering system to ensure your plants survive vacation periods.

✳ Group potted plants together in a shady spot so that it's easy for caretakers to water your plants all at once. Place indoor plants in the shower – they can be watered all at once by turning on the shower, they're out of direct sun, and your caretaker doesn't have to worry about overwatering and have water dripping on your carpets.

Easy fix   An automatic watering system is also an option for people who have little time or inclination to water plants on a deck or balcony regularly.

TAKE CARE

It's not a good idea to overwater plants before going away on vacation in an attempt to get them through until you get back. Overwatering plants at any time can cause root rot.

Choosing OUTDOOR PLANTS

The first impression visitors have of our home is the front entrance so we want to make it as inviting as possible – ideally with flowers, foliage plants and shrubs, planted in garden beds or grown in pots or tubs. Plants are not only attractive but can provide privacy and protect us from the wind.

✳ Your home's balcony or deck is the transition space between its indoor and outdoor living areas. An imaginative selection of plants here can create the impression of sitting out in nature, all the while being comfortably sheltered.

Your balcony or deck is the transition space between your home's indoor and outdoor living areas.

✳ When it comes to choosing the right plants for a particular spot, the same rules apply outdoors as indoors. How much light does the space receive at different times of day? And how many hours of sunlight does it receive in total throughout the day? Make sure you know the answer to these questions before you start buying plants. How much sun a deck or balcony sees is mostly determined by the direction it faces. But check what is located next door or across the street – a tall building or tree can cast a shadow and turn what should be a sunny south-facing balcony into a semi-shaded environment. East-facing positions will receive morning sun but will be shady for the rest of the day; west-facing spots will bear the brunt of the sizzling afternoon summer sun.

MAKE THE FRONT ENTRANCE INVITING WITH FLOWERS AND FOLIAGE PLANTS IN GARDEN BEDS OR POTS.

✳ There are pros and cons to having a roof over a balcony, deck or front entrance. A roof provides shelter from the wind but it can also limit sunlight hours, prevent rain from reaching plants and allow heat to build up.

✳ Once you have a clear idea about your balcony's climatic conditions, think about its structural considerations. Plants, pots, planter boxes, potting mix and outdoor furniture all add a considerable amount of weight. Added to that, of course, is the weight of all the people who will be using the space. Bear in mind that a generously filled planter can easily weigh 100 lbs. or more and will become even heavier after watering and rainfall. As a general rule, the load on a balcony should not exceed 500 lbs per 10 sq ft. If you are in doubt, seek advice from a structural engineer.

MOUNT PLANTER BOXES ON THE INSIDE OF BALCONY RAILINGS SO THEY CAN'T FALL ONTO THE STREET BELOW.

✳ There are a few other important safety concerns for outdoor plants. When mounting planter boxes on balcony railings, hang them inside the railing so that, if they ever fall, they'll land on the balcony rather than the street below. Make sure to fit any hanging pots on your balcony, deck or entrance securely to prevent a strong gust of wind from tumbling them down. Keep in mind, too, that hanging baskets will become heavier over time as the plant grows.

Easy fix Plants in hanging baskets look great, but the trouble is that they dry out quickly. Make watering easier by equipping them with a pulley system to raise and lower them. Another option is to use a watering wand to reach up to the plant.

Insider's hack It can be especially challenging to choose the right mix of plants that will look good in a sloping front garden. One technique is to put taller plants at the bottom of the slope with shorter ones closer to the house. This will lessen the visual impact of the slope.

A bunch of FRESH FLOWERS

You don't need to wait for a special occasion to express your affection and appreciation for someone with a bunch of flowers. The sight of a beautiful vase of cut flowers is a source of pleasure any time. Whether bought from a florist or picked from your own garden, flowers in a vase should stay fresh and beautiful for a decent amount of time, and not wilt and fade after only a couple of days. Stick to these basic rules to enjoy cut flowers for longer.

✳ When buying or picking flowers, make sure the buds are fully developed but have only just opened. Flowers from your own garden will keep longest if you pick them in the morning. To ensure the stems soak up water when in the vase, cut them with a sharp knife to avoid crushing them. When buying flowers, check that the stems look strong and don't have any brown patches.

✳ Before arranging flowers in a vase, remove any leaves from the lower part of the stems as the leaves will decompose rapidly in water. With a sharp knife under running water, cut all the stems at an angle. This is because a flower can only take up as much water as the cut surface of its stem allows – an angled cut will expose a greater surface area than a straight one. Cutting under running water means the new cut won't be exposed to air (and bacteria that cause blooms to decompose), and ensures a good supply of water reaches the flower.

Cut all the stems at an angle using a sharp knife under running water.

✳ Once the stems are cut, place the bouquet straight into the vase. Initially, the water in the vase should be lukewarm; you can add a special preservative for cut flowers if you like. Available in liquid or powder

TAKE CARE
Never use scissors to cut flowers as you will crush the delicate vascular system inside a flower's stem.

form from a florist and sometimes included with your bought bunch of flowers, these products slow down the decomposition process and keep your flowers from wilting too quickly. To finish, top off the vase with distilled water. If you are not using a preservative agent, change the water every day (don't just top off what's there). Cut the stems again each time you change the water.

✳ The cooler you can keep cut flowers, the longer they will last. At the very least, put your flowers somewhere cool at night – you can put them back out on display during the day. Remove wilted leaves and flowers, which give off ethylene gas. Ethylene has a ripening effect and will cause the remaining flowers to wilt more quickly.

Save money Even if you don't have a large garden you can still enjoy cut flowers at home without spending a fortune. Good-quality flowers at reasonable prices can sometimes be found in supermarkets. Pick up a few different kinds and arrange them into a bouquet yourself.

BEST VASES for bouquets

It's a good idea to own a few different vases so that you can choose just the right one when you receive or buy flowers. Tall slender vases suit long-stemmed flowers, a medium-sized round-bodied vase will

ADD PRESERVATIVE TO THE WATER IN A VASE TO KEEP FLOWERS FROM WILTING TOO QUICKLY.

CREATE A LOVELY SHABBY CHIC EFFECT BY TEAMING A TEAPOT WITH A SMALL BUNCH OF FLOWERS.

hold a great big bouquet, and smaller vases are best for little posies or a single exotic bloom. If your bouquet has been carefully arranged by a florist, put it in the vase as is rather than untying it. If the flowers are loose, on the other hand, you can arrange them yourself. Conical vases, which are wider at the top than at the base, are good for this. A rule of thumb to achieve an elegant, classic look is to use a vase that is between one-third and half the height of the flowers.

✳ Sculptural vases can hold flowers but are also decorative items in their own right. Use these vases to add a point of interest to a room, with or without flowers. Choose an uncluttered position that shows your vase to its best advantage, such as a bookshelf, coffee table or sideboard.

✳ A large floor vase can also work as a room ornament, especially in a prominent position such as beside a fireplace or in the corner of a room. Enhance the visual impact by filling the vase with textural plant material such as bamboo canes or corkscrew willow branches.

✳ Don't limit yourself to dedicated vases for your flowers. Use other vessels, such as teapots and water jugs, for a lovely shabby chic effect. There are some great finds in charity shops, second-hand shops or flea markets. Also look for old bottles and urns.

✳ A new trend is to use a gift bag as a decorative cover for a vase. This simple trick takes advantage of the fact that gift bags these days come in a variety of attractive designs. It's simply a matter of arranging the flowers in any old container and placing everything inside a gift bag.

BIRDS in the backyard

It's hard to imagine what the world would be like without birds and birdsong. Even if you don't have an extensive garden, all you need to enjoy regular avian visits is a balcony or courtyard filled with plants. Make these feathered friends feel welcome by being accommodating to their needs.

✳ Provide places where birds can sleep, nest and take shelter. Plant shrubs and hedges if you have enough space. Vines and creepers growing up walls and façades, or even on a balcony, also provide a good habitat for birds.

✳ Flowering shrubs that produce berries, seeds or nectar are an important source of food; you can grow them in pots on a balcony or terrace.

✳ A bird feeder or bird bath will fit on even the smallest balcony. In temperate climates, birds will be happy to have an additional source of food during cold winter months. Position a bird bath where cats cannot reach it and keep it filled with fresh water.

✳ If you want to put up a bird nesting box, locate it away from direct sunlight at a height of at least six feet to ensure it stays cool and safe from cats.

BUILD A BIRD NESTING BOX

To make this nesting box, you will need: a plank of rough-sawn wood or untreated 1/4 in. outdoor plywood (sawn as shown below), drill, some nails, hammer, brass hinge or strip of rubber such as an old bicycle inner tube, brass catch (optional).

BACK	BASE	ROOF	FRONT	SIDE	SIDE	STEP 1
13 3/4 in.	4 3/4 in.	8 1/4 in.	7 3/4 in.	7 3/4 in.	9 3/4 in.	

1 Make cuts for each of the sections of the box, then drill a few 1/3 in. drainage holes in the base.

2 Nail the side sections to the base and then the back section to the sides. Four nails should suffice to join each side to the back.

3 Before you attach the front section, use a space drill bit (a wide drill bit) to create an entrance hole. The bottom edge of the hole must be positioned at least 5 in. up from the base so that young birds can't fall out. Line up the nails centrally with the section beneath.

4 Nail on the front section, then attach the lid with a brass hinge, or a strip of inner tubing. Fix a small brass catch to the roof, if using. The inside wall below the entrance hole should be rough to help young birds clamber up and out. A hinged lid allows you to open the box to clean it in autumn.

5 Hang your box using a nylon bolt or wire. A piece of hose around the wire will prevent damage to the tree. Position the box facing between north and east and tilt down to protect it from direct sun and rain. Place the box high enough to escape the attention of cats.

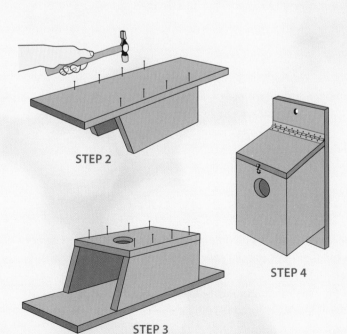

STEP 2

STEP 3

STEP 4

Once you've built your box, let your imagination run wild with how you decorate it.

FLOWERPOTS aren't just for plants

Basic earthenware or terracotta flowerpots come in all shapes and sizes, from tiny mini-pots to giant tubs for large plants. With a bit of creative thinking, you'll find there are many more things you can do with pots, both old and new, than simply put plants in them.

A POT OF PENCILS

Terracotta pots about 3 to 4 in. high are not only great for seedlings, they are the perfect size for pens and pencils. Line up a few on your desk and use them to stash all your home office supplies.

A CASCADING WATER FEATURE

Nothing is more soothing than the gurgling sound of running water in the backyard. Given that we all can't live beside a stream, you can build your own one-of-a-kind fountain from an oversized feature pot. Pots with rough textures or glazing work particularly well with the water running over the surface. You'll need to plumb in a water pump and set up a waterproof reservoir for the pot to sit in.

EASTER WITH A DIFFERENCE

If you are entertaining for Easter breakfast, why not use tiny terracotta flowerpots as eggcups. Just make sure you wash the unglazed, untreated pots thoroughly with hot soapy water. Another idea is to bake chocolate cupcakes inside the mini-pots. Line the pots with cupcake liners first then bake your favorite cupcake recipe inside. Ice with chocolate "soil" icing then decorate the tops with a flowery motif – an Easter garden in a pot.

TIERED JEWELRY TREE

Flowerpots and saucers come in many beautiful glazes and in all shapes and sizes. Use this to your advantage when you find a glaze you love by selecting three saucers in different sizes and two small pots. Stack the saucers in diminishing size with the pots upturned in between to make a decorative stand for your everyday jewelry. Alternatively, you can buy plain terracotta or earthenware pots and paint with your choice of acrylic paint. Also consider lining the saucers with decorative scrapbook paper to dress it up further.

Simply beautiful ideas

Give your rooms a distinctive personal touch with tasteful decorations to create the look you want and turn your house into a place where you truly feel at home.

Splash out with SOFT FURNISHINGS

Soft furnishings such as cushions and throws do more than provide comfort and warmth; they also tie a room together visually. Bright cushions can liven up an otherwise dull-looking couch, they're an inexpensive way to try out a new decorating trend, and they can improve the look of an awkwardly proportioned furniture arrangement.

✳ Cushions create impact through their size, shape, color or fabric. Give a glamour boost to a monochrome sofa that doesn't quite set the room on fire with cushions in varying patterns, colors and sizes.

✳ Turn a plain-colored cushion cover into a one-of-a-kind decorator item by adding stencilling. You can buy ready-made stencils from a fabric shop or cut out your own design from cardboard. Attach the stencil to the fabric and apply fabric paint over it. Allow to dry before removing the stencil carefully. The paint will appear only in the cut-out areas of the stencil.

✳ Create an especially distinctive look with your cushions by sticking to a single color but choosing contrasting patterns.

✳ A loosely folded throw or blanket can serve a similar purpose: creating a new look, emphasizing certain features or concealing others. Of course, a blanket is also great for snuggling under when reading or watching television. There is a wide range of colors and fabrics available, from crocheted or knitted cotton to luxurious cashmere. Especially fashionable at the moment are reversible blankets, which have a patterned fabric such as silk on top and a soft, fleecy or mink-like material on the underside.

CREATE A DISTINCTIVE LOOK WITH CUSHIONS OF A SINGLE COLOR BUT CONTRASTING PATTERNS.

Create coziness with CANDLES

Although we no longer rely on candles to provide light, we still appreciate the decorative, pleasant glow cast by their soft, warm light – and not just at Christmas and birthday parties. Candles look great on a balcony or terrace in summer, creating a romantic mood on warm nights. And when the weather cools down, candlelight creates a cozy ambiance indoors.

Instead of lighting candles with a match, use a long lighter designed for barbecues.

✳ Candles come in a range of colors and sizes to suit your decor and reflect different times of the year. Traditional white candles always look good and suit a festive table. Tea lights in spring or autumn colors look good in their respective seasons, but opt for candleholders in understated colors and materials; otherwise your decoration may look over

BEESWAX CANDLES, OR ORDINARY WAX OR SOY CANDLES WITH SCENT ADDED, ARE POPULAR.

the top. Take care also not to go overboard with elaborate arrangements of multiple candles – you don't want to turn your living room into a temple.
✳ Genuine beeswax candles have a beautiful scent. There are also ordinary wax or soy wax candles with scent added, which are popular.
✳ To create an unforgettable table setting, fill a glass bowl with water, then add artificial water lilies and floating candles.
✳ A fire-safe alternative to candles are LED candles. Either battery powered or rechargeable, LED tea lights and candles cast a similar glow and even flicker like the real thing. Plus, you can put them in glass jars without fear of them shattering, or on wood furniture without the risk of wax marks or heat burns.

Insider's hack Instead of lighting candles with a match or cigarette lighter, use one of the long lighters designed for lighting barbecues. This will save you from burning your fingers.

HANDLING CANDLES with care

Candleholders should be stable and made from non-flammable materials. Stick a candle adaptor (available online), a dot made from sticky wax, on the bottom of each candle to hold it firmly in place.
✳ Don't ever light a candle that is not standing up straight. It may fall over or break off.
✳ Tea lights are typically made from mineral paraffin and cannot be extinguished with water. Blow them out or cover to extinguish instead.
✳ Tea lights produce a considerable amount of heat so don't group them together. Place them no less than 4 in. apart; otherwise flammable gases can accumulate over the candles and ignite suddenly.

PICTURES and photographs

Whether you want to hang family photos, vacation snapshots, oil paintings or graphic art on your walls, finding the right frames, appropriate lighting and a harmonious arrangement are all necessary to present your pictures in the best possible way.

✳ Tradition holds that large pictures should have a thick frame while small pictures should have a narrow one. But this isn't always the best way to go – small oil paintings, for instance, may benefit from having a thick frame to prevent them from disappearing against the wall.

✳ Other ways you can help your small pictures stand out include grouping several of them together, or choosing a narrow section of wall for a small picture. Large pictures, on the other hand, look good on their own as the centerpiece on a large expanse of wall, and often look best without a frame at all.

✳ When hanging pictures, a good height is a few inches above the average person's eye level. Before you start drilling holes in the wall, lay your pictures out on the floor to test the arrangement you had in mind.

✳ If you have several pictures of similar shape and size, you can group them together in a strong geometric pattern. If your pictures are different sizes, you can achieve harmony in the arrangement by aligning pictures with their top and bottom edges, or through their vertical or horizontal centers.

MAKE PLANT STAMPS

A cut above the average potato stamp, there are many arresting patterns to be found in plant cross-sections, which you can use for wrapping paper or gift tags. What you'll need: your choice of vegetable (see box below for ideas); stamping ink pads, plain wrapping paper, art paper and blank cards; cutting board and knife; paper towel; old dish towel.

1 Celery, okra, radicchio, Brussels sprouts, peppers, bok choy and starfruit all create wonderful patterns. To make a stamp, first cut crosswise to reveal the cross-section. Stand, cut side down, on paper towel to blot excess liquid.

2 Cover cut side with stamping ink. First, make a few practice stamps on scrap paper. Then lay a folded dish towel under the paper or card to soften the surface. Stamp a repeat pattern over paper for gift wrap, or a single stamp for a card.

3 A bunch of celery makes a rose-shaped stamp (boxes front and back), and okra's cross-section produces tiny round flower shapes (small box far left). On the cards, radicchio (top) and celery (bottom) make striking single motifs.

✳ If you are unsure about which color frame to choose, here are two ideas that may help. If you have dark-colored wood furniture in the room, a matching dark wood frame will look good. Otherwise, you can let the frame color be guided by the colors in the picture itself. For instance, if a picture includes a distinctive shade of dark red, a frame in that color can work well.

✳ When it comes to deciding on the style of frame, you don't have to match the decor in the rest of the room. In fact, it can be a more interesting design decision to choose something that is in stark contrast to the rest of the room. A baroque-style gilt frame, for instance, can be a real eye-catcher in a room with otherwise minimalist modern decor. If you

want to be really daring, why not put such a frame around an abstract painting, or graphic print? The only rule is: if you like it, do it.

A baroque-style gilt frame can be a real eye-catcher in a room with otherwise minimalist modern decor.

✳ Photos, graphic art, drawings and watercolors should be framed behind glass; oil and acrylic paintings should not be. There are two schools of thought on the best kind of glass to use. Some people prefer non-reflective glass, which prevents glare from windows or lamps; others find that non-reflective glass makes a picture appear dull because of how it scatters light. Check out both options in a framing shop and make up your own mind as to which one you prefer.

✳ Ensure your pictures are properly illuminated. Pointing a spotlight directly onto a picture will cause annoying reflections so is not the way to go. Rod-shaped picture lights are a better way; these lighting strips cast gentle, glare-free light on your photos and artworks from above.

✳ For a clever twist on a picture frame that's sure to make a statement, recycle an old window. If someone in your neighborhood is renovating, keep an eye out for old window frames with multiple panes of glass that may be destined for the tip. Use this to frame a selection of black-and-white photos, or even one large favorite print.

IF YOU HAVE SEVERAL PICTURES OF SIMILAR SHAPE AND SIZE, YOU CAN GROUP THEM TOGETHER IN A STRONG GEOMETRIC PATTERN.

Living with pets

Pets bring life into a home and add variety to our everyday routine. They are a source of comfort or a friend to play with, but you should keep a few things in mind so you get the maximum enjoyment out of living with a pet.

Should I OWN A PET?

Before you decide on owning a pet – whether it's a dog, cat, rabbit or bird – consider what life might be like with a new companion in your home. While pets are a source of joy, they also bring certain responsibilities with them.

❋ You first have to consider whether your house or apartment is suitable for keeping a pet. Is there enough space? Do you have valuable or delicate furniture, carpets or curtains? You can count on a pet – especially a cat, rabbit or rodent – to scratch or nibble on upholstered furniture and hardware. Pets also create additional mess. If you are renting, check with your landlord or building administration to see if pets are allowed in the property.

❋ Pets need care, attention and activity, which means you need to invest time in them every day. You cannot rely on your children saying they will do it. Ultimately, responsibility for a pet falls to the adults in the house.

❋ All the members of a household must agree about getting a pet because a pet represents a new and, in some cases, rather demanding occupant of the household. Some pets, such as cats and dogs, can live for 15 years or more. You also need to be sure that no one in the family is allergic to animal hair (especially cat or dog hair).

❋ There are various costs associated with owning a pet – food, straw, a cage, kitty litter and so on. Pets can get sick, meaning there will be vet's bills to pay. Putting your pet in a boarding facility while you are away on vacation can also be expensive. Dog owners may also face registration and liability insurance costs, not to mention visits to the groomer or obedience school.

Easy fix To avoid disappointment and potential problems trying to return a pet, talk to people you know who have pets to get an idea of their experiences living with one.

PETS NOT ONLY BRING YOU JOY, BUT ALSO RESPONSIBILITY ... WHICH ULTIMATELY FALLS TO THE ADULTS IN THE HOUSE.

WHICH PET is right for me?

Just about every child wants a pet at some point and many adults, too, can scarcely imagine life without one. But which is the right pet for you? Do you leave the house to go to work every day? Do you have children and are they old enough to be around a pet? If you and your companion animal are going to get along well over the long term, there needs to be a good match between what the animal needs and what you want in a pet.

✳ Owning a dog is like having another member of the family. Dogs are social creatures and like being in the company of people. For a dog, the family is like its pack and there needs to be a clear sense of hierarchy. There can be doubt about who the leader of the pack is – and it certainly must not be the dog itself, otherwise it will not obey your commands. Some breeds of dog – certainly not all – are well suited to families with young children, but under no circumstances should you leave it up to your children to care for and train a dog. A dog will suit people who have a reasonable amount of free time to spend with their pet, people who like going for walks even in the wind and rain, and people who

are also prepared to invest time and effort in training their pet. If you live alone and don't always have time, you could ask your neighbors if they would be prepared to take your dog for a walk. There are also dog sitters who can walk your dog on occasion for a reasonable hourly rate.

✳ If you leave the house for work, you'll need to make your dog accustomed to your absence, or have someone reliable to look after the dog while you're not there. If you often go away on business trips, you should seriously consider whether a dog is the right pet for you.

✳ An important point about dogs is that the bigger they are, the more challenging they often are to own as pets. Some breeds are also easier to train than others. Only those who are experienced with dogs should consider owning a large or "stubborn" breed.

✳ Cats tend to be fairly individual creatures who like their freedom. They don't mind close contact with people and they will cuddle up against their owners, but don't expect the same level of loyalty or devotion from them as a dog. Cats are good for people who have a certain amount of time to spend with an animal, and who want to develop a rapport

A DOG WILL SUIT PEOPLE WHO HAVE A REASONABLE AMOUNT OF FREE TIME AND WHO LIKE GOING FOR WALKS.

RABBITS DON'T LIKE BEING BY THEMSELVES.

with their pet but also appreciate that animal's independence. Cats are also good for children to cuddle and play with, but small children need to learn that cats will make it very clear when they don't like certain things!

✳ Cats need regular feeding and a clean litter box. Otherwise, you can leave them on their own and they will keep themselves entertained.

RABBITS, HAMSTERS, birds and fish

Rabbits are timid creatures suitable for people who are calm and gentle with their pets. Although they may look very sweet, rabbits are not cuddly toys and they don't especially like being picked up. When you first bring a rabbit home, give it time to settle down and adapt to its new surroundings, before you start stroking and playing with it. Rabbits are suitable for older children who can be responsible for feeding them and cleaning their hutch. They need a fair amount of space – allow about 32 sq. ft. for two or three rabbits. You can leave rabbits by themselves for several hours without a problem provided they are in the company of other rabbits; they do not like being by themselves.

✳ If you get along well with rabbits, you will also like guinea pigs. These cuddly-looking animals also need a fair amount of space. Although they are quite sociable, they need a place to withdraw – a little

box placed in their hutch works well. Guinea pigs are suitable for children provided you make it clear to your kids that the little creatures are not toys but companions that need looking after. If possible, you should have at least two guinea pigs – they do like the company of their own kind and a rabbit is not a substitute!

✳ Hamsters are nocturnal creatures. They're awake while you sleep, busily scurrying about; and when morning comes, it's time for them to curl up in their little den. If a hamster is disturbed from its slumber, it can become quite disagreeable and may even bite. As hamsters are not especially cuddly and are only active at night, they don't make great children's pets. But they will suit adults who come home late at night when the little rodents are most active. A hamster is also a good option for people who have limited time and space but would still like a pet.

✳ Parakeet owners already know that their pets can be quite noisy. They are social creatures and it's essential that parakeets have the company of their own kind, otherwise they will be lonely and bored.

PARAKEETS CAN BE VERY TAME AND SOME MAY EVEN LEARN TO SPEAK.

FISH ARE EASY TO CARE FOR, BUT THERE IS A BIT OF WORK INVOLVED IN MAINTAINING A FISH TANK.

If an owner has plenty of spare time to spend with their parakeet, however, the bird can thrive on its own. They can be very tame and some may even learn to speak. Older people with reduced mobility can gain a lot of pleasure out of owning a parakeet. The birds are also suitable for children, although parents should help with looking after them.

✳ Aquarium fish are typically freshwater fish from the tropics. No one could say that fish are noisy pets, and their diversity of shapes, sizes and colors makes them quietly captivating creatures. Many people find fish relaxing or calming to look at.

✳ Fish are easy to care for, demanding only food and clean water. However, there is a bit of work involved in maintaining a fish tank. Ask the staff at a pet or aquarium store for advice on how to set one up properly, and what you need to do to keep your fish healthy and alive for a long time. Fish are a good choice for people who like the idea of having an animal to look after but don't want noise or mess in the house.

Save money Instead of buying that expensive pedigree kitten from a breeder, why not take home a healthy, fully vaccinated young cat from an animal shelter? You will save money and be doing a good deed at the same time.

WHAT'S IN STORE with a pet

Whether it's a dog, a cat or a rabbit, if you have an animal with long hair it's important to check and maintain its coat. Cats are very clean and only long-haired breeds need brushing. Many breeds of dog, on the other hand, require quite a lot of grooming. All animals should have their ears checked and claws or toenails clipped regularly. If you own rabbits, check their coats and the undersides of their hind feet frequently to ensure they are clean, and trim their nails regularly, too.

✳ Dogs eliminate waste outdoors, while house cats, rabbits, guinea pigs and similar pets use litter indoors, which requires daily cleaning. Animals

Expert advice

Protecting your unborn child from toxoplasmosis

If a cat is infected with the parasite *Toxoplasma gondii*, it will excrete the parasite's eggs in its feces. Infection in humans causes virtually no symptoms and leads to subsequent immunity. However, the parasite poses a particular risk to pregnant women who do not have pre-existing immunity as it can cause serious harm to the fetus. Women of child-bearing age should have a blood test to see if they have antibodies against toxoplasmosis and follow their doctor's advice if they do not have immunity.

that are kept in an enclosure need a clean place to rest and sleep. Cages should be cleaned out once a week. The litter or sand should be changed every two to three days.

✳ Good hygiene is particularly important when you have a pet. Dogs, cats, guinea pigs and parakeets can all transmit various diseases to humans. Make sure to take appropriate precautions, especially with pets you enjoy cuddling up with.

✳ Many dog owners love their animal so much that they'll give it a kiss on the muzzle, but for hygiene reasons, it's better to refrain. Our four-legged furry friends have a habit of sticking their noses in all kinds of places, including dirt, animal droppings and trash – the smellier the better – so you risk picking up all kinds of germs when you kiss a dog. They may not make you sick every time, but the possibility is certainly there.

✳ Pet owners sometimes wonder whether they should wash their hands after every time they pat their animal. That would be overdoing it, but it's certainly advisable to wash your hands before cooking or eating.

✳ Opinions vary on whether you should allow your pet to sleep in the bed with you. Some owners love to snuggle and will happily share the bed with their cat or dog. But doctors warn that doing this is a health risk, by increasing the chances that any ticks or fleas on your animal will jump across to you. Apart from this, germs carried by animals, as well as their dander, can irritate your airways.

✳ Pay close attention to hygiene when pets and children come into contact with each other, as

THE LITTER USED BY HOUSE CATS, RABBITS, GUINEA PIGS AND SIMILAR PETS REQUIRES DAILY CLEANING.

children are often more susceptible to disease than adults. Make sure your child does not kiss or get licked by your pet. If your child is slobbered on by an animal, wash the affected area with soap and water right away.

✳ In addition to practicing good hygiene, it's important to take your pet regularly to the vet for regular check-ups and vaccinations. Deworm your animal, and apply flea and heartworm treatment to ensure children and adults alike can be in contact with your pet without risking their health.

✳ It's also important to think about things in the house that pose a potential risk to your pet. For tips on minimizing these risks, see page 195, "Preventing danger for pets."

Insider's hack Cats should be neutered, unless you specifically aim to breed them. Castrating a male cat will stop it from marking the house with unpleasant-smelling scent. If a female cat has not been spayed, it will go into heat, attracting all the male cats in the neighborhood.

TAKE CARE

Don't pat an animal you don't know. You can never be sure if a dog is ill-tempered or not and some dogs will snap simply out of fear. Strange dogs may also be carrying ticks or diseases.

Informal entertaining

There are all kinds of occasions when it's great to have people over. Good planning is essential to ensure everything goes smoothly and your guests have a good time. And when visitors arrive unexpectedly, there are a few tricks to help you breeze through it.

Make every PARTY A SUCCESS

Before you start inviting people, be clear in your own mind about the scale of the event. It's important to plan the whole thing well to prevent a pleasant occasion from becoming a source of stress.

✳ If you are inviting a lot of people to a big event, such as a wedding, it is worth hiring professional help such as a catering service. This will allow you, the host, to enjoy the party, too. For smaller events, you can manage the preparations yourself.

✳ Once you have decided to organize an event and set a date, it's time to start inviting people. For large events, you should send out invitations in writing at least four weeks ahead of time. If the occasion is especially significant, such as a wedding or an anniversary celebration, you should allow even more notice so people can send RSVPs and make travel arrangements as necessary. For a small get-together, such as an afternoon coffee date, you can just ask them in person.

✳ Once you have received your guests' RSVPs and you have the final number of people attending, it's time to begin planning the event in detail. Start by checking you have enough dishes, cutlery, glassware, napkins and chairs. If you are going to be preparing food yourself, you should finalize your menu no later than a week before the event so that you have plenty of time to shop for all the necessary ingredients.

Easy fix If you are having family or good friends over, you can make it a potluck where each person brings a dish to share. Some planning is still required to ensure you don't end up with two or three plates of the same thing.

GOOD PLANNING WILL PREVENT A PLEASANT OCCASION FROM BECOMING A SOURCE OF STRESS.

What PARTY FOOD to eat?

Food is at the center of major celebrations in just about every culture. As a host, you should put some thought into what to serve your guests.

✳ For a group of six to eight people, a dinner party is a great way to spoil your guests. It's common to serve three courses: appetizer, main dish and dessert. For really special occasions, you can serve extra courses between these. In general, main ingredients should not appear more than once in the meal – if you have a fish appetizer then serve meat, poultry or a vegetarian dish for the main course.

✳ If you like cooking, you'll relish the opportunity to conjure up something special. But if the culinary arts are not your strong point, don't feel obliged to do all the cooking yourself. Aside from catering services, you can also hire an in-home chef, who will prepare all the food in your kitchen and even bring their own cookware. If you can then add something homemade, such as a deliciously fragrant chicken soup, your guests will appreciate it all the more.

✳ Together, the meal and the table decorations provide a feast for the eyes, making it clear to your guests that this is a special occasion.

TOGETHER, THE MEAL AND TABLE PROVIDE A FEAST FOR THE EYES.

Expert advice

A smorgasbord of options

For large parties – especially when your dining table doesn't have enough room to serve a formal meal – a buffet can be the way to go. You can set it up either inside the house or, if the weather is nice, on the balcony, deck or out in the garden. If you use caterers, they will advise you on the selection and quantity of dishes to provide.

★ If you are going to prepare food for a buffet yourself, be guided by this rule of thumb: for around 20 people, you should prepare three to four appetizers (including soups and salads), two main dishes with two sides each, two to three desserts, and a cheese plate with five kinds of cheese.

★ When it comes to how much of each dish to prepare for a buffet, these per-person amounts are a general guide:

1 cup soup; 1 cup appetizer/salad;
4 to 5 ounces fish/meat; 1/2 cup rice/pasta;
4 ounces vegetables; 1/2 cup or 2 ounces dessert;
2 ounces cold meats and cheeses; one piece of fruit;
an assortment of bread.

Summertime calls for
OUTDOOR CELEBRATIONS

When the weather warms up, your balcony, deck or garden is ideal for entertaining guests. The simple pleasure of sitting outdoors underneath a clear sky is in itself enough to create a convivial atmosphere.

✳ When family, neighbors, friends or coworkers come over, you don't need to make a lot of fuss. All you need is something to drink and a few snacks – unless of course you feel inclined to fire up the barbecue.

✳ If you would like to make more of an effort, say if you are entertaining your boss and their partner, you can set up a refreshments table with a white tablecloth. Set out cold dishes such as salads, cold cuts, an antipasto platter, a cheese plate, a variety of bread and fruit. Have several bottles of good-quality wine or some non-alcoholic cocktails on hand to offer your guests.

✳ As darkness starts to fall, use mood lighting to create a charming atmosphere and allow the conversations to flow for as long as the balmy night air allows.

WHEN FAMILY, NEIGHBORS, FRIENDS OR COWORKERS COME OVER, YOU DON'T NEED TO MAKE A LOT OF FUSS.

When company ARRIVES
UNANNOUNCED

You're just settling in to enjoy some peace and quiet when the phone rings and your friends announce they want to drop by. At moments like these, the house is often not looking its best. But don't panic! You can pull it all together at the last minute.

✳ Your front hall and coat stand will look tidier in an instant if you gather up all the coats, jackets and shoes, and make them disappear into the bedroom and shoe rack.

✳ Grab everything that's lying around on the couch or living room floor, put it all in a basket and stash it away in the bedroom, too.

✳ Guests often like to gather in the kitchen. If there are dishes out on the counter, put them in the dishwasher. Replace dish towels with fresh ones.

✳ There are often tubes and little bottles floating around in the bathroom. Put them away in the medicine cabinet. Hide the dirty-laundry basket in the bedroom. Then don't forget to shut the door!

✳ Keep a supply of snacks and drinks in the pantry so there will be something to offer guests who drop in on short notice.

Easy fix If you have enough space in your freezer, keep a supply of favorite snacks that you can easily pop in the oven, such as mini-pizzas, mini eggrolls and assorted quiches.

Insider's hack Sometimes visitors turn up without any warning at all. When this happens, just relax and don't feel the need to apologize for any untidiness.

Guests who STAY THE NIGHT

If you like having family and friends over to your place, then you will probably have overnight guests from time to time. It can happen when someone has a glass too many, they live far away, or bad weather prevents them from travelling. Whatever the reason, it's good to be prepared and be able to offer your guests somewhere to sleep.

✳ If you have a spare room, you can turn it into a permanent guest room with a comfortable bed. If you only have people stay overnight once or twice a year, it's a good idea to use the room for another purpose as well – such as a study that doubles as a guest room, perhaps with a sofa bed.

✳ If you don't have a guest room, there are plenty of other options for guest bedding. A sofa bed in the living room is a popular choice. Many living room furniture sets include pull-out or fold-out sofa beds,

IF YOU HAVE A SPARE ROOM, TURN IT INTO A PERMANENT GUEST ROOM.

which are just as comfortable as a normal couch or bed for sitting or sleeping. If you find pull-out mattresses too thin, an alternative is a day bed with a futon mattress.

✳ Alternatively, you can choose a couch that has an extra-deep seat, which you can use as a bed without needing to pull or fold out a separate section. Make sure the couch has appropriate back and side cushions so you can sit on it comfortably without getting a sore back. When you want to sleep on it, you simply remove these cushions.

✳ If your children want to have friends sleep over, a trundle bed in your child's room can work well. Comfortable and space-saving, a trundle bed simply pulls out from underneath the main bed.

✳ Folding beds or camp beds are solutions for people who are not prone to lower back pain. The advantages of these options are that they will fit in just about any room, they are quick to set up and pack away small when not in use.

Save money An air mattress is fine for younger guests. They are cheap and take up very little space when deflated.

chapter 4

Take Care of What You Wear

Know your textile fibers and fabrics

Clothing fabric is made from natural or synthetic fibers, or a mixture of these. Different fibers have different properties, and if you look after them well, they'll last for a long time.

NATURAL AND SYNTHETIC fibers

The list of materials you find on many clothes labels can leave you guessing as to what sort of fiber you are actually looking at. The following tips will help you navigate the labyrinth of fibers on the market.

✳ Natural materials are made from animal hair or plant fibers. Both the thick hair of sheep and the fine hair of goats, camels and llamas make excellent wool, and silk is obtained from silkworms, which are the larvae of the silk moth. Silkworms spin their delicate silk into cocoons, which are unravelled to make silk threads for exquisite fabrics.

✳ The most important plant fiber we use for fabric is cotton, which is spun from the downy fibers inside cottonseed capsules. Linen is made from flax (linseed) plants, which have pretty blue flowers. Also producing plant fibers are hemp plants (hemp), coconut palms (coir) and agave cacti (sisal).

✳ Artificial fibers, which are manufactured by industrial processes, are divided into two categories: cellulose and synthetic fibers. The base substance for cellulose-based synthetic fibers is, as the name suggests, cellulose, a natural material that is converted into so-called textile pulp by means of chemical processes. The pulp is then spun into fibers such as viscose, rayon and acetate. With synthetic fibers, the textile pulp is extracted chemically from petrochemical products. Common synthetic fibers include nylon, polyester, polyamide, acrylic and Lycra, among others.

Material PROS AND CONS

Many people check what fibers clothes are made from before buying, and often prefer natural fibers because they believe they're better for our skin and

OBTAINED FROM SILKWORMS, SILK MAKES THREADS FOR EXQUISITE FABRICS.

health, and are environmentally friendly. In the past, synthetic fibers were indeed not very pleasant to wear: the fabrics felt uncomfortable on the skin and caused perspiration, in both summer and winter. However, modern technology makes for a more sophisticated manufacturing process, which produces fabrics whose quality is usually at least equivalent to and sometimes even better than that of natural fibers. One example is modern, fully synthetic microfibers.

✳ With regard to environmental concerns, clothes made from natural fibers are nowhere near as environmentally friendly or healthy as most people believe. We want wool sweaters that aren't itchy, silk dresses that don't crumple and cotton T-shirts that hold their shape and don't pill. And in glorious colors, of course! To achieve this, natural fibers are processed extensively, and these refining and dyeing processes rely on the use of chemicals that may affect our health by, for example, causing allergies.

Most modern fabrics contain a small percentage of Lycra to give them a little bit of stretch.

✳ Most people who prefer wearing "natural" fabrics buy cotton clothes, but they should be aware that commercial cotton cultivation employs chemical fertilizers and pesticides to maximize yield, which causes a significant environmental burden and exposes cotton pickers to health risks. However, the textile industry has now created special standards to ensure that consumers are not exposed to any harmful substances (see page 131, "Have confidence in your textiles.")

✳ In terms of consumption of natural resources, the production of cotton and chemical fibers ranks fairly evenly: while manufacturing synthetic fibers requires more energy, growing cotton uses vast quantities of water.

✳ To make the most of each fabric's properties, it is common to combine natural and synthetic fibers. Most modern fabrics contain a small percentage of Lycra, for example, because we find clothes with a bit of stretch to be more comfortable. This is particularly true for many denim fabrics. And as synthetic fibers are stronger and hold their shape better than natural fibers, they are frequently combined with natural fibers to improve their durability and ease of care.

WE WANT WOOL SWEATERS THAT AREN'T ITCHY AND COTTON T-SHIRTS THAT HOLD THEIR SHAPE.

COTTON IS SPUN FROM THE DOWNY FIBERS INSIDE COTTONSEED CAPSULES.

Easy fix Don't remove the care labels on your clothes so you'll always know what material they are made from and how to wash and iron them. Cut out any bothersome labels and put them into a small envelope with a brief description of the item, such as "wrap-around blouse, light blue."

Insider's hack If you want to make sustainable choices, take the durability of clothing into account. Whether they're made from cotton, silk or synthetic fibers – the longer you wear clothes, the better it will be for the environment. Also, think about shopping in second-hand or charity shops, where you can often find high-quality clothes in very good condition.

Save money Buy good-quality T-shirts made from long-fiber ("long-staple") cotton. These are not only softer and easier to iron, but also retain their shape and color better so you don't need to replace them as often. Ultimately, this approach will turn out cheaper.

Modern MICROFIBER fabrics

Microfiber is a generic term for fabrics made from extremely fine, usually synthetic, fibers. On average, each microfiber (dozens of which are spun together to make a single thread) is one-tenth the thickness of a human hair. Microfiber fabrics are soft, dry

quickly and retain their shape well. You can find modern microfibers almost everywhere in the form of upholstery, towels, curtains, bed covers, mops and cleaning cloths, among others (see also page 161, "Microfiber cloths in the kitchen.")

✳ This "miracle fiber" has become firmly established for both outerwear and underwear, as microfiber fabrics are supple, soft to the touch, yet tear-resistant. People with allergies or sensitive skin tend to tolerate microfiber well, which is also breathable and therefore makes excellent sportswear. It comes as no surprise then that microfiber textiles are becoming more and more popular.

Each microfiber is one-tenth the thickness of a human hair.

✳ The quality of different microfiber fabrics can differ substantially, however; that's why it pays to check for high-quality materials and finishes to ensure that you will enjoy maximum benefit from this special fiber.

✳ Always read care labels to ensure your microfiber textiles last. As a rule, you only need to use a little laundry detergent and you can machine-wash them at low temperatures. Always hang up microfiber fabrics as soon as the laundry cycle is finished to prevent creasing. Microfiber clothes usually do not need ironing; if they have wrinkled, iron them inside out at a low setting only.

TAKE CARE
Avoid using fabric softener with microfiber fabrics. Softeners attach to the surface of the fiber and prevent it from functioning as intended, as far as moisture wicking and breathability are concerned.

How fibers BECOME FABRICS

There are three main processes for turning fibers into fabrics and textiles: weaving, weft knitting and warp knitting.

✴ Weaving involves a weft yarn being interlaced with parallel warp yarns. How these yarns then interlace with each other (the "weave") determines the look of the final fabric. The simplest weave is plain linen weave, in which the weft is guided over and under the warp yarns in a regular criss-cross pattern. Woven fabrics usually do not stretch, unless a Lycra thread is woven into them.

✴ Weft-knitted fabrics consist of interlaced loops or stitches of yarn, with the horizontal yarn forming the loops. Types of knitted fabrics include interlock, rib, purl and jersey or single-knit. Knitted fabrics in general stretch very well. Pantyhose is, for example, knitted from tiny loops.

✴ Warp-knitted fabrics are also made from loops, but in contrast to weft knitting, the loops are added in vertical columns instead of rows due to a special

MICROFIBER IS BREATHABLE AND THEREFORE MAKES EXCELLENT SPORTSWEAR.

Expert advice

Have confidence in your textiles

The OEKO-TEX® Standard 100 is a globally uniform testing and certification system for textiles: the raw materials, as well as intermediate and final products, are tested at all stages of production, with the aim of completely eliminating harmful substances.

★ The tests conducted for harmful substances cover substances that are prohibited or regulated by law and chemicals that are harmful to health, as well as testing parameters that are included as a precautionary measure to safeguard health.

★ OEKO-TEX® tests are carried out exclusively by authorized, independent textile research and test institutes with proven expertise. The tests are based on the OEKO-TEX® modular principle: certification is possible at every stage of the textile manufacturing chain and existing certificates from earlier stages are recognized.

★ A textile that has successfully passed the test may then be marked with the OEKO-TEX® label.

CONFIDENCE IN TEXTILES
Tested for harmful substances according to Oeko-Tex® Standard 100
00000000
Institute

way of guiding the yarn. It can produce fabrics with complicated patterns, colors and textures. Warp knitting creates fabrics that are less stretchy but also less prone to running than weft knitting.

What do those CARE LABELS mean?

Whether made of natural or synthetic fibers, clothes will only give you lasting pleasure if they are cared for properly. Always stick to the recommendations on the care labels to ensure your T-shirts and blouses retain their color, your sweaters stay soft and fluffy and your pants don't shrink. Yet this is sometimes easier said than done: while some care symbols are quite obvious, others look like some sort of alien code. Refer to the summary below to make caring for your clothes easier.

Washing instructions **1** **2** **3** **4** These four symbols relate to the different options you have for washing an item. Symbols 1 indicates that an item can be machine-washed; one dot (symbol 2) specifies cold water, two dots (not shown) suggest

warm water, and three dots (not shown) suggest washing in hot water. Symbol 3 means that an item is delicate and should only be handwashed in lukewarm water using a mild detergent. Symbol 4 means that an item is dry-clean only and shouldn't be washed (such as evening gowns, some woollens, and men's and women's suits).

Ironing instructions **5** **6** **7** Seeing an iron on a care label means that an item may be ironed. The dots in the center (symbols 5 and 6) indicate the highest ironing temperature that may be used, one dot being cool iron, three dots being hot iron. If the label shows symbol 7, that item must not be ironed.

Dry-cleaning instructions **8** **9** If the care label shows symbol 8, an item must be dry-cleaned professionally, while symbol 9 indicates that the fabric is not suitable for dry-cleaning.

Bleaching instructions **10** Textiles marked with symbol 10 don't tolerate chlorine bleaching; that is, to remove stains or brighten whites.

Drying instructions **11** **12** Symbol 11 indicates that an item is safe for the drier. A single dot in the center means that it can be dried only at low heat; three dots (not shown) specify high heat. Textiles marked with symbol 12 shouldn't be tumble-dried.

THESE LABELS MAKE IT EASIER FOR YOU TO CARE FOR YOUR CLOTHES. ALWAYS COMPLY WITH CARE INSTRUCTIONS.

New uses for old PANTYHOSE

Pantyhose, which is generally made from a delicate polyamide/ Lycra knit, snags and runs easily. Pantyhose with a run is often just thrown into the trash. That doesn't always need to happen, as this material has many other household uses.

TOY STUFFING MATERIAL

If a soft toy has lost any of its stuffing, cut some old pantyhose into thin strips, bunch these up and use them as new stuffing. The benefit over synthetic fiber stuffing is that pantyhose strips do not become lumpy.

A SWEET-SMELLING CLOSET

Here is an easy way of storing mothballs or homemade sachets of potpourri in your closet: cut off the foot of your old pantyhose and place the mothballs inside. Tie the top into a knot around a closet rod.

EASY-CLEAN HAIRBRUSHES

Pull a strip of pantyhose tightly around the bristles so that they pierce the fabric. Tie the pantyhose together at the back of the brush. Hairs will then stick to the fabric, which you can eventually simply pull off and replace as needed.

FIND LOST TRINKETS

Have you ever tried searching through a carpet for a lost gemstone, contact lens, or some other tiny, precious item? Try this solution: Cut a leg off an old pair of pantyhose with the toe section intact, and cover the nozzle of your vacuum cleaner with it. Secure the stocking in place with a tightly wound rubber band. Turn on the vacuum, carefully move the nozzle over the carpet, and you'll soon find your lost valuable attached to the homemade filter.

SHINY SHOES

Apply shoe polish to your shoes as usual, but then polish it away with old pantyhose. This works so well that you probably will never use a shoe-shine brush again.

Stains, a problem that never goes away

Whether grease, blood or grass – stains on clothes are always a nuisance. But while they may be unavoidable, there are a number of ways to deal with them effectively.

Stain-busting GROUND RULES

You generally want to treat stains while they are still as fresh and damp as possible – this makes it easier to remove them fully. Launder washable textiles after stain treatment and have other fabrics dry-cleaned. There is a wide range of sprays and gels for pre-treating stains available, and you can also pre-treat or even remove many stains using home remedies (see also page 19, "Solving a problem carpet stain.") The best way to remove stains depends on both the type of stain and the material to be cleaned: delicate fabrics cannot be treated with hot water or harsh cleaning agents, for example. Always check care labels first.

MUSTARD, TOMATO SAUCE and milk

Gently rub soapy water or ammonia into mustard stains to remove. You can soak older mustard stains with glycerine: apply and leave to absorb for an hour, then launder the item or have it dry-cleaned.

✳ Tomato sauce stains are common on children's clothes. Use a paper towel to absorb as much of the sauce as possible, then dab the stain with lukewarm water before carefully rubbing it out with salt water (1 teaspoon table salt in 2 cups water).

✳ Milk stains are relatively easy to remove: simply treat fresh stains with warm soapy water. For dried milk stains, soak the item in warm soapy water before laundering it as usual.

CAREFULLY RUB TOMATO SAUCE STAINS WITH SALT WATER.

BALLPOINT PEN, ink and felt pen

Markers and pens often leave marks on our clothes – not just those of schoolchildren.

✳ Lemon juice is an effective treatment for ballpoint pen stains. Drizzle fresh stains immediately with lemon juice and then launder the item according to its care instructions.

✳ You can treat fresh ink stains by sprinkling the stained area repeatedly with salt and rinsing under running water. Alternatively, drizzle stains with lemon juice before laundering as usual.

✳ Remove felt-pen stains by dissolving the ink with alcohol and turpentine. Repeat several times, then launder as usual. If your stain was made by permanent marker, however, save your effort – this will be almost impossible to remove.

DRIZZLE INK STAINS WITH LEMON JUICE BEFORE LAUNDERING THE ITEM AS USUAL.

FATS AND OILS, coffee and tea

Remove oil stains from textiles by sprinkling them immediately with cornstarch, allowing the starch to soak up the oil then brushing it out. Baking soda is another alternative. Most fresh oil stains can also be scrubbed with hot water (over 140°F) and dishwashing liquid, but note that synthetic fibers do not tolerate high temperatures.

You can treat fresh ink stains by sprinkling repeatedly with salt and rinsing under running water.

✳ Use a different approach for dried oil stains. If they are on delicate fabric, cover the stain with parchment paper and iron over the stain. Have the setting just hot enough so that the oil melts and is soaked up by the paper.

✳ You should pre-treat greasy dirt, for example found inside collars, by rubbing a citrus-based stain-removal spray or laundry (available from at supermarkets or online) into the stain and leaving it on for a little while before washing the item as per its care instructions.

✳ For thick grease, use a spatula or a dull knife-edge to remove the excess grease. Lay the fabric, stain side down, on a cloth and blot dry-cleaning solvent from the inside to force the stain out.

✳ Soak coffee stains on clothes immediately in cold salt water; alternatively, pour sparkling mineral water into a cup, add a few drops of dishwashing liquid and dab at the stain repeatedly using a cotton swab. The carbon dioxide contained in the mineral water will dissolve the stain. Treat old coffee stains by dabbing on glycerine before washing.

✳ Remove tea stains by simply washing the item in warm water; alternatively, soak the clothing in mineral water solution (as for coffee stains) before laundering as usual.

TAKE CARE

Before using a cleaning solution on a garment or upholstered furniture, test it on an inconspicuous spot first to make sure the fabric can tolerate it.

BLOOD, RED WINE and grass

The golden rule for blood stains in clothes is to rinse them immediately with cold water. Never use hot water, as it causes the protein in blood to coagulate, making it more difficult to remove. Soak stubborn and/or dried blood stains in salt water or with an oxygen alkaline stain remover (if the fabric is colorfast). Treat dried blood additionally with laundry soap.

✳ Don't sprinkle fresh red wine stains with salt or cornflour (for delicate fabrics) and try to brush the stain out: the salt will absorb the liquid, but the reddish-brown color will remain. Instead, rinse the stain under warm running water or mineral water to remove as much wine as possible, then machine-wash the item immediately. Take items that cannot be machine-washed to the dry-cleaner and hope for the best.

✳ Dried red wine stains are much more difficult to treat. Try applying glass cleaner: spray on, leave it to soak for 15 minutes, then wash (see also page 19, "Solving a problem carpet stain.")

DRIED RED WINE STAINS ARE DIFFICULT TO TREAT — TRY GLASS CLEANER.

✳ Rub fresh grass stains on delicate fabrics gently with liquid laundry detergent. Use ammonia or denatured alcohol for more robust fabrics. Cover old grass stains in a mixture of egg white and glycerine (1:1), then launder clothes as usual.

SWEAT, WAX and glue

Make sweat stains disappear by applying a solution of 1 tablespoon vinegar to 3 tablespoons water; you can also treat non-delicate fabrics with a half-strength solution of ammonia and water.

✳ For wax stains, first scrape off as much of the wax as possible; then place the fabric between two layers of parchment paper. Iron the spot at the highest setting possible for the fabric until the paper has absorbed the stain. Colored wax may leave a residual stain, which can be treated by dabbing on denatured alcohol; any residue should vanish with dry-cleaning.

✳ Glue is best removed as quickly as possible. For clear glue stains, apply Eau de Cologne or an oil-free nail polish remover; in other cases try turpentine,

FOR WAX STAINS, PLACE THE FABRIC BETWEEN TWO LAYERS OF KITCHEN PAPER THEN IRON AT THE HIGHEST SETTING POSSIBLE.

denatured alcohol or lighter fuel. As most of these products are quite aggressive, you should try them on an inconspicuous spot first.

Avoid and remove
MOLD STAINS

Mold and mildew cause yellowish and brownish discoloration on fabrics. These fungi thrive in conditions where there is little air circulation, such as when clothes and linen are hung up or stacked very tightly. (Mildew stains in books develop in a similar way.) To prevent mold stains, air closets and bedrooms regularly, especially when it's dry outside, and occasionally unfold and re-stack all of your folded clothes and linens.

✳ If you discover mold stains, you can sometimes remove them by soaking affected items in vinegar before laundering as usual. Soaking in buttermilk can also be helpful. Use chlorine-based bleach only with great care and according to instructions, as it can cause colors to fade.

✳ Treat mold stains on silk or viscose by gently dabbing on borax (available from supermarkets or hardware stores) and washing at the highest possible temperature for that fabric.

Save money Air moldy clothes or linen in full sun, as UV light kills mold and mildew spores. Then launder at 140°F or even 190°F, if possible. However, there is no guarantee of success.

CHOCOLATE and chewing gum

The general rule that stains should be treated as quickly as possible does not apply to chocolate or chewing gum stains. Quite the contrary – allow these to dry first.

✳ Leave chocolate stains to harden and then scrape off as much as possible using the back of a knife. Soak the item in soapy water for about 30 minutes before washing it with an enzyme-based detergent. Alternatively, rinse with clear water after soaking, drizzle the stain with lemon juice, leave on for a little and then rinse again with clear water.

✳ For non-washable fabrics, first scrape away the chocolate as before, then use a damp sponge to blot at the stain, being careful not to over-wet the area.

✳ Unfortunately, it is easy to pick up chewing gum stains on pants or skirts from park benches or restaurant chairs. Chewing gum is, of course, highly annoying, but fortunately is not difficult to remove, especially from denim. Place the item in a plastic bag and put it in the freezer, as you can scrape off frozen chewing gum quite easily. Brush off any residue before laundering the item as usual.

Leave chewing gum stains to firm up in the freezer as you can scrape off frozen chewing gum quite easily.

✳ If you do not have a freezer, apply ice cubes to the stain, then proceed as described above once the gum has firmed up.

LEAVE CHOCOLATE STAINS TO HARDEN AND THEN SCRAPE OFF AS MUCH AS POSSIBLE WITH A KNIFE.

Store clothes properly

Your dresses, coats, skirts, pants, shirts and sweaters all need a suitable home, where they will be well protected. Most of the time the best place for them will be in your closet.

OPTIMUM USE of your closet

The closet is not only a place for storing clothes and accessories, but it also protects clothes against wrinkles and dust. If you keep your closet organized, you won't have to search for your favorite clothes. This is easy if you approach the task systematically (see also page 53, "Bedroom storage strategies.")

Sift out any clothes that haven't been worn in about five years to create space in your closet.

✳ First, get a good overview of all the clothes you have. This will let you decide how much and what kind of storage space you will need; for example, hanging rods for dresses, skirts and shirts, shelves for sweaters and T-shirts, and drawers for underwear and accessories. Sift out any clothes that haven't been worn in about five years to create space in your closet.

✳ A systematic approach will make it easier to find things: keep your favorite, frequently worn clothes

SPACE IS IMPORTANT FOR STORING CLOTHES – AVOID HANGING CLOTHES HANGERS TOO TIGHTLY.

accessible – hang them at the front of the closet or place them on easily reachable shelves. Items that you don't wear regularly should be stored in the top shelves or hung in the back.

✳ Space is important for storing clothes – avoid hanging clothes hangers too tightly, do not stack too many sweaters and T-shirts on top of each other, and do not overload drawers. Otherwise you may rummage through everything just to get to one item.

✳ Set your clothes rods at different heights to make the most effective use of your closet space. You will need a high rod for long items such as dresses, and two rods placed at a shorter distance from each other for shirts and skirts or pants. Tiered hangers are useful for small closets.

✳ If your bedroom space is limited, it is a good idea to get a closet with sliding doors. Invest in a high-quality model with ball bearings; otherwise you may soon find yourself struggling with doors that catch or are difficult to move.

Save time To avoid rummaging through a big pile of socks to find what you want, line your sock drawer with two or three open shoe boxes. Sort dress socks, casual socks and sports socks into the appropriate compartments so you'll be able to find what you're looking for in a flash.

Easy fix There is a straightforward way to prevent your closet from bursting from its seams: every time you buy something new, give away or discard an old piece of clothing.

Insider's hack Do you like hanging your pants on coat hangers with a horizontal bar, but find that the bar creases them? Simply wrap the bar with a few layers of bubble wrap held in place with adhesive tape to solve this problem.

Save money Revive the drawers of an old unused dresser as under-bed storage. Attach casters to each bottom corner (look for space-saving ones) to make a rolling storage compartment.

CLOTHES HANGER PERFECTION

1 Buy hangers that are the same width as the shoulders of your tops to prevent unsightly hanger stretch marks.

2 Plain plastic hangers are lightweight and take up less space than wooden hangers; they are best for your shirts, blouses and tops.

3 Choose high-quality, shaped wooden hangers to keep heavy coats and jackets in shape. These hangers have thick, rounded ends that fit inside the shoulders of clothes.

4 Avoid metal hangers unless made from stainless steel or coated with plastic or fabric; otherwise they may cause rust stains.

Chemical-free protection from CLOTHES MOTHS

If you wish to avoid an unpleasant surprise when getting your warm wool sweaters out for winter, you'll find learning about moths and how to prevent or address a moth problem helpful.

✳ Clothes moths are troublesome pests whose larvae feed mainly on animal hair. That's why clothes made of wool, silk, fur and leather are particularly at risk for infestation. Moths eat the fibers of sweaters, shirts and coats, leaving numerous holes; they can also infest blended fabrics with a wool or

Expert advice

Walk right in

Do you have a bedroom in your home that's lying empty because your children have left home? Consider converting it into a walk-in closet to create more space in your bedroom.

You could take two different approaches when setting up a walk-in closet:

★ Buy a simple, white modular closet system minus the doors (remove them if included) for easy open access to all your clothes. Install the units according to the manufacturer's instructions.

★ Fit shelves and clothes rods to the room itself. Attach shelves to the walls with screws and fasten clothes rails to the walls or ceiling, depending on the system chosen. Make sure you attach shelves with a suspended rod underneath firmly, as they will have to support a lot of weight once clothes are hung on the rod.

MOTHS DO NOT LIKE THE SCENT OF LAVENDER; USE LAVENDER SACHETS TO HELP KEEP THEM AWAY.

silk base. The only fabrics they reject are those made purely of plant materials, such as cotton, hemp or linen.

✳ Your best protection against moths is prevention. Moths love skin flakes and the scent of sweat, so try to only hang clean, washed clothes in your closet. Store valuable, at-risk items inside cotton pillow cases or sealed in vacuum storage bags.

✳ There are plenty of proven home remedies to prevent moth infestations. These annoying pests do not like the scent of lavender, cloves or cedar wood, for example, so placing a sachet of lavender or cloves (available from health-food shops, supermarkets or online) or cedar-wood balls inside closets helps to keep them away. Replace these regularly before their scent vanishes.

✳ Check your clothes, air your closets and re-stack or rehang clothes regularly, as moths do not like movement. Also make sure that vulnerable clothes are stored somewhere cool and dry, because moths like warm, moist environments.

`Insider's hack` Once cedar balls start losing their scent, rough up the surface with sandpaper to release more of their scent. You can also add some drops of cedar oil.

IF YOU DISCOVER MOTHS IN YOUR CLOSET, YOU'LL NEED TO TAKE INSTANT ACTION.

MOTH INFESTATION!
What can you do?

If you discover moths in your closet despite all precautions, it's time to take instant action.

✳ Empty the closet entirely and check in all corners, the floor and any crevices to find any nests, larvae and moths. Vacuum and wipe the closet thoroughly, and leave it open to air for two or three days. Keep the windows open in dry weather. Then clean the closet once more.

✳ Check clothes for moth damage and consider whether any need to be thrown out. Everything that is still salvageable needs to be washed at a temperature of at least 140°F (if the fabric permits) as the high temperature will kill off eggs and larvae. Hang clothes outside in full sun, as moths cannot tolerate direct sunlight. Alternatively, iron fabrics at high heat (if possible). Delicates that can only tolerate a warm wash should be dry-cleaned.

✳ If these measures don't get rid of clothes moths, try using a clothes moth trap. Note, however, that these products may contain insecticides that damage our health and the environment. Scented sachets and sprays containing essential oils are a more natural alternative, but while less harmful, they can cause headaches and skin allergies in sensitive people.

`Easy fix` As well as sunlight, moths can be killed by cold temperatures. Shake clothes out thoroughly, wrap them in a plastic bag and place them in your freezer (this temperature hovers around –4°F). Most moths and larvae will be dead within a week, but leave the clothes in the freezer for up to four weeks to be safe.

`Insider's hack` If you have pets or small children, you should avoid using traditional moth balls, as naphthalene, one of the active ingredients, is highly toxic if inhaled or swallowed.

Dealing with MOLD AND MILDEW

If your closet has a musty smell, or you discover clothes covered with a whitish or greenish coating, these are signs of mold and mildew.

✳ Mold and mildew usually develop when you put away clothes or linens in the closet before they are properly dry. Once the closet doors are closed, humidity remains trapped inside, allowing mold and mildew to grow.

✳ Another reason for moldy and mildewed clothing can be if your closets are located in front of a cold external wall. This can cause condensation forming at the back of the closet, which creates an environment where molds thrive (see also page 217, "The right ventilation.")

✳ If you suspect there is mold in your closet, clear out and inspect all of your clothes and linens. Use your sense of smell too – take action even if there is

only a musty smell without any visible signs of mold. Air all clothes and linens thoroughly in the sun before washing them or having them dry-cleaned to remove the musty smell. Meanwhile, clean the closet thoroughly.

✳ A cleaning agent with citric acid as the active ingredient is particularly useful in the fight against mold, as it will eliminate small mold stains and leave a pleasantly fresh scent. If there is a lot of mold with a slimy coating formed, you may need a vinegar cleaner. After cleaning, leave the empty closet open to allow it to dry out and air properly for a few days – even consider placing a fan inside or just out front – before putting your machine-washed or dry-cleaned clothes and linens back inside.

✳ If you find mold on your clothes, you need to act quickly, as only relatively fresh, small mold stains are removable. Rub soap or lemon juice into the stains using a soft brush before machine-washing the items at 140°F or hotter, if possible, and allowing them to dry in full sun. The UV light from the sun will kill any remaining mold spores.

✳ You can treat mold stains on white cotton with a chlorine-based bleach. Machine-wash using the hottest cycle and leave to dry in the sun.

TREAT MOLD STAINS ON WHITE COTTON WITH A CHLORINE-BASED BLEACH, THEN DRY IN THE SUN.

✳ For high-quality clothes such as suits and dresses that aren't machine-washable, beat mold stains out in the fresh air before having the items dry-cleaned.

✳ If you can't remove mold stains with any of these measures, then the clothing or accessory can't be rescued. You will need to discard it, no matter how hard that may be.

✳ Moldy leather handbags and belts can generally not be rescued and need to be discarded.

TAKE CARE

Never shake out or beat clothes affected by mold without wearing a particle face mask (available from hardware stores or online), as the mold spores are harmful to your health.

Treat your shoes well

We all have several pairs of shoes, and we want to enjoy them for as long as possible, especially as good-quality shoes are expensive. Take care of your footwear to keep it in tip-top shape.

SHOE STORAGE solutions

Our feet release a lot of moisture every day, which is absorbed by our shoes. While leather and other natural materials allow feet to breathe, they also retain moisture, which can cause odor or even mold. That's why it is best to leave shoes to air before putting them away.

✳ Use shoe trees to keep your shoes in shape. Damp leather shoes are prone to losing their form.

✳ Shoes that you wear only rarely will gather dust over time. Store them in fabric bags to keep them clean, or place them individually inside old stockings or socks. Never store leather shoes in plastic, which will cause them to go musty.

✳ Shoes are best stored in a shoe rack or cabinet, but make sure they are clean, dry and well aired before putting them away.

✳ If you are going to buy a new shoe cabinet, check that it has ventilation slots to let air circulate. Look for cabinets that have height-adjustable shelves or compartments – ideal for accommodating sandals, pumps and men's shoes. Fold-out shoe cabinets are not very practical if any family member has large feet, as the compartments are usually too small for shoes above size 11.

Save money Quality shoe trees, such as red cedar ones, come at a price, but you can use scrunched-up paper towel as a cheap alternative. Place rolled-up magazines inside boot legs to keep them straight and in shape.

A SHOE-CLEANING primer

Well-cared-for shoes not only look good, they also last longer. That's why it is worthwhile knowing how to clean shoes properly.

✳ Use a firm brush to remove coarse dirt from smooth leather shoes, then wipe off any remaining residue with a damp cloth. Apply shoe polish with another cloth; reserve a different cloth for each color polish. Buff off the polish with a very soft brush and reserve two separate polishing brushes for light- and dark-colored shoes.

MAKE SURE SHOES ARE CLEAN, DRY AND WELL AIRED BEFORE PUTTING THEM AWAY.

TAKE CARE

Never place wet leather shoes on a heater for drying; this will make the leather hard and brittle, and prone to cracking.

✳ Clean suede and nubuck leather shoes with a special suede or rubber brush (available from shoe stores or shoe repair shops). They are usually double-sided – use the brush side to clean and the rubber pile side to raise the leather nap.

✳ Water marks on smooth leather shoes are best removed by rubbing at the marks with the cut side of half an onion or a little lemon juice. Leave on briefly, then brush off. Remove water marks from suede leather by rubbing them off with salt.

✳ Talcum powder or cornstarch are both effective treatments for smelly shoes. Sprinkle on and leave overnight. Shake out well, then dry with a blow dryer.

Easy fix Fabric sneakers are machine-washable. It is best to wash them together with towels to prevent the shoes from beating against the drum of the washing machine.

Insider's hack An easy fix for colored shoes that stain socks and stockings is simply to spray hairspray inside the shoes. Leave to dry well before wearing the shoes next. There will be no more stains.

Save money There's no need to discard dried-out shoe polish. Gently warm the polish on a heater or in the sun to make it soft and smooth again.

Don't neglect RUBBER BOOTS

What should you do with wet rubber boots after gardening or a rainy-day walk? If you leave them outside, they won't dry. If you take them off inside and leave them in the hall, they can fall over, soil the floor and look messy.

✳ An easy solution is to repurpose a plastic laundry basket as a catch-all for all things muddy and to keep your hall clean and tidy.

✳ To clean rubber boots, simply mix up a solution of warm water and dishwashing liquid in a spray bottle. Spray on, leave for a few minutes then buff off with an old rag.

✳ Place a packet or two of silica gel inside each boot to dry them out quickly before they start smelling. Silica gel comes in small pouches of highly absorbent granules; you'll find them inside the packaging of new shoes, electronic goods or handbags. You probably used to throw them out, but waste them no more!

Insider's hack If rain or water somehow gets inside your boots, scrunch up some sheets of newspaper and stuff these into the boots. The dry paper will quickly absorb the moisture and save you from moldy boots.

REPURPOSE A PLASTIC LAUNDRY BASKET AS A CATCH-ALL FOR ALL THINGS MUDDY.

Look after jewelry

We value our jewelry, not only because of its exquisite materials, but also because it often reminds us of precious moments in our lives. Treat your keepsakes with care.

Protect your PRECIOUS PIECES

Whether you love elegant gold or silver jewelry set with gemstones, or prefer trendy fashion or ethnic pieces, you should always store it appropriately to make it last.

✳ Pearls are delicate and should be kept separate in a jewelry box inlaid with velvet or another soft fabric. This is also true for gold, which is a relatively soft metal that scratches easily. Pure gold is usually alloyed with another metal to make jewelry, and the higher the gold content the softer the material. Check the metal stamp for the gold content: if it says 750, for example, the alloy contains 750 parts gold per 1000 parts in total. This is equivalent to 18 carat gold (where pure gold is expressed as the maximum of 24 carats).

✳ Decorative fashion jewelry is generally made of glass or plastic – or materials such as wood, leather, porcelain and non-precious metals – which is less delicate than "genuine" jewelry. You can store these items in bowls or boxes, or hang them up on hooks or jewelry stands.

✳ Silver can oxidize (turn black) if it is not worn for extended periods. It is therefore best to wrap your silver rings, earrings, necklaces and bracelets in aluminium foil or a silver cleaning cloth. Another option is to keep a piece of chalk with your silver jewelry to prevent oxidation.

Save time Pull thin necklaces that tangle easily through individual drinking straws. Close the clasps outside the straw to make sure each and every one is always ready to be worn.

STORE VALUABLE JEWELRY FROM GOOD JEWELERS IN ITS ORIGINAL CASE TO ENSURE IT RETAINS ITS FULL VALUE.

Easy fix Can't get a ring off your finger? Simply spray the finger with a little window cleaner, and the ring will slide off easily.

Insider's hack Store valuable jewelry from good jewelers in its original case. This not only provides optimal protection, but adds to its value if you want to sell it or give it as a gift later on.

DIY JEWELRY cleaning

If your jewelry has become tarnished or dirty over time, despite your most careful storage efforts, there are a few simple home remedies to clean and restore it to its full glory.

✳ Simply wipe fashion jewelry with a damp cloth, as detergents may damage the material. Sprinkle soiled jewelry with baking soda and gently scrub it with a soft toothbrush, then rinse with warm water and pat dry.

✳ Place gold jewelry into a kitchen strainer for cleaning (clean pieces individually so they do not become scratched). Add a little dishwashing liquid and hold the strainer under running hot water. You can also clean solid gold jewelry (that is not merely gold-plated) with baking soda: first apply the powder to a damp cotton pad, wipe the piece carefully and then rinse.

✳ Onion juice will perk up gold jewelry that has lost its shine; leave it on for about three hours, then polish away with a soft cloth.

✳ Clean tarnished sterling silver jewelry with aluminium foil: cover a deep plate or bowl with foil, place the jewelry on top, sprinkle with salt then pour boiling water over it. Leave to stand for an hour, then polish the pieces with a soft cloth to restore their full shine. Alternatively, wrap the jewelry in aluminium foil, place in a saucepan of water and briefly bring to a boil. Be careful, though: don't use the foil method if silver jewelry has intentionally blackened parts that create an antique finish, as it will brighten these, too. Also avoid this method if your jewelry contains porous precious stones such as turquoise or pearls. A gentler alternative is to place the jewelry in a saucepan of water, add half a teaspoon of dishwashing liquid and boil it for two to three minutes.

ORGANIZE YOUR EARRING COLLECTION

It is not easy to store earrings in a way that is tidy, keeps pairs together and prevents them from becoming tangled, but here is a surprisingly simple and decorative idea. You can turn those jewels into a piece of art worthy to hang on a wall!

1 Buy a wooden picture frame and some wire mesh. Cut a piece of mesh to fit the outside dimensions of the frame.

2 Place the mesh on the back of the frame and fix it in place with small tacks.

3 Hang the earring frame on a wall, or stand it on a bedside table, and push your earrings through the mesh in pairs.

✳ Gemstones must be treated with care. Use a fine brush to remove dust and clean hard gemstones such as diamonds, rubies and sapphires with pure alcohol or a solution of 1 quart water and 2 tablespoons ammonia. Remove soap, grease and cosmetics, which may accumulate in claw or prong settings, with a soft toothbrush, then rinse and pat dry with a microfiber cloth.

✳ Opals are very delicate – only polish them with a microfiber cloth. To clean, gently wash opals in warm water with mild detergent and a soft brush or microfiber cloth.

Easy fix If you need to clean your jewelry or glasses regularly, it may be worthwhile investing in an ultrasonic jewelry cleaner. Inexpensive, they are available to buy online.

Insider's hack For precious gemstone jewelry, you may want to have it cleaned professionally by a jeweler, who will also check whether the settings are still in good condition. Have scratched gold pieces professionally polished by a goldsmith.

Caring for AMBER, PEARLS and coral

Amber, pearl and coral jewelry needs special care, as these non-mineral materials are more delicate than gemstones and most jewelry stones.

✳ Clean soiled amber with lukewarm water and pat dry immediately. A few drops of olive oil buffed onto amber will restore shine. Spread white chalk on grease stains, leave on for a few hours and then wipe off with a soft cloth. Amber is affected by heat so it's best not to wear it while cooking.

✳ The best care you can give pearls is to wear them often, as skin contact makes them retain their luster. However, remember to give them a wipe with a soft wool cloth after each wear. Periodically remove dust, sweat and grime by dabbing the pearls with a

AMBER, PEARL AND CORAL JEWELRY NEEDS SPECIAL CARE, AS IT IS DELICATE.

cloth dipped in a dilute solution of alcohol and water. Re-dip the cloth in fresh water to wipe clean, then buff dry with a soft cloth.

✳ Clean coral jewelry in sudsy water, rinse under clean water and polish with a microfiber cloth. Avoid soaking coral jewelry in liquid as it can absorb moisture and look dull. As coral is a soft stone, store jewels separately to avoid scratches.

✳ You should think twice about buying new coral jewelry, but by all means keep wearing existing pieces. While only a few species of coral are covered under the Washington CITES agreement, all coral reefs are threatened habitats. It is almost impossible to verify the type and origin of commercially sold coral, so it is best to avoid it altogether if you do not want to contribute to the destruction of reefs.

Insider's hack Take care not to let amber air-dry when you clean it, as you risk turning the stone cloudy. Air-drying is fine for pearls and coral.

chapter **5**

Great Ideas in the Kitchen

Grocery shopping know-how

You can save a lot of time and money if you stop and think about what you really need before you go shopping. Make a list. It's a good way to stop yourself from buying things you don't need or buying too much of what you do need.

Be a SAVVY SHOPPER

The following tips can help you get the shopping done quicker, save money and come home with fresh, top-quality groceries and produce.

✳ Lower-priced products are often placed on the lower shelves in supermarkets. Knowing this can save you a lot of money. If you are not in good shape physically or have back problems, ask a staff member to help you.

✳ Supermarkets often have products in bulk packs at significantly better prices than smaller-sized packages. Check the label for the item cost per ounce or pound to compare if you're not sure. If you are shopping for a small household only, consider splitting a bulk pack with neighbors or friends.

✳ Always check the weight of fruit and vegetables sold by the container as another shopper may have picked individual pieces out of the container.

✳ Make sure packaging is in good condition before you buy. Dented cans are best left on the shelf. Don't buy dairy products if the lid is bulging upwards, even if they are still within the expiration date, as this is a sign that the contents may have spoiled. Take care when buying frozen foods, too. The supermarket's freezers should not have a thick build-up of ice, and the products should have no sign of freezer burn.

✳ Fresh beef should be rich red in color, pork should be a paler pinkish red. Signs that fish is fresh include a mild scent with moist flesh.

✳ Keep a stash of reusable shopping

my weekly menu planner

monday
breakfast
oatmeal

lunch
sandwich

dinner
no-meat Monday!

tuesday
breakfast
muesli

lunch
salad

dinner
lasagna

wednesday
breakfast
toast at work

lunch
leftover lasagna

dinner
fish & salad

thursday
breakfast
cereali

lunch
lunch out

dinner
· pumpkin soup
· bread rolls

friday
breakfast
toast at work

lunch
pumpkin soup

dinner
· chicken breast
· carrots
· beans
· potatoes

saturday
brunch
breakfast at diner

afternoon
cheese and fruit

dinner
dinner with Beryl

sunday
brunch
quiche and muffins

afternoon
picnic at the park

dinner
· leftovers
· avocado toast

lunch box extras
rice crackers

drinks
· juice boxes: OJ & apple
· wine

snacks
dips for picnic

baking

WHEN YOU GO SHOPPING, TAKE YOUR LIST WITH YOU. IT COULD BE BASED ON YOUR WEEK'S MENU PLAN.

TAKE CARE

Never go to the supermarket when you're hungry. If your stomach is growling, there is a much greater chance you'll buy things you don't need – and end up spending more. Have a meal or a snack first, then go shopping!

bags handy in the trunk of the car, or a couple of foldaway ones in your everyday bag, for when you go grocery shopping so you can say "no" to plastic bags at the checkout.

✳ As much as you can, keep to the perimeters of the supermarket. This is where you'll find the fresh and frozen foods – packaged and processed foods dominate the center aisles.

Insider's hack Keep an eye on pantry supplies so you can stock up as needed on long-lasting products such as canned foods, dried foods, long-life milk and soft drinks. Do a big shop once a month and take advantage of bulk buys or "two for one" deals.

Save money Supermarkets often reduce the price of food that is close to its expiration date. Make the most of this if it's something you're likely to eat quickly or you can freeze for later. You'll also often find good deals at farmers' markets towards closing time.

A SHOPPING LIST

TAKE YOUR TIME	Compile your shopping list over time. Put the list up in a conspicuous place in the kitchen so you can add to it every time you notice you've run out of something. If you write your list just before you go shopping, you usually won't remember everything you need.
THINK ABOUT MENUS	Before you head out to the shops, come up with a rough menu plan for the week to come. Check your pantry and fridge for the ingredients you'll need for these meals; if you don't have them, add them to your shopping list.
DON'T FORGET YOUR LIST	This tip might seem obvious, but plenty of people get to the shops only to find that their carefully prepared shopping list is still at home. With no list, you're likely to forget half of what you need, so make a mental note to always check your bag or pockets before you leave the house. Or keep your shopping list on your smartphone, either as a note or in a shopping list app, so it's always with you.

KEEP REUSABLE SHOPPING BAGS HANDY SO YOU CAN SAY "NO" TO PLASTIC BAGS AT THE CHECKOUT.

Choose LOCAL PRODUCE in season

If you have a farmers' market near you, this is a great place to find fresh, high-quality fruit and vegetables in season. Typically, the produce at these markets is sold directly by growers from nearby farms. It's a chance to ask growers about their farming methods – they may not have organic accreditation but still use organic methods, for example. Eliminating long-distance transport means the food arrives fresher, and can be better environmentally, too.

✳ You may also be able to find locally grown produce in some greengrocers and supermarkets – the boxes that fruit and vegetables are packed in will usually indicate the place of origin.

"BEST BEFORE" and "use by" dates

Manufacturers must provide a "best before" date on packaged food. This is the date up until which a product will not deteriorate in flavor or quality, provided it is stored under appropriate conditions. A product will not necessarily have spoiled once its best before date has passed, and it may still be sold so long as it is in sound condition.

✳ Perishable foods such as meat, poultry and dairy products must be marked with a "use by" date as opposed to a "best before" date, and the packaging must also include information about the required storage conditions. Food marked with a "use by" date may not be sold once that date has passed.

✳ A "sell-by" date helps the stores determine when products should remain on shelves. Once this date has passed, the store should no longer display the product for sale.

The language of FOOD LABELS

Wherever you're buying it, to be sure that a food is really good, you have to look behind fancy packaging and clever wording to identify the essential facts. Learn to spot the words that may give a product a halo of quality but guarantee no such thing – and make a point of ignoring them.

✳ Many familiar terms seen on food packaging may have no legal definition whatsoever. Watch out for: "artisan," "traditional," "pure," "fresh" and "natural." Some products do live up to the promise, but you can't take that for granted. Similarly, a label on the front may feature mouth-watering pictures of food, or idyllic images of green fields and happy animals. Be sure to read the fine-print nutrition information label on the back, with the hard facts.

A FARMERS' MARKET IS A GREAT PLACE TO FIND FRESH PRODUCE AND IT'S USUALLY GOOD VALUE FOR MONEY, TOO.

✳ Many food manufacturers are well-practiced in placing phrases on their packaging to suggest that the product has a healthy nutritional profile, which may not be the case. A product with a "low fat" label might sound healthy, but that product could be loaded with sugar, processed starches or salt.

✳ "No added sugar" sounds promising, but a food or drink with this on the label may contain an artificial sweetener that might be controversial health-wise. The phrase "as part of a balanced diet" might suggest you can eat a product freely, but strictly means you must take its ingredients and calories into account. "Supplies your energy needs" is just a clever way of saying that a food has calories: it certainly doesn't mean that it's a particularly healthy food.

✳ Remember that a higher price doesn't equate to better taste or quality. If you have any doubts, buy a few different brands, strip off the packaging and do some blind tasting to test your choices objectively.

A LABEL MAY PROMISE MOUTH-WATERING FOOD BUT THE FINE PRINT ON THE BACK WILL CONTAIN HARDER FACTS.

Expert advice

Decoding the nutrition information label

Ingredients Listed from greatest to smallest by weight. Check if the first few ingredients are items high in saturated fat, sodium (salt) or added sugar.

Check servings and calories Look at the serving size and how many servings the package contains. If you eat one serving, the label clearly outlines the nutrients you get. If you eat two servings, you double the calories and nutrients, including the Percent Daily Value (% DV). The Daily Value is how much of a specific nutrient you need to eat in a day. Percent Daily Value tells you how much of a nutrient is in one serving of food compared to the amount you need each day.

Know your fat Opt for foods low in saturated fats, trans fats, and cholesterol for good health and to reduce your risk of heart disease. Total fat intake should be around 25% to 35% of calories. Food that have 5% DV or less are considered low in fat, those with 20% sDV or more are high.

Fiber Aim for 3 g or more per serve.

Sugars Be sure that sugar is not one of the first 5 ingredients. Names for sugar include *sucrose, glucose, high-fructose corn syrup, corn syrup, maple syrup* and *fructose*.

Sodium (salt) Keeping sodium under 1,500 mg per day is ideal but be sure to stay under 2,300 mg per day. A low sodium food contains 140 mg sodium or less per serving.

Use your refrigerator effectively

Once the shopping is done and you've got it back home, you'll want to put the perishables in the fridge as quickly as possible. Choosing the right part of the fridge for each item will have a big impact on how fresh it stays and how long it lasts.

FOR EACH TYPE OF FOOD, THERE IS AN OPTIMAL POSITION IN THE FRIDGE WHERE THE TEMPERATURE IS BEST.

A WELL-ORGANIZED fridge

To keep everything fresh and know what's where, it pays to be a little organized. The temperature inside a refrigerator varies from one shelf or compartment to the next. For each type of food, there is an optimal place in the fridge, where the temperature is best to keep that food fresh and in good condition for as long as possible.

✳ When you have designated spots for each type of food, your fridge will stay tidier and you'll have a better overview of what you have on hand and what needs to go on the list for your next shopping trip.

WARMER AT THE TOP,
cooler at the bottom

As a general rule, the temperature inside a standard refrigerator is higher at the top than at the bottom. Food will be kept coldest when placed towards the back of the glass shelf at the bottom of the fridge because colder air is denser and sinks to the bottom.

✳ Temperatures are milder in the doors, on the top shelf, and in the fruit and vegetable drawers, which are separated from the rest of the fridge by a shelf. There is typically a 1°F to 2°F difference between the warmest and coldest parts of a fridge.

✳ Temperatures inside a fridge should typically be 40°F. There is a thermostat inside every fridge. Check your user manual to find out which setting

TAKE CARE
Don't overload your fridge to the point where air cannot circulate freely around the food as this will impair its ability to keep things cool.

will give the fridge an average interior temperature of 40°F. The natural circulation of cool air within the cabinet will vary the temperatures elsewhere in the fridge. You may want to purchase a freestanding appliance thermometer to assure your refrigerator maintains the proper temperature.

Save money Sticky, syrupy residues can drip down the fridge door and cause it to stick, which may damage the seal. Prevent this potential repair bill by wiping the fridge seal down regularly with a sponge and warm water only. Be careful not to use dishwashing liquid or other detergent as it may damage the seal.

Easy fix Take care not to allow items to rest against the back of the fridge, where they can become frozen onto the surface. Ripping them off can damage the packaging or the item itself, and it's a nuisance to have to defrost the fridge just to get one thing loose.

Insider's hack Don't keep food in the fridge in an open container. Use an appropriately sized glass or plastic storage container with a lid, or cover dishes with plastic wrap.

Save time If you're cooking dishes ahead of time to refrigerate and eat later on, set up an ice bath in the sink with cold water and ice cubes to rapid chill what you've cooked before transferring to the fridge. Also divide up large portions into smaller, shallow containers so they cool more quickly, which saves an additional power load on the refrigerator.

WHAT BELONGS WHERE IN THE FRIDGE?

1 **Door compartments** Butter, margarine, cheese, mayonnaise, mustard, salad dressing, tomato sauce, non-perishable sauces such as ketchup, barbecue sauces and hoisin sauce, jellies and jams, opened beverages

2 **Top shelf** Cream cheese, soft cheese, butter, cakes

3 **Middle and lower shelves** Milk and dairy products such as yogurt, cream, buttermilk and cottage cheese; leftovers and pre-prepared (cooked) meals

4 **Bottom shelf (glass)** Fresh meat and meat products (sausages, cold meats, etc.), fish, poultry and other perishable foods

5 **Fruit and vegetable drawers** Fruit and vegetables that can withstand refrigeration include salad greens, carrots, celery, cruciferous vegetables such as broccoli and cauliflower, fennel, beets and more. Apples, pears, citrus fruits, melons, berries, pineapple all do well in the fridge. (Note that some produce, such as tomatoes, basil, potatoes, onions, garlic and avocados, bananas, are sensitive to cold and are best kept in a cool, dark place.)

Make the most of YOUR FREEZER

Most refrigerators include a freezer compartment, which best at a temperature of 0°F. Apart from making ice cubes and keeping store-bought frozen foods, you can use your freezer to freeze cooked meals and fresh food.

✳ Freezing is a means of preserving food. To get the best results, it's important that any fresh or cooked food you intend to freeze should be as fresh as possible. The longer you leave food before freezing, the more it will lose freshness and quality. In the case of store-bought frozen food, be guided by the information on the package.

✳ If you intend to freeze your own food, you need to know how long it will keep. The following is a guide to how long various foods can be kept when maintained at an ideal freezer temperature of 0°F:

Vegetables 3–12 months
Meat and fish 3–12 months
Herbs 3–4 months
Fruit 9–12 months
Sausages 1–6 months
Cheese and butter 2–6 months
Baked goods 1–3 months
Home-cooked meals 1–3 months

✳ If you like the idea of preserving a large supply of frozen food, you should consider buying a stand-alone freezer. The same storage principles apply as for an ordinary freezer compartment, but the additional space will allow you to buy up a lot of produce when it is in season or even freeze fruit and vegetables from your own garden, enabling you to enjoy near-fresh quality all year round.

> For best results, any fresh or cooked food you intend to freeze should be as fresh as possible.

Insider's hack Wiping the insides of your freezer with cooking oil or glycerine (this is available from pharmacies) can prevent it from icing up too quickly and also make the ice easier to remove when you do eventually defrost the freezer.

Keep your fridge a GERM-FREE ZONE

Many of us only clean our fridge when we have to, usually when something spills and creates a mess. But experts recommend that we clean our entire

Expert advice

Things that shouldn't go in the freezer

Freezing food is a practical way to ensure you always have something on hand to feed the family, but not all foods are suitable for freezing.

★ Whole eggs, raw or cooked, should not be frozen, but egg yolks and beaten egg whites can be.

★ With the exception of butter and cheese, dairy products are not suitable for freezing.

★ Tomatoes, onions, salad greens and other vegetables with a high water content become soft, lose color and look unappetizing when thawed after freezing.

★ Tropical and exotic fruits will not tolerate being stored in the freezer. Citrus will become blotchy and bananas will turn brown if frozen.

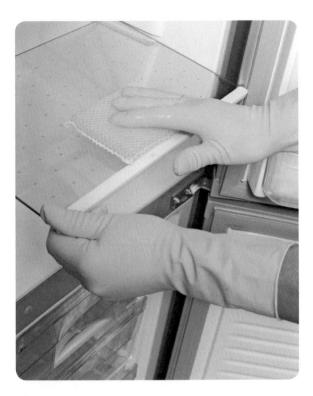

CLEAN YOUR ENTIRE FRIDGE REGULARLY TO PREVENT GERMS FROM BUILDING UP.

THE PRE-VACATION TO-DO LIST

LEAVE THE FRIDGE CLEAN	When you're getting ready to go on vacation, there's lots to do to get your house cleaned before you go. It's especially important to leave the fridge clean and tidy. A foul smell in the kitchen is really not the best thing to come home to.
DISCARD ANYTHING THAT HAS BEEN OPENED	Throw out any partially used containers of perishable food or take them on your trip with you. You don't want nasty surprises waiting for you when you get back.
TURN YOUR FRIDGE OFF	If you are going away for a longer period, empty your fridge out completely, turn it off and clean it out. This will save you money, as your refrigerator is one of the most energy-hungry appliances. Make sure the fridge door stays open to prevent mold from growing inside the cabinet.

fridge regularly, especially if there are young children in the house, who are less resistant to germs than adults.

✳ Significant populations of undesirable micro-organisms live and grow inside a typical household refrigerator. This may seem hard to believe, given that the cool temperature inside a fridge is supposed to prevent the growth of mold and bacteria. But there is a range of nasties that don't mind the cold and will happily proliferate, regardless of the chilly conditions inside your fridge.

✳ Once they have settled in, these germs multiply rapidly, covering the interior surfaces of the fridge with a film invisible to the naked eye. The bottom line is that you should keep your fridge clean as an essential part of good food hygiene. You don't need to use a special cleaning product for the fridge. It's enough to wipe out the interior regularly with a conventional household cleaning solution. Make sure you use a clean cloth or sponge to wipe off surfaces thoroughly.

✳ If there is a bad smell in your fridge, first locate the source and dispose of it. Then it's time to give the fridge a thorough clean. This is easiest if you clear everything out first, then wipe the fridge out with vinegar, which is good at neutralizing odors.

Hygiene in the kitchen

It's essential to handle food carefully to prevent the spread of germs. This means keeping work surfaces and utensils clean, and paying proper attention to personal hygiene as well.

Wash YOUR HANDS first

Germs are everywhere. Micro-organisms commonly end up on our hands when we touch doorhandles, handrails or money. To prevent germs from being passed on, always wash your hands thoroughly with warm soapy water before you start preparing food. Dry your hands with a separate hand towel, rather than the dish towel you use for the dishes.

✳ Remember to wash your hands between different stages of food preparation, especially after handling raw foods such as meat, poultry or salad greens. If you have an open cut on your hand, ensure it is covered with a waterproof dressing or wear a pair of disposable gloves.

WASH YOUR HANDS THOROUGHLY, ESPECIALLY AFTER HANDLING RAW FOOD.

Avoid that dreaded HAIR IN THE SOUP

No one likes finding a hair in their soup. The kitchen is not the place to wear your hair down – tie it back or cover it with a headband or cap when cooking. You should also take off any jewelry because, even if you wash your hands, germs can still be lurking underneath and end up in your food. Your jewelry can also be damaged when cooking.

✳ Even when we are healthy, we carry a certain amount of bacteria in our nose and throat. If you need to cough or sneeze, turn away to prevent any germ-carrying droplets from landing on the food. Avoid cooking altogether if you have a cold or gastrointestinal illness. The bugs that cause these illnesses are tough and can withstand even the best hygiene practices.

Keep work SURFACES CLEAN

Kitchen counters and sinks are the perfect spots for germs to breed. From food scraps to potato peels, or the juice from defrosting a chicken – it all lands on our countertop or sink, harboring countless micro-organisms that can end up on our food. This is why it's absolutely essential to keep these areas meticulously clean. Even when a countertop has been thoroughly cleaned and looks immaculate, there will still be around 1,700 germs per sq. in. on the surface.

✳ But this doesn't mean you have to sterilize your kitchen. Cleaning your counters and sink with hot water and ordinary dishwashing liquid is sufficient.

Using a vinegar solution is another good option for cleaning countertops (see page 41, "Kitchens and bathrooms").

✳ Your kitchen trash can is a real hotbed for germs. Empty the can at least every week and wash it out with hot water and all-purpose cleaner. If you use plastic can liners, you should still check that the can is clean as the bags can have holes or tear, with food scraps sometimes ending up between the bag and the can. If this happens, give the can a thorough scrub and clean.

Insider's hack After a meal, put dirty dishes into the dishwasher rather than leaving them stacked on the counter, providing idyllic conditions for all manner of micro-organisms to multiply. If there is not enough in the machine to be worth running a normal wash cycle, give the dishes a quick rinse before putting them in, or run the machine on a short pre-rinse cycle.

Dirty dishes stacked on the counter provide idyllic conditions for micro-organisms to multiply.

EVEN WHEN A COUNTERTOP LOOKS THOROUGHLY CLEAN AND IMMACULATE, THERE WILL STILL BE GERMS.

CLOTHS, SPONGES
and dish towels

We use cloths and sponges throughout the house for cleaning, but you need to take special care with how they are handled in the kitchen. Large numbers of bacteria can take up residence in cloths, sponges, scrubbing brushes and dish towels. There are a few important rules to follow to prevent these germs from being transferred to your food.

✳ You should change the cloths used for washing dishes daily and wash them on your machine's hottest cycle (usually 170°F). This will kill just about any germ and the cloth will be ready to use again without worry.

✳ Sponges and sponge cloths are a popular choice for their capacity to absorb. You can wash them at on hot or sanitize or put them in the microwave on full power for a few minutes to rid them of most germs, but they should be disposed of after a few week's use.

✳ Hang dish towels on a hook or rail rather than leaving them scrunched up on the counter. Wash them on your machine's hottest cycle.

Easy fix It's not hard to keep a scrub brush clean. Simply put it in your dishwasher each time you run the machine.

The best material for
CUTTING BOARDS

The humble cutting board is an item that needs careful consideration when it comes to hygiene in the kitchen. Your cutting board is used several times a day and soon becomes covered with cuts and scratches. This can make it difficult to clean the board properly, providing an ideal opportunity for germs to grow.

The scratches on a cutting board provide an ideal opportunity for germs to grow.

✳ Expert opinion differs on which material is the most hygienic choice for a cutting board. Some say plastic boards are best while others prefer wood. While plastic boards are easier to clean than wooden boards and are less likely to absorb odors or colors from food, micro-organisms thrive in knife marks on the plastic. Some laboratory tests have shown that germs grow more slowly on wood; in other tests, however, both materials performed

TO REMOVE CARROT STAINS, SMEAR A LITTLE VEGETABLE OIL ON YOUR CUTTING BOARD BEFORE WASHING. THE PIGMENT IN CARROTS IS FAT SOLUBLE.

equally well. At the end of the day, it doesn't really matter which material you choose. As far as good kitchen hygiene goes, what counts is cleaning your board properly.

✳ Wash used wooden cutting boards with hot water and dishwashing liquid after use. You can put plastic boards in the dishwasher.

✳ Use a soft scrubbing brush to remove particles of food. Abrasive cleaning products and scourers will scratch the board – whether wood or plastic – providing new focal points for germs to grow.

✳ Never leave wooden cutting boards soaking in water as the wood will swell. This will cause cuts in the surface to close over, preventing any germs lurking within from being removed when the board is cleaned. As the board dries out, these cuts will open up again and the germs will be free to come into contact with your food.

✳ Brush your wooden cutting board with cooking oil once every couple of weeks. This will reduce the board's tendency to absorb moisture and limit the growth of microbes.

Easy fix If you have a granite countertop, you don't need to use a cutting board at all. Just make sure you keep your counters clean, and be aware that cutting

TAKE CARE
Don't place a wet wooden cutting board on a heater to dry as this will cause cracks to appear in the surface.

directly onto the granite surface can make your knives blunt and will eventually dull the polish of the granite.

Insider's hack Orange stains left on a cutting board after cutting carrots can be almost impossible to remove by washing in water. As the pigment in carrots is fat soluble, a much more effective approach is to smear the board with vegetable oil before washing. Leave it for a while and then wash with warm soapy water.

Maintain a COLD CHAIN

Chilled and frozen foods must be kept under the right conditions at every step of their journey from manufacturer to wholesaler to carrier to retailer and, finally, to us as consumers. Maintaining a "cold chain," which means keeping food within a given temperature range at all times, is essential to prevent the growth of bacteria that can occur if food warms up or begins to thaw. It is a crucial part of good food hygiene that chilled and frozen foods do not increase in temperature significantly on the way from the

FROZEN FOOD MUST NOT BE ALLOWED TO THAW BEFORE YOU GET HOME.

shop's dairy cabinet or display freezer to your own fridge or freezer at home.

✳ To keep chilled foods cool and prevent frozen foods from thawing on the way home, use a couple of the insulated bags you can buy at the supermarket or take your own cooler. Put these foods in the fridge or freezer as soon as you get home.

Expert advice

Microfiber cloths in the kitchen

Cloths made from microfiber have extremely thin (usually synthetic) fibers, which gives the weave of the cloth a very large surface area, allowing it to pick up dirt much more effectively than conventional materials. With a microfiber cloth, you only need to use a tiny amount of cleaning product, or none at all.

★ Microfiber cloths should be washed between 100°F and 140°F. Do not use fabric softener! Microfiber tends to pill in the washing machine so always put your cloths in a washing bag.

★ There are special microfiber cloths for cleaning glassware that do not shed fibers. This will give your glasses streak-free results.

★ Wash dark-colored microfiber cloths separately as the polyamide fibers – an essential component of microfiber materials – don't hold their dye well.

★ Take care when using a microfiber cloth to wipe down surfaces with a high-gloss finish. As the cloths grab hold of every tiny crumb, they can leave scratches quite easily.

Reheating and keeping
FOOD WARM

Whenever possible, it is preferable to cook food fresh, but sometimes we need to reheat a meal. In principle, this should not pose a problem and, in fact, some dishes, such as stews and curries, often taste better when reheated. Stick to the following guidelines and you shouldn't have any worries with reheated food.

✳ Allow freshly cooked food to cool down as quickly as possible, in smaller portions if necessary, then put it in the refrigerator right away.

✳ To prevent airborne microbes from settling and multiplying, don't leave cooked food exposed to the open air for longer than two hours. Ensure food is covered or put in an appropriate container and kept cool.

✳ Don't just give food a quick warm-up. Ensure it is heated through thoroughly to a temperature of at least 165°F to kill off any germs that may be present.

✳ In addition to how thoroughly you reheat a meal, it's also important to be careful about how long you keep it warm. It's recommended to keep reheated food at a temperature of 165°F, and to consume food within a maximum of two hours of reheating. Any longer than that and heat-resistant microbial spores will start to germinate.

✳ Traditional culinary rules dictating that you shouldn't reheat foods like spinach or mushrooms probably date back to times when there was no refrigeration. As with any other cooked food, dishes containing spinach or mushrooms should be covered and put in the fridge, rather than being left at room temperature for long periods. Reheating these dishes to a minimum of 165°F will kill off any harmful micro-organisms and ensure they can be enjoyed safely.

MOLD in the kitchen

A major culprit in foods spoiling is mold; it can also pose a health risk. Be aware that the toxic substances produced by molds (mycotoxins) are found not only in the visible mold filaments on the surface but also deeper within mold-affected food where they cannot be seen. Here's how you can prevent the food in your fridge and the bread in your pantry from being attacked by microscopic mold spores.

✳ Buy the freshest possible food in small quantities that you will use up quickly. This will greatly reduce the risk of a mold outbreak.

✳ Choose fruit and vegetables that are in good condition, free from bruising and other damage.

✳ Keep food in clean, cool, dry conditions. This means giving bread boxes and other food storage containers a weekly cleaning, making sure you remove any crumbs of bread or little cheese scraps that are prime breeding grounds for mold.

Insider's hack Whether it's sliced or unsliced, you should throw out bread that shows any sign of mold. It is not enough to simply cut away the visibly affected part – assume that the entire loaf has spoiled.

AVOID EATING RAW MEAT AND RAW EGGS TO PREVENT SALMONELLA.

The hazards of SALMONELLA

Around half of all cases of foodborne illness are caused by salmonella. Infection with salmonella bacteria, known as salmonellosis, is a notifiable disease, and can be dangerous for people with a weak immune system, including babies, the elderly and those already suffering from another illness. Prepared meals and raw ingredients that have a high protein and water content are especially susceptible to salmonella contamination. This includes meat (especially poultry), fish, eggs and processed meat products. These items should be put away in the refrigerator as soon as possible after purchasing and kept apart from other foods. Ensure they are eaten promptly, especially when the weather is warm.

✳ To prevent salmonella infection, avoid eating raw meat and raw eggs, as well as any dish prepared with either of these ingredients. When thawing frozen poultry, it's extremely important to keep any juices away from other food and dispose of it hygienically. Wash anything the juice comes into contact with – including your hands – with hot soapy water.

✳ Salmonella is not affected by freezing and will survive subzero temperatures unscathed. The bacteria multiply rapidly at temperatures between 70°F and 100°F, but will be killed by heating food for several minutes at temperatures of 165°F or higher.

Easy fix Food-borne pathogens can survive on kitchen surfaces for several days but instead of worrying every time you handle raw chicken, wipe down your counters with citric acid solution. This will kill salmonella. Just give your stone counter-tops another wipe with a clean damp cloth, to avoid the acid solution eating into the surface.

FRUIT FLIES and houseflies

Common houseflies and fruit flies are among the most frequent insect visitors to our homes (see also pages 209–10, "Not-so-harmless flies" and page 212, "Tiny, irritating fruit flies"). Houseflies are not only

AN ORANGE STUDDED WITH CLOVES CAN HELP KEEP FRUIT FLIES AWAY.

annoying, they also carry disease. They love to land on animal droppings and rubbish in the garden or on the street, where they pick up germs before flying into our homes and landing on our food. Whether it's just a few cookie crumbs or your evening meal, flies are drawn to food so keep your meals covered, clear leftovers away promptly and don't leave dirty dishes lying around.

✳ Overripe fruit is especially attractive for fruit flies so keep it covered or throw it away.

Easy fix If you like to keep a bowl of ripe fruit in your kitchen, you will probably end up with a swarm of fruit flies to go with it. An orange studded with cloves may be the solution – the best place to put it is on the windowsill. Fruit flies will be drawn to the orange as citrus fruit is one of their favorite places to lay eggs. It will cost you a piece of fruit a day as you will need to dispose of the orange and replace it with a new one, but you will soon be rid of the fruit flies as you will break their breeding cycle.

Insider's hack Fly paper is effective against houseflies in the kitchen. It may not look very nice but it is free from toxic chemicals.

Long-life pantry staples

With many supermarkets these days staying open until all hours, you might not see the need to keep a well-stocked pantry. But when it comes to whipping up a meal when we simply don't have time to go shopping, the pantry is as important as ever.

FOODS WITH A LONG SHELF LIFE INCLUDE FLOUR, SUGAR, PASTA, COFFEE AND BEANS.

What belongs IN THE PANTRY?

While fresh foods such as fish, meat and dairy must be kept refrigerated, a cupboard or walk-in pantry is where to keep all those products collectively referred to as "dry goods." These products, such as flour, rolled oats, cereals, pasta, rice, sugar, salt, chocolate, coffee and tea, all have a long shelf life. You can also keep canned food, jam and honey in the pantry, as well as mineral water, fruit juice, soft drinks and spirits.

✳ If you have a walk-in pantry, it will typically be a little cooler than the rest of the kitchen. A walk-in pantry is therefore suitable for storing different types of fruits and vegetables, including bananas, citrus fruit, melons, pineapples and mangoes, along with cucumbers, zucchini, tomatoes, potatoes and capsicums. A cool pantry can also be a good place to keep white wine if you don't have a cellar.

Easy fix In most cases, it's fine to keep red wine in an ordinary kitchen cupboard as red is usually drunk at room temperature.

Ensure LONG-LIFE PRODUCTS go the distance

Long-life products have simple storage requirements, needing only to be kept at room temperature in a kitchen cupboard or slightly cooler in a walk-in pantry. As a general rule, dry goods need protection from moisture and large variations in temperature.

Store food appropriately and keep an eye on what's in your pantry to prevent things from spoiling any sooner than normal. Keeping your pantry clean and tidy will deter pests and make it easier to keep track of what you have on hand.

Dry goods need protection from moisture and large variations in temperature.

✳ To keep common pests such as moths and weevils out of your pantry, don't leave dry goods such as flour, cereals, pasta, rice, beans, nuts and dried fruit in their original packaging once they have been opened. Transfer the contents to a resealable container such as a screw-top glass jar.

✳ Products in glass jars, bottles or clear plastic containers need to be kept in a dark place.

✳ Pay attention to the "best before" date on packaged foods, but keep in mind that a product that has gone beyond this date may still be all right. This date simply indicates the minimum shelf life, that is, the date until which a product is guaranteed not to deteriorate in flavor or quality (see also page 152, "Best before" and "use by" dates).

✳ Adopt this technique used by supermarkets: put newly bought products towards the back of your shelves. This will encourage you to use the older things at the front first.

✳ If you make your own jams or preserves, it's essential you label the jars with a date – the year is all that's needed. If you make a lot of preserves, also include the month or a batch number so you can keep track of what you've made.

Easy fix If you want to put something such as flour into a container with a narrow opening and you don't have a funnel handy, simply fold a sheet of aluminum foil in half several times and roll it into a cone shape.

HOW LONG CAN DRY GOODS BE KEPT?

6 MONTHS	Flour, semolina, cocoa
1 YEAR	Pasta, rolled oats, tea, coffee, beans, cornmeal, cooking oil, dried fruit, cookies, spices, honey
1–2 YEARS	Canned food (fish, meat, soups, fruit), dried potato products, jams and chutneys
2 YEARS	Rice, canned vegetables
3–4 YEARS	Sugar, salt

LABEL HOMEMADE PRESERVES WITH A DATE OR BATCH NUMBER.

Stopping PANTRY PESTS in their tracks

Common pantry pests such as moths, weevils and mites will happily make their home in foods such as flour, cornmeal, sugar, nuts, dried fruit and various cereal products. An infestation of these pests can occur no matter how clean you keep your kitchen. In many cases, it begins because the eggs of an

CHECK THE FOOD IN YOUR PANTRY REGULARLY FOR PESTS. AT THE FIRST SIGN OF A PROBLEM, THROW THE AFFECTED ITEM OUT.

MINIATURE HERB GARDEN

Strawberry pots are ideal for culinary herbs, as you can plant trailing varieties in the side holes and more compact plants in the top. Include a central core of fine gravel to improve drainage. You'll need: strawberry pot, PVC pipe or cardboard tube, vegetable and herb potting mix, assorted herbs, gravel or small pebbles, liquid seaweed solution.

1 Position an cut of PVC pipe in the center of the strawberry pot. Hold the pipe steady on the base of the pot, then fill around it with potting mix as far as the first planting holes.

2 Add trailing herb varieties to the side holes of the pot, poking the herbs through from the inside and firming the potting mix around them. Work your way up, adding plants and potting mix until you reach the top.

3 Pour gravel into the pipe to the level of the potting mix, then ease out the pipe, leaving the core of gravel behind. Make planting holes and then add herbs to the top of the pot. Water everything in well with liquid seaweed solution.

unwelcome guest are already present in a product when we buy it. Take care when shopping to choose products that are in sound condition and that have undamaged packaging.

✳ Check the food in your pantry for pest infestation about once every four weeks. At the first sign of a problem, throw the affected item out. If an item is obviously infested, you will need to clear out the entire shelf or, better yet, the entire pantry. Dispose of all the food first, then wash out the pantry with a solution of vinegar and hot water.

✳ To prevent a plague of pests, keep food in well-sealed containers in dry, cool conditions. Clean and air out your pantry regularly.

✳ Pests contaminate food with their droppings, strands of silk and shed skin. This can cause skin irritation, allergies and gastrointestinal illness. Pests can also carry fungi, bacteria, viruses and parasites. For all these reasons, affected food should not be consumed under any circumstances.

TAKE CARE

Don't use chemical insecticides against pantry pests under any circumstances. If you are unable to get on top of an infestation, call in a professional exterminator.

CANS AND JARS keep for years

When there's a gaping void in the fridge, having a few cans or jars of food in the pantry will help you put a quick meal on the table. The shelf life of preserved food is around 12–18 months but many products will last significantly longer than that. In some cases, preserved food can still be edible after 10 years or more, although it will lose its consistency, color and flavor over time.

✳ Preserved food can spoil if the vacuum seal of a glass jar fails or a can gets dented, creating a crease in the metal where rust is more likely to occur. If an unopened jar's lid is bulging upwards, it's a sign the contents have spoiled and the jar should be disposed of. If you are unsure, open the container and have a sniff. If it smells doubtful, throw it out.

✳ If you only use part of the contents of a glass jar, simply screw the lid back on. For cans, on the other hand, it's safest to transfer the unused portion to a container with a lid even if the inside of the can has a synthetic coating. In most cases, you can keep the unused contents of a can or jar in the fridge for up to three days.

Save money Supermarkets sometimes discount cans or jars of preserved food that have gone past their "best before" date. These products can still be purchased and consumed without concern.

THE SHELF LIFE OF PRESERVED FOOD IS AROUND 12–18 MONTHS BUT CAN BE LONGER.

Kitchen waste

More than half the garbage that gets thrown in the trash can and transported to landfill is organic kitchen and garden waste. Whether it's potato peels, vegetable scraps or salad greens that have gone past their prime, food waste is too good to be thrown out in the regular garbage. Put your food waste on a compost pile or in a composting bin so it can be turned into valuable garden nutrients.

WASTE NOT, want not

Households in developed nations commonly throw out as much as a third of the food they buy. We throw away food for one of two reasons: because we've prepared too much, or because it's gone bad. Both of these situations can be remedied with just a few simple, sensible strategies.

✳ It may sound old fashioned, but planning the week's meals and then preparing a shopping list is one of the most effective ways of reducing waste. Check the fridge, freezer and pantry to see what you already have on hand before buying more.

✳ Cooking or preparing more food than is necessary is a common problem: a couple of cups of rice when only one is needed, or a 2 pounds of ground meat gets cooked when half a pound would do. One solution is to use the leftovers for other meals, and the other is to get the portions right in the first place – so notice which foods you routinely end up throwing out.

✳ Chilled foods will spoil sooner than they should if your refrigerator isn't cold enough. If your milk, butter or cheese regularly go bad before the use-by date is reached, then your fridge thermostat is probably set too high. All refrigerators should be set to 40°F or lower.

✳ When you come home with meat, only store what you intend to use in the next 24 hours in the fridge and put the rest in the freezer to be defrosted when you need it. That way you won't have meat spoiling in your fridge before you get around to cooking it.

✳ The freezer is great for bread, too. Unless your household goes through bread very quickly, when you bring home a loaf, it's a good idea to put half of

TAKE NOTE OF WHICH FOODS YOU ROUTINELY THROW OUT – CAN YOU USE THE LEFTOVERS FOR OTHER MEALS?

A DESIGNATED COMPOST BIN IN A CORNER OF A BACKYARD WORKS JUST AS WELL AS LARGER SET-UPS.

it in the freezer. Enjoy the plain bread while it's fresh, then use the frozen bread for toasting.

✳ Know where fresh food is best kept. A bunch of grapes in a bowl on the counter can spoil within a couple of days, but in the fridge they'll last a week or more. Store potatoes in a cool place in the dark so they don't turn green, and don't store potatoes and onions together or the potatoes will spoil. Cutting the leafy tops off vegetables such as carrots and beets adds to their storage life. And fresh meat stored in a ventilated container in the fridge will last for a day or two longer than fresh meat that's wrapped in plastic.

Start a COMPOST BIN

Putting your kitchen (and garden) waste into a compost bin or a worm farm instead of putting it in the bin can reduce your household waste by as much as half.

✳ Passionate composters use set-ups that include multiple bins, but a designated compost pile or bin in a corner of the backyard works just as well.

✳ Toss all the fruit and vegetable scraps into the compost, except for onion and citrus peels, which should be limited. Add coffee grounds, tea bags, eggshells, clippings and prunings from the garden, and torn-up newspaper. Don't add dairy foods, fats or meat, however, as these can attract maggots, rats and other vermin.

✳ Compost is ready for use when it is crumbly and earthy smelling, but you shouldn't be able to spot many identifiable bits of food. Dig it into garden beds as an organic fertilizer, use it as a top dressing for lawn or mix it 1:1 with garden soil as an alternative to store-bought potting mix for container plants.

✳ There are alternatives to composting yourself – local gardening clubs may take your food waste, or ask your town to introduce a food waste recycling program. You could also try approaching local cafés and restaurants – some are already recycling food waste back to farms.

✳ Worm farms are a great solution if you live in a small house or apartment where a compost pile is just not practical. The worms live in the top part of the farm, along with their bedding and their food (food scraps). Mash or shred scraps to help the worms break them down faster. Don't add onion, shallot or garlic scraps, or citrus peels, because worms are sensitive to them and won't eat them. And avoid adding meat scraps or dairy products, as they'll attract maggots.

TAKE CARE
While it's fine to add most tea bags to your worm farm, remove the labels first as they can be laminated in plastic.

Take care of cookware

Pots and pans are among the most important pieces of kitchen equipment and are available in an enormous range of materials. When it comes to using and caring for cookware, it pays to know the pros and cons of each material before you decide what to buy.

GO EASY on your cookware

Each material – whether stainless steel, enamel, copper or cast iron – needs to be treated differently. If you stick to a few general principles, you will avoid damaging your cookware and it will be easier to care for it.

✳ Don't use metal utensils (spatulas, spoons) when cooking as they can damage the surface of your cookware. Wooden spoons and plastic utensils are a better option. This is especially important for non-stick pots and pans, but holds true whatever material your cookware is.

✳ Wash pots and pans with a sponge or scrubbing brush in hot water and ordinary dishwashing liquid. You can use steel wool judiciously on heavily soiled stainless steel and some enamel cookware (but follow the manufacturer's recommendations). To avoid scratching, however, the scouring side of a sponge scourer is a safer alternative.

✳ Dried or burnt-on food is easier to remove if you let it to soak overnight in water with a little salt added. The next day, put the pan on the stove and bring the water to the boil. Allow to cool and the residue should wipe out easily. To finish, wash with dishwashing liquid.

Insider's hack Choose darker colored plastic cooking utensils over white ones as white utensils will quickly develop a yellowish discoloration. While this is harmless, it is unsightly and virtually impossible to remove.

Virtually indestructible
STAINLESS STEEL

Many people prefer using stainless steel cookware as it is robust, impervious to rust and discoloration, completely food safe and easy to look after. If you

WOODEN SPOONS ARE A BETTER OPTION WHEN COOKING, BECAUSE METAL UTENSILS CAN DAMAGE THE SURFACE OF YOUR COOKWARE.

TAKE CARE

Don't put wooden cooking utensils or pots and pans with wooden (or plastic) handles in the dishwasher. The wood will swell up and eventually be ruined.

treat your stainless steel pots and pans properly, they will give you many years of satisfaction.

✳ Cooking salt can attack the surface of stainless steel, so make sure you rinse out your cookware immediately after use. When cooking pasta, for instance, wait until the water is boiling before adding salt. The salt will dissolve immediately and won't affect the surface.

✳ Stainless steel cookware is easy to clean. You should only need to resort to a special stainless steel cleaning product to deal with stubborn marks that can't be removed by ordinary washing up. Stainless steel pots and pans are completely dishwasher safe.

Stainless steel pots and pans are completely dishwasher safe.

✳ Stainless steel pans vary in price depending on quality. At the upper end of the price range, pans are heavier and have handles that remain cool to the touch so you don't need pot holders to pick them up. As stainless steel does not conduct heat well, high-quality pans also have cleverly designed bases consisting of several layers of metal to transmit heat quickly and evenly. Premium models feature a layer of copper at the core of this sandwich base.

Easy fix Cooking spinach in a stainless steel pan will kill two birds with one stone. Not only will you have a healthy serving of greens, you will also restore

HIGH-QUALITY STAINLESS STEEL PANS HAVE A SANDWICH BASE MADE UP OF SEVERAL LAYERS OF METAL.

the shine to your pan. The oxalic acid in spinach will give the steel a thorough clean. Using oxalic-acid-rich rhubarb will give you the same result.

Insider's hack To make a stainless steel pot shine like new, fill it with water, add a tablespoon of baking soda and bring to the boil. To remove scale deposits, rub the pot with vinegar or lemon juice.

SEASON A NEW CAST-IRON PAN BY BRUSHING IT WITH OIL AND PLACING IT IN A HOT OVEN.

Expert advice

Removing rust from cast iron

Small spots of rust can appear on cast-iron pots even when you clean it well and store it appropriately. Citric acid, which occurs naturally in lemons, is an effective rust remover. Mix a tablespoon of citric acid with 2 cups water. Dip a scrubbing brush into the solution and scrub the rust spots away. To finish, wash the item up as you normally would.

Traditional CAST IRON

Heavy cast-iron cookware has outstanding heat-conducting properties, which enable it to deliver excellent cooking results. Cast iron is especially good for searing foods such as steak at high heat to achieve crisp yet juicy results. The material is also long lasting, especially if you clean and care for it properly.

✳ Cast-iron cookware needs to be seasoned before its first use. For pots and pans, clean thoroughly, rub the surface generously with vegetable oil and place in a 375°F oven for 1 hour. Allow to cool before wiping out with paper towel.

✳ Wash cast-iron pots and pans in hot water after use (avoiding detergent if you can), dry thoroughly and then rub a little oil into the surface.

Insider's hack To prevent cast-iron cookware from rusting, store it in a cupboard away from cooking vapors.

Beautiful COPPER COOKWARE

Copper is vastly superior to cast iron or stainless steel in its ability to conduct and retain heat, and copper cookware is prized for how well and evenly it distributes heat. As copper reacts with acidic foods to form toxic green-colored copper carbonate (verdigris), the inside of your copper cookware is usually lined with another metal. Traditionally, copper pots were lined with aluminum but stainless steel is becoming increasingly as common and aluminum linings have a limited life and can be damaged by overheating. Nevertheless, many professional cooks still swear by aluminum-lined copper cookware.

✳ Before using new copper cookware for the first time, soak it in boiling water and let stand until the water has cooled.

✳ If you have unlined copper cookware (which certainly still exists), keep it spotlessly clean and remove food as soon as it's cooked rather than

COPPER POTS HAVE AN OUTSTANDING ABILITY TO CONDUCT AND RETAIN HEAT.

letting it get cold in the pot. Also avoid using it for cooking acidic foods, such as tomatoes and lemons.

✳ For safety's sake, wash your copper pots and pans by hand rather than in the dishwasher. Use a special copper cleaning paste to keep the beautiful surface in top condition.

✳ Cooper cookware is not suitable to use on an induction cooktop.

Easy fix Use a cut lemon sprinkled with salt to polish tarnish spots off copper.

Save money Copper cookware is a significant investment. If the aluminum lining wears out, it's worth asking the manufacturer if they can resurface them. If you can't find this service in your local area, look online for a coppersmith.

Popular but controversial ALUMINUM

Many people enjoy using aluminum cookware as it is lightweight and conducts heat well. Opinions vary, however, on the health impact of the minute amounts of aluminum that end up in your food afterwards. If you want to keep using aluminum cookware, stick to the following rules:

✳ Don't cook fruit or vegetables in aluminum as the acids in these foods will react with aluminum

to form harmful compounds.

✳ Don't leave aluminum pots and pans soaking in water for too long and don't store food in aluminum cookware. Both these things can cause unsightly discoloration and pitting (tiny spots of corrosion).

✳ Never use washing soda (sodium carbonate) to clean aluminum cookware and never put it in the dishwasher. The best way to clean it is with soapy water and steel wool. To make steel wool last longer, wrap it in a piece of aluminum foil.

NON-STICK pots and pans

Cookware with a non-stick coating has two main advantages: you can cook foods using minimal fat or oil, and food will not burn onto the surface. Provided that you don't overheat non-stick pans, they don't pose any health risks. The coatings will degrade and give off toxic fumes only at temperatures above 600°F, which is beyond the range of normal cooking.

✳ Non-stick skillets are popular because frying in conventional pans typically requires a lot of oil. The main disadvantage of some non-stick pans is that they scratch easily.

TAKE CARE
Never use a wire scourer or steel wool on an aluminum-lined copper pan as this will absolutely destroy the lining.

STYLISH AND COLORFUL, ENAMEL COOKWARE DOES NOT AFFECT FLAVOR. IT IS EASY TO LOOK AFTER AND LONG LASTING.

baking soda to the boil. Pour the liquid out and wipe the pan thoroughly.

Insider's hack If you want to stack non-stick pans inside each other, place a layer of paper towel between each one to prevent scratching. Hanging pans up is another good way to store them.

Colorful and hard-wearing ENAMEL

Enamel cookware is a healthy, energy-efficient option that does not affect the flavor of the food you cook in it. Enamel is nickel free (important for people with a nickel allergy), easy to look after, long lasting, and available in a wealth of stylish colors. High-quality, heavy enamel cookware can be quite expensive but there are less expensive options that are also perfectly serviceable.

✳ The rule that applies to pans made of any other material is especially important for non-stick pans: never use metal cooking utensils.

✳ Don't overheat non-stick pans – and avoid heating empty pans – as excessive heat can damage the non-stick coating. Temperatures of 400°F to 500°F can be enough to cause a problem.

✳ Clean non-stick pans with water and dishwashing liquid only. Finish by coating the surface with a drop of cooking oil.

✳ To remove dried-on food from a non-stick pan, bring a solution of 2/3 cup water and 3 tablespoons

Expert advice

Cleaning a kettle

Removing water deposits from your kettle will not only make your tea and coffee taste better, it will also help save electricity.

★ Various products are available from stores but water and vinegar or citric acid (a gentler option) will do the job, too. Fill the kettle halfway with equal parts water and vinegar (or halfway with water plus a couple tablespoons citric acid) and bring to the boil. Let the solution work for a few hours before rinsing out the kettle thoroughly.

★ Another effective way to clean the kettle is to use lemon juice and baking soda.

★ Placing a pebble or marble chip in your kettle can help prevent the build-up of minerals.

TAKE CARE

Never pour cold water into a hot enamel pan which can cause the enamel to crack or flake away from the surface.

✳ To enhance the hard-wearing qualities of enamel cookware, you can treat it with a solution of salt and vinegar before first use. To 1 quart water, add 2 tablespoons salt and 2 tablespoons vinegar, bring to the boil and simmer for an hour.

✳ Enamel pots and pans are dishwasher safe but if your cookware has plastic handles, check the manufacturer's guide to confirm if these are also dishwasher safe.

Enamel cookware is energy efficient, nickel free and easy to look after.

✳ If your enamel cookware becomes discolored, soak it overnight in a strong solution of washing soda (sodium carbonate).

Save money When rhubarb is in season, save the trimmings from rhubarb stalks and boil them up to remove deposits from the surface of enamel cookware. Rinse thoroughly afterwards.

How to CLEAN THE OVEN

If your oven does not have a self-cleaning function (see page 234, "The oven, heart of the kitchen"), cleaning it can be a challenging task. Fats, sugars and pan juices burn onto your oven's metal surfaces at high temperatures, and it takes a lot of work to remove the build-up. You should never use wire brushes or scourers to clean an oven as they will damage the surface. Oven spray can be useful but it's not always effective. If you would prefer not to use harsh chemicals, try the following techniques using common household products.

✳ The best solution for a thick, crusty build-up on your oven's bottom is salt. Cover with a 1/2 in.-thick layer of coarse rock salt, turn the oven on at 200°F and leave it to work for half an hour. Allow to cool, vacuum up the salt, then wipe over the oven with a damp cloth.

✳ Baking soda is good for cleaning ovens, too. Heat the oven to 150°F (or the lowest setting), dampen several pieces of paper towel with lukewarm water and sprinkle them with a thick layer of baking soda. Place the pieces of towel on the bottom and sides of the oven (it will stay in place because it's damp). Use a spray bottle to re-moisten the paper towel if it dries out. Once the layer of greasy build-up has softened, remove the paper towel and wipe out the oven with a damp cloth.

✳ You can also try the same salt and baking soda techniques on your baking pans and sheets to remove baked-on residue.

Save time If you have a dish that may overflow (such as a fruit pie baked on a flat tray), line the bottom of the oven with aluminum foil to save yourself a time-consuming cleaning-up job.

Insider's hack Prevent mess by using parchment paper, oven bags and roasting pans with lids.

CLEAN YOUR OVEN WITH A THICK LAYER OF COARSE ROCK SALT.

Make cooking a breeze

With some planning and a dash of skill and creativity, you can save time and money, and make cooking easier. Should a culinary mishap occur, a bit of improvisation and a few tricks up your sleeve can help get things back on track.

Good options for QUICK MEALS

While many people enjoy cooking elaborate meals, just as many of us simply don't have the time or inclination. But that doesn't mean we have to resort to a pizza delivery or Chinese takeout. You just need to keep a supply of food on hand that is quick and easy to prepare. There are products on the market these days that bear no resemblance to the dreary frozen dinners of times past. Fresh pasta and parboiled rice are quick to cook, while frozen herbs, peas and broccoli don't need to be washed or chopped.

✳ Frozen vegetables are a big help when you're in a hurry. Fresh produce is snap frozen, which means it remains rich in vitamins and nutrients.

✳ Combine frozen vegetables with ready-made pastry or dough to make a quick vegetable quiche or spinach pizza that everyone will love.

Insider's hack Many homemade meals are fine to freeze. If you have a freezer, cook double or triple the amount of your favorite recipes and freeze the excess in individual portions. Then all you need to do is defrost and reheat. You will spend less time cooking and will always have a delicious meal on hand. You can also cook extra potatoes and pasta, then store the excess in the fridge for one or two days. A quick reheat is all it will need.

FROZEN VEGETABLES ARE IDEAL FOR QUICK MEALS.

JUST LIKE A TV CHEF, LAY OUT ALL YOUR INGREDIENTS AND UTENSILS BEFORE YOU START COOKING.

Save money Prepared or processed vegetables can save you time but they also tend to be more expensive. Fresh carrots or potatoes are better value and you can speed up the cooking time simply by cutting them into small cubes.

BANISH CLUTTER from the kitchen

Some people think that there is a link between clutter and creativity but that doesn't hold in the kitchen, where it pays to know where things are. If you keep your kitchen counters and stovetop tidy, you won't have to clear off a whole lot of junk every time you want to cook. Leave only those things you use all the time – such as salt and pepper, oil, herbs, wooden spoons and pot holders – within easy reach.

※ Before you start cooking, lay out all your utensils and ingredients, just like a TV chef would. This will save you from forgetting vital ingredients or digging around in the cupboard for a utensil while something is burning or boiling over on the stove.

Easy fix We often need to wipe our hands when cooking so keep a roll of paper towel handy. If you are handling raw meat, however, always wash your hands thoroughly with soap and water afterwards (see also page 158, "Hygiene in the kitchen").

Save money If you need boiling water when cooking, use a kettle as it will boil faster than a pot on the stove. When the kettle boils, simply pour the water into your pot and continue cooking.

Practical KITCHEN AIDS

Employing some small, practical appliances can make cooking tasks easier and help save you time in the kitchen.

※ A small electric chopper can chop onions faster than a knife and an electric mixer kneads dough faster than by hand. If you often make casseroles or stews, an electric pressure cooker is a worthwhile investment as it cooks food gently and saves both time and energy.

TAKE CARE

Don't put good-quality kitchen knives, including those with metal handles, in the dishwasher even if they are labeled as being dishwasher safe. The chemicals in dishwasher detergent attack metal. Over time, this will not only blunt your knives but can also cause them to corrode.

※ Make sure your kitchen knives are of good quality and sharpen them regularly. A well-honed knife will let you cut more quickly and with less effort. It is safer, too, because you are less likely to slip and cut yourself when you don't need to apply a lot of pressure.

Overcoming kitchen CATASTROPHES

Things don't always go according to plan in the kitchen – roasts may burn, soups turn out too salty and sauces just won't thicken. Here are a few tricks to help you overcome some of these obstacles.

※ If a roast gets burnt, cut away the affected part and put the meat back in the oven in a clean pan with a little fresh oil. You can also simply slice the meat, add gravy and serve.

※ If a baked dish gets burnt, carefully remove the overcooked layer and sprinkle with grated cheese, breadcrumbs or ground nuts. Add a few dabs of butter and put it back in the oven to finish it off.

TO SAVE A BURNT ROAST, CUT AWAY THE BURNT PARTS AND PUT IT BACK IN THE OVEN WITH A DASH OF FRESH OIL.

※ If you burn a pot of boiled potatoes, take all but those on the bottom out of the pot and put them in a fresh pot of salted water to finish cooking. The salt will remove the burnt flavor.

※ You can dilute too-salty soups or sauces with water, wine, milk or cream. For creamy soups and stews, reduce the saltiness by adding a little grated potato. Two tablespoons of rice wrapped in cheese-cloth and placed in the soup pot for 15 minutes will also absorb salt and achieve a similar result.

※ If a meat stock is too salty, add one or two raw egg whites and allow to cook in the broth. As it cooks, the egg white will take up salt; you can then remove it by pouring the broth through a sieve.

※ If the crust on a roast is too salty, you can salvage it smearing the crust with honey to give it an exquisite flavor.

※ If beaten egg white won't stiffen, add a few drops of lemon juice and a pinch of salt. To prevent the problem from occurring in the first place, don't use a plastic bowl, make sure your bowl and beaters are free from fat or oil, and be sure there is no trace of yolk in the egg white.

※ Gauging the heat of fresh chillies is not easy and sometimes you can end up with a dish so hot it's barely edible. Try adding a little milk, cream or yogurt, as the fat in dairy products helps temper the heat. Adding more liquid, vegetables or tomato paste can also achieve the same result.

※ If you have added too much garlic to a dish, bundle some finely chopped parsley in cheesecloth and place it in the pot until you have balanced out the strong garlic flavor.

※ If a sauce gets too thick, thin it with water, stock, milk or cream. Check the seasoning: you may now need to add more.

✳ Thicken soups or sauces that are too thin with a teaspoon of cornstarch, tapioca starch or arrowroot. Take the saucepan off the heat. In a small jug, mix the thickening ingredient with cold water and stir until smooth, then add to your soup or sauce. Return to the boil and season to taste.

If you have added too much garlic, make a cheesecloth bundle of finely chopped parsley and place it in the pot.

✳ To make a lumpy sauce smooth again, run it through a fine sieve. If a sauce separates, add a little cold butter and mix thoroughly with a hand blender.
✳ If the shell cracks while you are boiling an egg, quickly add a dash of vinegar to the water. The egg white will solidify immediately, and it can be enough to seal up the crack in the shell.
✳ If pasta sticks together while cooking, drain it and place the colander over boiling water to allow the steam to separate it again. Prevent pasta from sticking in the first place by using plenty of water (about 1 quart per cup) and stirring occasionally.
✳ If you have rice that's cooked but mushy, place in a colander and run under cold water, separating the grains with your fingers. If it's too far gone, however, save it for rice pudding and start again.

COOKING ECONOMICALLY

1 The type of cooktop you choose makes a difference. Gas is more economical than electric. If you are going to get an electric cooktop, choose ceramic-glass because they are more efficient than electric coil cooktops. Induction cooktops are expensive and you may need to buy new pots and pans to use with it, but they are more energy efficient and the investment may be worthwhile in the long run.

2 Use pots with lids that fit properly. Your food will cook more quickly as the heat is better retained.

3 If the bottom of a pan is buckled or uneven, the surface will not distribute heat evenly and energy will go to waste. When cooking with uneven pans, the cook time will increase taking longer to get meals on the table.

4 When using an electric cooktop, turn off the heat at an appropriate moment and make the most of the residual heat to finish off dishes such as rice or pasta.

IT ISN'T EASY TO GAUGE THE HEAT OF FRESH CHILLIES. THE FAT IN MILK OR YOGURT HELPS TEMPER THE HEAT.

✳ If a sauce has become too fatty, lay a piece of paper towel or a few lettuce leaves over the surface to soak up excess fat.

✳ If gelatin becomes lumpy, put the mixture through a fine sieve and heat gently while stirring to dissolve the lumps.

✳ If the top of a cake has burnt, allow it to cool then cut off the burnt areas and cover the cake with icing. No one will ever know!

✳ If you've overcooked a cake, but it's not burnt, spread melted butter over the top of the cake while it's still hot. This will soak in and return some moisture. You can also save a freshly baked loaf cake, such as banana bread, that has become too dry. Poke holes all over the top of the cake with a toothpick and then sprinkle a little fruit juice over it.

Prevent blocked DRAINS

If your kitchen sink does not have a strainer, you can pick one up from a supermarket or hardware store (either plastic or stainless steel) and place it over the drain hole. They come in different sizes to fit most conventional drains. The right size strainer is important so that it completely covers the drain in your sink. Clean out the strainer regularly.

✳ If your sink's drain is a non-standard size and you can't find a strainer that will fit, cut a piece of window screen to size and place it over the drain.

✳ Pour boiling water down the drain from time to time to help keep your pipes clear. It's kinder to the environment, as it can save the need to resort to chemical drain cleaners to clear a blockage. What's more, chemical drain cleaners don't always work and they can damage your plumbing.

TAKE CARE

Don't pour hot cooking fat down the sink. When it cools, it will stick to the insides of your pipes, eventually causing a blockage. Allow fat to cool and solidify in the pan, spoon it out onto some newspaper, then wrap it up and put it in the trash.

Expert advice

Prevent kitchen mishaps

★ Stop milk from sticking to a saucepan by rinsing it out with cold water first, leaving a few drops behind.

★ When parboiling sausages, add a little milk to the water to prevent them from bursting.

★ Keep a roast from getting tough and leathery by basting with hot water or stock.

★ To prevent custard-based desserts from sticking to the pan, smear the bottom with butter first.

★ Butter burns easily when you use it for frying. To prevent this, add a splash of a neutral-tasting vegetable oil (such as sunflower oil).

★ If an egg has a cracked shell, keep it wrapped in aluminum foil for cooking at a later time.

★ For firm whipped cream, put everything (cream, bowl and whisk) in the fridge to make it nice and chilled before you begin.

★ When you put pasta, potatoes or soup on the stove, place a wooden spoon between the pot and the lid to prevent the pot from boiling over.

★ If a cake is a couple of days old and starting to go stale, you can make it taste fresh again. Brush the top with milk and warm it in the oven for a few minutes, or give it a short burst in the microwave.

Your COFFEE FILTER'S hidden talents

When Melitta Bentz, a German homemaker, invented the coffee drip filter from blotting paper in 1908, she couldn't have imagined how many different uses her creation could be put to, not only in the kitchen but around the home.

DRAIN EXCESS LIQUID

A coffee filter comes in handy when you want to add cottage cheese or yogurt to a creamy sauce or filling but the product is too watery for your desired consistency. Place a filter into a sieve and fill with cottage cheese or yogurt. Suspend the sieve in a bowl and let stand in the fridge for a few hours to allow the excess liquid to drain.

A FERTILE START FOR FLOWERS

Once you've made your morning coffee brew, save the used grounds that are in the filter paper. Use the used filter papers to line the inside base of a flowerpot before filling it with potting mix. The filter paper will stop any potting mix falling out the drainage hole, and the coffee grounds contain beneficial minerals that help to fertilize plants.

BOUQUET GARNI

If you don't have any cheesecloth, you can place herbs for flavoring soups and stews in a coffee filter and tie it together with kitchen twine. Place the bundle in the pot while your dish is cooking then simply remove and throw away when you are ready to serve. This will save you fishing out bits and pieces.

A MAKESHIFT FUNNEL

If you need a funnel but don't have one handy, a coffee filter will work in a pinch. To transfer sugar, flour or coffee from one container to another without losing any over the side, just cut a hole in the bottom of the coffee filter. Both cone-shaped and basket-shaped filters are suitable for funnels.

Smart solutions

We often need to improvise in the kitchen – a missing ingredient or something that needs to be used up, or when hungry guests arrive unannounced. With some creative thinking, you'll get a "thumbs up" from family and friends and save yourself time and effort, too.

Make SOUPS, STEWS and salads go further

When a few extra friends show up unexpectedly at dinnertime, you can make many dishes go further to ensure everyone gets enough on their plate. The challenge lies in making it happen fast. If you have a soup or stew on the stove, you can't just add water because your meal will end up losing flavor. Dried onion flakes (available from the supermarket and a handy pantry staple) will help put some pep back into a soup that has been thinned out with water. Dried mushrooms or a dash of sherry will also do the job nicely. Mixing in some broth cubes or powder and instant mashed potato flakes is another way to bulk out a soup.

✳ Make a salad stretch further by adding fruit, nuts, olives, boiled eggs or tuna. Croutons, made with bread spread with garlic or herb butter, then cubed and toasted in a pan, are also delicious sprinkled over the top of a salad.

When there's TOO MUCH of a good thing

Sometimes we buy too much of a particular fresh ingredient and just can't use it all. Here are some tips on how to use up food before it goes bad.

✳ Make the most of fruit and vegetables in season. Towards the end of summer, for example, locally grown produce tends to be cheap and plentiful. Ripe tomatoes in particular can be puréed with a hand blender or food processor and then put in an ice cube tray to freeze. This will enable you to have fresh tomato on hand to make appetizing sauces right through the winter. You can puree and freeze other vegetables this way to use later in soups, too.

✳ This technique is also great for parents with babies who prefer to prepare food themselves rather than buying baby food in jars. Carrots, parsnips,

MAKE THE MOST OF FRUIT AND VEGETABLES IN SEASON, WHEN LOCALLY GROWN PRODUCE IS CHEAP AND PLENTIFUL.

sweet potato, pumpkin, beet and spinach can all be puréed and frozen in an ice cube tray. Store the frozen cubes in freezer bags with the date written on. Once thawed, add any other ingredients your pediatrician might recommend, such as butter or coconut oil.

✳ Fruit can be used to make jams or compotes that have a long shelf life. Puréed fruit, such as strawberries, is also good for freezing for use in desserts or to be served with ice cream. Many fruits, such as apples, pears, peaches, nectarines and other seasonal delights, are also easily stewed, puréed and frozen in ice cube trays.

✳ Ground meat that you are not going to use right away can be browned and then kept in the freezer. This will allow you to whip up a bolognese sauce or chilli con carne at short notice.

✳ Leftover beverages can also have a second life. Use flat mineral water to make tea, and wine that has slightly oxidized can stand in for vinegar in salad dressings.

Natural FLAVOR ENHANCERS

Fresh mushrooms that you are not going to use right away are perfect for puréeing with a little stock, then freezing to use later on to enhance the flavor of sauces and soups. Mushrooms are high in glutamic acid, which is a natural flavor enhancer. Other sources include: mature cheeses (such as Parmesan); fish sauce and soy sauce; ripe tomatoes and tomato paste; cruciferous vegetables such as broccoli and Chinese cabbage; walnuts; and slow-cooked braised meats and bone broths.

CREATE GORGEOUS GARNISHES

A well-chosen garnish will contrast with a dish in color and texture. It should enhance both its look and its taste.

Savory garnishes These can be as simple as slices of lemon cut into butterfly shapes, parsley sprigs or a sprinkling of fried breadcrumbs. Or try using croutons or fried sage leaves.

Cucumber twists To make cucumber twists, use a small sharp knife to cut the cucumber into thin slices. Make a single radial cut from the edge to the center of each slice, then twist either side of the cut in opposite directions.

Radish roses Remove the stalk and slice across the base so the radish stands upright. Make partial scalloped incisions in the radish. Place in iced water for an hour then dry.

Frosted treats Brush fruit such as grapes, cherries (with stems), sprigs of red currants, edible flowers or mint leaves with lightly beaten egg white, dredge with granulated sugar then dry on wire racks.

Dipped fruit Half-dip fruit such as strawberries or cherries into melted chocolate and place on parchment or wax paper to dry.

Citrus strips Remove the peel from lemons or oranges without pith and cut into thin strips. Boil peel in a sugar syrup, drain and dry.

IF YOU DON'T HAVE A PROFESSIONAL PIPING BAG, MAKE DO WITH A SMALL FREEZER BAG WITH ONE CORNER CUT.

✳ Transform your leftover hollandaise sauce (a perfect accompaniment for asparagus) into a béarnaise sauce with the addition of finely chopped shallots and tarragon. To this, add a little tomato paste to create choron sauce. Both are excellent with grilled meat such as steak.

✳ When making jam, adding the juice of one or two lemons to the fruit will help retain its color.

Easy fix If a soup or casserole recipe calls for sprigs of rosemary or thyme, bay leaves, whole cloves, cardamom pods, cinnamon sticks or star anise, you'll want to spare yourself the tricky task of picking these ingredients out of the dish when it's ready (not to mention avoiding an unexpected bite). Simply place your herbs and spices into a tea infuser and put the infuser in the pot during cooking. All you need to do afterwards is pull the infuser out before serving.

MAKING DO in a pinch

You're all set to cook a favorite dish or bake a cake but you're missing an ingredient. Don't panic! You can substitute many ingredients with something else. Even when you're missing a particular cooking utensil, there is often something else that will do the job fine in a pinch.

✳ If you have run out of flour to make a roux, you can thicken soups and sauces with cornstarch or tapioca flour. Alternatively, blend in a beaten egg.

✳ Make your own icing sugar by grinding ordinary white sugar to a fine powder in a food processor or well-cleaned coffee grinder.

✳ How do you get your pancakes to hold together when there isn't a single egg in the house? Just stir a heaped tablespoon of semolina into the mix. When baking, substitute 1 teaspoon ground chia seeds or flaxseed mixed in 1 tablespoon water for one egg. (But if the recipe calls for more than two eggs, choose a different recipe or go to the store!)

✳ Grind oatmeal or nuts (such as almonds) for an easy and tasty alternative to breadcrumbs for cauliflower cheese or a gratin. Or make your own breadcrumbs by blending some day-old bread in the food processor.

✳ If you don't have fresh cream on hand for that creamy sauce, evaporate milk or shelf-stable cream will work just as well.

✳ If your rolling pin has gone missing, a wine bottle will do the job. Just remove the label and wash the bottle thoroughly first.

Insider's hack If your cookbook keeps snapping shut, or you don't have a stand or enough space on the counter for it, clip it to a pants hanger. Then you can hang this at a convenient height, such as on a kitchen-cupboard door handle or the handle of your microwave.

Save money It's not worth the hassle of buying a professional piping bag if it's not something you will use all that often. You can make do with a small freezer bag with one corner cut off. This trick will also work if you don't have a funnel.

Don't let leftovers go to waste

Even with careful planning, it's inevitable that we end up with leftover food from time to time. It pays to make the most of leftovers as food is expensive and too good to go waste.

Classic BAKES AND GRATINS

You can turn pretty much any kind of leftover food into a bake or gratin. Meat dishes, sausages, ham or ground meat, potatoes, rice or pasta, all kinds of vegetables, fish – the list goes on. The basic method is to layer all the ingredients in a greased ovenproof dish and cover with white sauce, which you can make from simple ingredients you are sure to have on hand.

✳ Whisk three eggs into 1–2 cups cream (milk is also fine). Add salt, pepper and nutmeg to taste. Pour the sauce over everything in the baking dish.

✳ Béchamel sauce is a more challenging variation of white sauce. Melt 2 tablespoons butter in a saucepan and stir in 2 tablespoons flour. Cook for 2 minutes to cook off the flour taste. Remove from heat and gradually stir in 2 cups milk. Return the mixture to the heat and bring to the boil, stirring continuously, then simmer for 10 minutes. Add salt and pepper, and nutmeg if desired. Pour the sauce over the ingredients in the baking dish.

✳ To finish your gratin, scatter grated cheese over the top to finish, then bake in the oven until the cheese has melted and the sauce has thickened and started to form bubbles.

✳ While many people simply discard the hard outer edge of a block of parmesan as unusable, when it is added to a soup, casserole or risotto, the rind softens and infuses the whole dish with a gentle parmesan flavor. Store your leftover

BAKE YOUR GRATIN IN THE OVEN UNTIL THE CHEESE HAS MELTED.

parmesan rinds in ziptop bags in the freezer. Just remember that the rind doesn't dissolve, so fish it out before you eat the meal.

Insider's hack Chefs call it *mise en place*, meaning "everything in place" – while it usually refers to organizing your ingredients before cooking, you can also use this technique to prepare leftover fresh ingredients so they will keep for longer. Think of whipping up a fresh pesto with half a bunch of basil, or blanching and freezing excess spinach. And those leftover vegetables will make a great stock.

Leftovers with plenty of POTENTIAL

Starchy potatoes, pasta and rice are all popular accompaniments to meat and fish. We often prepare too much and end up with leftovers. Beyond simply frying up potatoes or rice, for example, there are one or two more sophisticated alternatives.

✳ To make a potato soup, puree leftover potatoes and thin out with stock. Enhance the soup by adding cream or diced bacon. Season to taste and garnish with chopped chives to serve.

✳ Boiled potatoes are a good foundation for a hearty country-style breakfast. To serve two people,

BEET AND MOZZARELLA SALAD

Beet leaves are similar in taste and texture to spinach, and can be used in similar ways. Steam them, sauté them, blend them in a green smoothie or toss them raw into this bright and colorful salad.

Serves 4 • Preparation 15 minutes

7 ounces beet leaves
1 bunch yellow baby beets, trimmed
  and thinly sliced
1 bunch red baby beets, trimmed
  and thinly sliced
1 English or other small cucumber,
  thinly sliced
2 fresh mozzarella balls (8 ounces), torn into
  bite-sized pieces
¼ cup fresh mint leaves
2 tablespoons fresh dill sprigs

DRESSING
2 tablespoons extra virgin olive oil
2 tablespoons lemon juice
1 teaspoon sugar
2 teaspoons horseradish
salt and freshly ground black pepper

1 Arrange beet leaves, yellow and red beets, cucumber, mozzarella, mint and dill on a serving platter.

2 To make the dressing, combine oil, lemon juice, sugar and horseradish in a small bowl. Season with salt and pepper and whisk until well blended. Drizzle dressing over the salad and serve.

whisk four eggs with four tablespoons milk and season well with salt and freshly ground black pepper. Slice the potatoes and pan fry in a little oil. Pour the egg and milk mixture over the top and continue cooking until it becomes firm. To add even more flavor, add bacon, onions, garlic, herbs and tomatoes or red peppers.

Make potato cakes from mashed leftover potatoes – coat them with breadcrumbs and fry.

✳ To make tasty potato cakes, mash some leftover potatoes and mix with an egg, finely chopped onion and salt and freshly ground black pepper. Shape the mixture into small patties, coat with breadcrumbs and fry in oil.

✳ Leftover cooked pasta (particularly short spirals or shells) is the perfect last-minute addition to a hearty minestrone soup. If you have any leftover herbs or cooked meats from the same meal, throw these in the soup pot at the end of cooking time, too.

✳ Pasta salad is the classic way to make use of leftover food. To leftover pasta, add a can of chunk tuna (separated into small pieces), a handful of baby arugula leaves, some diced oil-packed sun-dried tomatoes and black olives, cubes of feta and a dollop of pesto, toss to blend.

✳ There's lots you can do with leftover rice. How about a colorful, nutritious pilaf? Brown ground meat, onions, garlic and vegetables (such as celery, zucchini, peas, corn or carrots) over high heat, add peeled tomatoes and simmer until almost all the liquid has cooked off. Stir the rice through the mixture and season with salt, pepper and garam masala to taste.

✳ Instead of the same-old fried rice, try an Asian-inspired rice salad. Together with leftover steamed rice, add some baby corn, snow peas, red pepper, celery and scallion. Drizzle with a dressing made

INSTEAD OF THE SAME-OLD FRIED RICE, TRY AN ASIAN-INSPIRED RICE SALAD INSTEAD.

from sesame oil, soy sauce, rice vinegar and grated fresh ginger and scatter over a few cashews.

✳ Leftover rice is also perfect for sweet creations such as delicious rice pancakes. Combine leftover rice with flour, milk and eggs, and then pan-fry the mixture in individual portions. Sprinkle with sugar and cinnamon and serve hot. These pancakes also go well with jam or fruit compote.

Easy fix Cooked pasta will readily stick together into one big clump that has to be untangled before it can be reused. An easy way to solve this problem is to simply blanch the pasta in boiling water for about 10 seconds then drain.

Reclaim COOKED VEGETABLES

Is there a plate of leftover peas from last Sunday's roast sitting in your fridge, a few carrots that are starting to shrivel up, or a pepper that's past its prime? There's no need to throw these leftovers away as there many options for turning them into a decent meal.

✳ Turn leftover vegetables into a creamy purée. Reheat yesterday's cooked potatoes, peas or carrots in a little stock and purée with a hand blender. Stir in milk for a creamy consistency. To finish, add a teaspoon of butter and stir until it melts. Season to taste with salt, pepper and chopped herbs. This is great as a dip served with raw vegetable sticks.

✳ Leftover vegetables are also a perfect addition to a soup. Cut raw vegetables into small pieces, simmer in salted water and top up with vegetable stock. Add vegetables that are already cooked at the end. To give the soup a boost, add herbs, a dollop of pesto or cream.

TAKE CARE

Don't reheat leftovers of any dish containing shellfish, including shrimp, crab or mussels. Throw out any unfinished portion.

Breathe new life into STALE BREAD

When bread is no longer fresh, popping it in the toaster and slathering it with a butter is not always the most appealing option. You can make countless delicious dishes, both sweet and savory, with leftover bread.

✳ French toast is a childhood favorite. Whisk together milk, eggs and vanilla sugar. Dip slices of bread into the mixture, allow the excess to run off, and fry until golden brown. Sprinkle with sugar and cinnamon, or serve with fruit compote. For a decadent treat, serve French toast with vanilla ice cream or whipped cream.

✳ Any bread you have on hand, including white bread that has gone stale, can make a bread salad. Cut the bread into bite-sized pieces and toast in a pan with olive oil and some chopped garlic. Wash your salad greens – arugula is good but other types of lettuce work well, too – and scatter over the toasted bread and garlic. Add chopped walnuts, cubes of feta, cherry tomatoes or finely chopped sun-dried tomatoes (preserved in oil). A dressing of extra virgin olive oil, balsamic vinegar, honey, salt, pepper and chopped rosemary marries well with this salad.

✳ You can also use leftover bread to make a tasty baked dish. First toast several slices of bread. Then

FRENCH TOAST WITH CINNAMON AND SUGAR IS A CHILDHOOD FAVORITE.

sauté sliced mushrooms in a skillet with a little oil. Season the mushrooms with salt, pepper and nutmeg. Chop some scallions and a few slices of ham. Layer all these ingredients in a greased ovenproof dish with the bread on the bottom. Whisk together eggs, milk, salt, pepper and nutmeg and pour over the top. Sprinkle shredded or finely chopped cheese (Swiss or gouda) over the top and bake at 400°F for about 30 minutes.

If you have a lot of stale bread, make a large batch of croutons.

CROUTONS for soups and salads

Stale bread or rolls are perfect to make crunchy croutons to scatter over soups and salads. Simply cut the bread into small cubes with a sharp knife and toast in a pan with a little butter.

✳ If you have a lot of stale bread, make a batch of croutons. Cut the bread into cubes and toast over low heat in a non-stick skillet without oil until crispy. These croutons can be kept at room temperature for several weeks in an airtight screw- or clip-top container.

✳ When you are ready to use your croutons in a soup or salad, gently brown the desired quantity in a little butter. The advantage of using dried croutons is they will soak up considerably less fat than fresh ones.

TURN LEFTOVER CAKE INTO CAKE POPS

To make 20 sprinkle-covered cake pops, you will need: 1/4 cup butter, 4 ounces cream cheese, 1/2 cup confectioners' sugar, 10 1/2 ounces crumbled leftover cake, 14 ounces dark melting chocolate, 20 lollipop sticks, 1 cup colored sprinkles and a piece of styrofoam.

1 Mix the butter, cream cheese and confectioners' sugar with an electric mixer. Stir in the cake crumbs to create a dough. Shape mixture into 20 balls and chill in the refrigerator for 20 minutes.

2 Melt the chocolate. Dip the lollipop sticks into the melted chocolate then immediately stick one into each ball. Return the cake pops to the fridge until the chocolate sets. Then dip the cake pops into the chocolate and roll in the sprinkles.

3 Insert the cake pops into the styrofoam and allow the chocolate to set. You can also use coconut instead of sprinkles.

chapter *6*

Health and Safety

Accident-proof your home

Most people feel safe from danger at home, but this sense of security can be quite deceptive. Around a third of all accidents happen at home; however, there are ways to prevent potential risks and eliminate many dangers around the house.

CHILDREN AND SENIORS
most at risk

Children are the most likely to have accidents, simply because they are unaware of many hazards, not least of them chemicals (including cleaning agents and medications), electricity and open flames. This is where parents need to take care and inspect the home diligently from a safety perspective.

✳ Seniors over the age of 75 are also at higher risk of having accidents at home. More than half of all accidents they suffer occur in their own homes – most commonly falls after tripping or slipping. Possible causes include deteriorating vision and muscular strength, but the use of sleeping pills and sedatives also presents a significant risk.

✳ You can mitigate many potential accident sources in the home with a bit of thought and some minor modifications.

Remove trip hazards to
PREVENT FALLS

About 80 percent of all domestic accidents are falls. Falls can cause severe injury, including head injury, if people hit hard edges or surfaces when falling.

CHILDREN AND SENIORS OVER THE AGE OF 75 ARE PARTICULARLY ACCIDENT-PRONE.

Carpets, runners, bedroom rugs and bath mats are all potential trip hazards. On smooth floors, secure them with anti-slip mats or double-sided adhesive tape, and always ensure carpets don't have curled edges or bumps.

✳ Electrical and telephone cords on the floor are also dangerous. Route cords along baseboards or inside cable ducts, or attach them to the floor with adhesive tape or cable ties. A cordless home telephone is a better choice than a phone with an extra-long cord.

✳ Your stairs must have strong handrails. Teach children to hold on to the bars of the handrail when walking down stairs (they should never skip, jump or play around on stairs). You should secure any carpet on stairs to the treads. Ideally, apply non-slip rubber strips to the edges of wood steps to prevent slipping.

✳ If you need to go to the bathroom in the nighttime, make sure that there are no obstacles between your bedroom and bathroom such as chairs, bags, toys or laundry baskets.

Easy fix If you struggle to find the bathroom light switch at night, you could install a motion sensor, which will switch on the light automatically. Another option to consider is a dim LED strip light with integrated motion sensor, which will not disturb others when activated.

Insider's hack Are you considering renovating your bathroom? Choose smaller mosaic tiles over large floor tiles, as the grouting between small tiles helps prevent slipping. If paving or tiling a patio area, look for textured tiles that are specifically designed to be non-slip in rainy conditions.

Save money Put glow-in-the-dark stickers (such as little stars) on light switches and other objects you need to access at night regularly. Widely available from toy shops and craft stores, these stickers are an inexpensive substitute for special switches with built-in lights.

SLIPPERS WITH BACKS AND SOLES REDUCE THE RISK OF TWISTING YOUR ANKLE.

Avoid accidents with
NON-SLIP SLIPPERS

Backless slippers can be hazardous because they do not support the feet well. Buy slippers that enclose the foot, or slipper socks that have a sole, as they will reduce the risk of twisting your ankle, slipping on stairs or tripping over a raised carpet edge or an unexpected obstacle.

✳ Also look for slippers or socks that have treaded rubber or leather soles. These provide some traction and support even on slippery floors and, above all, on stairs. By contrast, smooth plastic slipper soles increase the risk of falling, especially on wet tiled or vinyl bathroom floors. While this holds true for all household members, it is most significant for seniors and young children, who are less sure-footed to start with.

TAKE CARE

When climbing up or down stairs, never carry anything that blocks your view of what lies ahead.

USE CHILD SAFETY GATES ON STAIRS AND SAFETY LOCKS ON WINDOWS.

as children can suffocate if they pull them over their heads.

❋ Good-quality baby changing tables have some form of roll-off protection, but this does not guarantee safety from falls. Falls, from changing tables and other furniture, are the most common cause of accidents involving babies and toddlers. Crib slats must be spaced closely enough (no more than 2 3/8 in. apart) to prevent children's heads or limbs from becoming trapped.

Falls from furniture are the most common cause of accidents involving babies and toddlers.

❋ Only use low-voltage (or battery-operated) lamps and toys in the nursery. Make sure any batteries, especially those small button batteries, are taped or screwed down securely, and thrown out as soon as they run out of charge.

❋ Install child safety plugs on all unused electrical sockets and ensure that no loose power cords are accessible to small children.

❋ Always unplug electric kitchen appliances after use when there are small children in the home. This ensures that children cannot accidentally switch on a blender, for example, and injure themselves. Never

CHILDPROOF from top to bottom

Keeping inexperienced youngsters safe from harm and potential risks is a top priority for families with small children, and must take precedence over the home's aesthetics or the adults' desire for prestige. When childproofing a home, take these hazards into account: never leave knives, scissors, needles, lighters, matches, cleaning agents, medicines, alcohol, paints and dyes, cosmetics or small objects of any kind lying around. Smokers must be particularly careful with their cigarettes – the nicotine contained in a single cigarette (or an e-cigarette refill) can be enough to kill a toddler. Keep these dangers in cabinets with childproof locks. Plastic bags are another significant menace,

TAKE CARE

Never allow little children to "help" you cook. They could hurt or burn themselves, or you could trip over them or their toys.

allow cords to dangle from your kitchen counter – children may pull on them and cause the appliance to fall on their heads.

✳ Secure nursery furniture to the wall with metal brackets to ensure that it will not topple even when toddlers try to climb on it.

✳ Use child safety gates on stairs and safety locks on windows. Safety gates on stairs can also be very helpful for the elderly, especially when they have poor vision, but you may need to install them higher than for children.

✳ Banish tablecloths, as children may pull on them. Move potted plants out of the house as long as children are small.

✳ Cover all hard furniture edges with corner protectors and fit safety locks on all cabinet doors, drawers and trash can lids.

Insider's hack Most parents-to-be know that big-ticket items only to be used for a short time, such as car seats, can be rented. But you can also rent high chairs, baby gates, changing tables and toys – a boon for parents travelling with infants or small children.

Dangers lurking in THE KITCHEN

Kitchens present many perils, again mainly for young children and seniors. If the phone rings or somebody knocks at your door while you are cooking, be aware that things may take longer than expected. Switch off your oven and cooktop, turn off the faucet, close the refrigerator door and make sure no child is left unattended in the kitchen.

✳ When using knives, especially very sharp ones, always slice away from the body, and only carry

WHEN USING KNIVES, ALWAYS SLICE AWAY FROM THE BODY.

PREVENTING DANGER FOR PETS

1 Protect your pets. Some dogs and cats like nibbling on potted plants, but many of these are poisonous, including azaleas, lilies, poinsettia, oleander and cyclamen.

2 Chocolate and cocoa, grapes and raisins, onions, garlic and nicotine are all toxic to dogs. Take a dog to the vet immediately if it has eaten any of these.

3 Cat owners need to keep their animals away from raw pork, which may contain viruses that can be fatal for them. Cats also cannot tolerate tea tree oil.

4 Medication intended for humans, such as aspirin, may be fatal to animals, as may all kinds of detergents and cleaning agents.

knives with the blade pointing downwards. Always hand them to somebody else handle first.

✳ Be careful when turning on faucets, as they may release scalding-hot water even on the cold-water setting, if they previously ran hot water.

✳ Turn pan and pot handles to point inwards on the stove, as it is easy for sleeves to catch on protruding handles, which could result in scalds or burns from hot oil or water.

✳ Watch out for kitchen wall-cabinet doors that have been left open, if you're working underneath. You may bump your head on the door corners – unfortunately this happens quite often!

✳ Always wipe up spilled liquids immediately – they are a slipping hazard!

Insider's hack Seniors should consider replacing old cooktops with modern induction ones. These only switch on when pots or pans containing iron or steel are placed on top; they switch off if not. Induction cooktops also remain cool if nothing is placed on top, because they heat by magnetizing the bottom of your cookware, not the cooktop itself.

CLEANING AGENTS,
a risky business

Quite a few domestic risks look entirely harmless at first glance, with their colorful bottles that promise to make cleaning tasks a breeze. These chemical cleaning agents may be helpful, but many of them are also hazardous.

✳ Ammonia, bleach and other cleaning agents containing solvents that are flammable, while drain cleaners and harsh bathroom cleaning agents can be downright dangerous: they often contain caustic ingredients that should not come into contact with skin. These products can cause skin irritation or worse, as some of them emit caustic vapors that irritate the respiratory tract and can even damage the lungs.

Clean regularly to avoid dirt and grime from becoming ingrained, and you will need to use fewer chemical cleaners.

✳ Your eyes are particularly at risk of damage from caustic agents. If you intend to clean a blocked drain with sodium hydroxide also known as lye or a similar substance, for example, make sure you always wear good goggles and rubber gloves. Even a tiny splash may cause irreversible eye damage.

✳ Chemical pesticides can also be hazardous to your health, especially if they are gaseous and can therefore spread throughout the home. They are best avoided altogether in living rooms, bedrooms

THE COLORFUL PACKAGING OF DOMESTIC CLEANING PRODUCTS PROMISES EASIER CHORES, BUT HIDES POTENTIAL RISKS.

TAKE CARE
Always leave cleaning agents in their original containers; never transfer them to drink bottles, as people may accidentally ingest them. This can be life threatening!

and kitchens. Try using baits or biological treatments (lures) instead to supplement proven physical measures such as sealing gaps in walls or floors, and vacuuming thoroughly.

✳ Water-based latex paints are relatively harmless, but any oil-based paints with an intense odor are an entirely different matter. If using such paints, ensure that you air rooms thoroughly for several days. That's why it is a good idea to save your paint jobs for the warmer months.

Insider's hack Clean regularly to avoid dirt and grime from becoming ingrained, and use more elbow grease when you do. You will then need to use fewer harsh chemical cleaners.

A GOOD LADDER is a must

Never climb on tables or chairs to hang up curtains, clean windows, change light bulbs or perhaps even paint the ceiling. For your safety, make the extra effort and get a ladder.

✳ Don't try to economize on the cost of a ladder: the most important criterion is quality. A good-quality ladder will be stable, have non-slip feet and bear a safety certificate. Read and follow all labels or markings on the ladder and use them to guide for your use of the ladder.

✳ Set up your ladder safely before climbing up. Place it on firm ground so that it does not wobble. Open out folding ladders fully and engage the safety catch to prevent the ladder from collapsing.

DON'T TRY TO ECONOMIZE ON YOUR LADDER; QUALITY IS MORE IMPORTANT.

TAKE CARE

Never use folding ladders as straight ladders. If you need both kinds, buy a special dual-purpose ladder.

✳ Don't position an extension ladder too close or too far away from the building – the ladder could topple back or slide down respectively.

✳ Always wear non-slip, supportive shoes when climbing a ladder, and only climb as far as you feel safe. Not everybody feels comfortable standing on the top platform!

✳ Avoid leaning out too far, as the ladder could topple, and always route power cords around ladders, not across the treads, as they constitute a tripping hazard.

✳ Carry any tools and equipment you will need for your job on the ladder in a tool-belt or bag to leave one hand free for support. Follow the 3-point philosophy, 2 hands and 1 foot or 2 feet and 1 hand on the ladder at all times.

Safety solutions for
REDUCED MOBILITY

There is no reason why, if your motor skills or abilities are limited or reduced, you should have to move out of your home. There is a whole range of dedicated products to assist you in maintaining your safety and independence at home.

✳ For people who have difficulty getting into and out of the bath, you can fit special handles vertically on the bathtub edge to provide firm support. If you're planning on remodelling your bathroom, it's worth considering installing a sunken bath, or if you have room, building in steps leading up to the bath. Another option may be a walk-in tub with a step of only about 4–8 in. These are usually a combined bath–shower, and may include a sit-down

FIT SPECIAL HANDLES IN THE BATHROOM TO PROVIDE FIRM SUPPORT FOR PEOPLE WHO HAVE DIFFICULTY.

bath. Walk-in baths can be good for children, who usually love getting into the bath through the "door."

✳ If people find it difficult to get up from the toilet seat, fit a plastic toilet-seat riser or handles on either side of the toilet. Many suppliers of bathroom products sell these.

✳ People using wheelchairs may have difficulty reaching standard sinks. They need special, accessible sinks with a narrow rim and shallow depth instead; these allow them to come in close with their chairs.

✳ You may require an adjustable bed in the bedroom. They are not cheap, so it's worthwhile checking whether your health insurance covers some of the expenses.

✳ Stairs should have handrails on both sides to improve safety for people with limited mobility. Extend handrails a little beyond the stairs to help them reach landings safely. If you have wood stairs, consider painting the risers a contrasting color, as this makes it easier to spot them with reduced vision. In certain circumstances, you may wish to install a stair-lift – these are customized for your home. While stair-lifts can cost upwards of several thousand dollars, your health insurance may pay part of this.

✳ Provide aids to make changing shoes easier in the hallway (a seat, shoehorn and boot jack, for example) and clear space for a walker, if necessary. Doorsteps may need to be made more accessible, too.

✳ It is a good idea to install emergency call devices at various spots inside the home (bathroom, toilet, bedroom and possibly also by a recliner or lounge

STAIRS SHOULD HAVE HANDRAILS ON BOTH SIDES TO IMPROVE SAFETY FOR PEOPLE WITH LIMITED MOBILITY.

chair). Phones should be easily accessible (cell phones are probably best) and easy to operate, with large buttons, a clear display and pre-set emergency numbers. These simple solutions can save lives in an emergency.

Easy fix All tank hot water heaters, both electric and gas, have a water thermostat which helps ensure that the water temperature is always within a pleasant range. Should the water no longer be heated to the normal temperature, look into replacing the water thermostat before having to replace the entire tank heater.

Insider's hack Enamelled bathtubs can be very slippery. You can place a rubber mat inside the tub, but it's not very hygienic. Acrylic bathtubs are less slippery than enamel, but a better option than both is an anti-slip treatment for enamel or porcelain bathtubs, or a non-slip enamel tub with a textured quartz/sand surface.

TAKE CARE

Avoid using stools in the bathtub – use a dedicated shower chair with armrests instead. Stools are not safe enough, as it is possible to miss the seat or to fall off in case of sudden weakness.

Electricity, a mixed blessing

Most modern industrial products are safe these days, as electricity has been around for a long time. Approach electricity with caution and take care to avoid potential hazards.

WE CAN'T DO WITHOUT THE POWER THAT GIVES US LIGHT AND HEAT, BUT WE MUST APPROACH IT WITH CAUTION.

HANDLE ELECTRICITY with care

There are two main dangers associated with electrical power: it may heat the wiring, potentially causing fires, and it may escape from power cords and appliances (mostly due to faulty insulation) and end up passing through the human body. Electric shocks are highly unpleasant and dangerous. They can cause burns or, in severe cases, respiratory paralysis or cardiac arrest, which can be fatal.

✳ Small appliances such as toasters, coffeemakers, and blenders make our lives easy but need to be handled with care. Plug all appliances into a ground fault circuit interrupter (GFCI) and unplug when not in use. Keep appliances away from the sink and the stove. Water can cause an electrical shock and heat may melt wires.

✳ Take particular care with cheap imports, or deals that seem too good to be true. Be careful when buying electrical appliances and keep your eyes out for telltale signs (see page 202, "How to identify poor-quality appliances").

Save time You must be able to switch off power quickly in case of an emergency. Label each fuse or

TAKE CARE

Never keep using damaged electrical appliances, even if they still work. Repair or discard them; otherwise they can cause a fire or electric shock hazard.

ROUTE POWER CORDS AND TELEPHONE CORDS ALONG BASEBOARDS OR INSIDE ELECTRICAL CONDUIT.

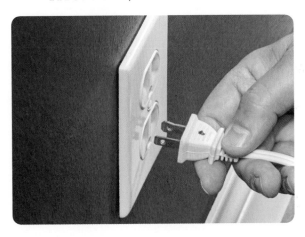

Electrical plugs generally have two flat prongs, with one slightly larger than the other.

circuit breaker in your main panel appropriately ("Bathroom," for example) to make it easier to find the right one when you need to, and ensure that everybody knows where the panel is located.

Insider's hack Teach your children about the hazards of electrical power and show them how to handle electrical appliances, plugs and outlets appropriately. Ask them questions to check whether they understand.

PLUGS, OUTLETS and
surge protectors

In North America, electrical plugs generally have two flat parallel prongs with one of the prongs slightly wider than the other. These can only be inserted into the outlet one way because of the different widths of the prong and the socket. These are reserved for double insulated devices that do not require "grounding." Three-pronged plugs have two flat parallel prongs with a round one below the two and this round prong is grounded. These protective plugs are very important for your safety, as they conduct electricity away or cause power to be disconnected if the device is damaged.

✳ Three-pronged outlets are required in all homes built after 1962. If your home still has two-pronged outlets, consider updating your home by having a licensed electrician install new outlets.

✳ There is an important difference between a surge protector and a power strip. Many power strips are simply extension cords with more than one socket. Surge protectors look like power strips but include built-in surge protection that shuts off if the strip is overpowered by too many connected devices or if the flowing current exceeds a certain level. They also prevent lightning power surges causing damage to electronics. Look for an Underwriter Laboratories approved surge-protector with a "UL 1449" label to ensure you are not purchasing a cheaper power strip. The label will be a holograph one to prevent counterfeit labels on cheaper and often imported products. An electrician can install a whole house surge protector device (SPD) in your circuit panel to eliminate the need for individual ones in many rooms throughout the home.

✳ The contacts of sockets and connectors should be somewhat elastic and spring back, allowing a tight fit; otherwise they can become deformed and fail to provide good contact. While an appliance connected to the socket may still work, as power continues to be supplied through the contacts, the safety feature of the socket may be severely compromised, or lost altogether if the plug is loose within the socket.

SAFE GFCIS SHOULD ALWAYS BE INSTALLED IN AREAS WITH HIGH HUMIDITY.

TAKE CARE

Never pull on power cords to remove plugs from sockets; always grab the plug itself, otherwise the cords will eventually break.

✳ Don't use an extension cord or power strip to insert a number of plugs to a single outlet if you plan to use them with powerful appliances that draw a lot of power, including electric fans, electric blankets, powerful lamps, vacuum cleaners, power tools and large kitchen appliances. Otherwise you run the risk of overloading the circuit and potentially causing a fire.

✳ If you discover a worn-out appliance and decide to throw it away, make sure it won't be picked up and used by somebody else.

Insider's hack Route all power cords inside electrical conduit or empty pipes, if you have rabbits or guinea pigs that you let roam through the house. These pets love to nibble on cords.

Save money Pull the plug on sensitive devices during thunderstorms and before going away on vacation to prevent any damage and potentially expensive repairs or replacements.

Safety with CIRCUIT BREAKERS

Arc fault circuit interrupters (AFCIs) greatly reduce the risk of fire by detecting small arc faults and then shutting off the power. AFCI protection is required (as of 2014 in the United States and 2015 in Canada) on all circuits in all living areas and comes in two forms: built into circuit breakers installed in the main circuit panel, or built into the outlets. Fuses protect cables and devices from overheating by disconnecting the power supply, if the power flowing through the circuit becomes too strong. However, they provide no protection against electric shock – keep in mind that even relatively weak electrical power can be fatal, if it passes through the human body.

✳ This is where ground faulted circuit interrupters (GFCIs) come in: they compare the electric current between the energized and the return conductor. If these two values do not match within a fairly narrow range of tolerance, there must be a current leaking somewhere, and leakage always indicates that there is a problem. The GFCI then immediately disconnects the entire power supply from the conducting wires, generally before the leaking current can cause any serious damage.

✳ GFCIs can become defective; therefore you should test them once a month by pressing the test button; alternatively, have them inspected by a qualified electrician. GFCIs are recommended (and required in newly installed or replaced outlets after 2017) in areas around the home where water is present such as kitchen countertops, bathrooms, laundry rooms and basements (damp skin conducts electricity better than dry skin). They can save lives in areas where there is a high risk of electric shock outdoors as well, such as pools and pond pumps. GFCIs are not particularly expensive to buy and they can be easily retrofitted by a qualified electrician.

Insider's hack Another way to keep children safe from electrical issues is to install tamper-resistant outlets. These outlets prevent curious kids from inserting objects like paper clips. Tamper-resistant outlets are required in all locations, so if you replace any outlet, use one labeled "TR."

USE ELECTRICAL APPLIANCES SAFELY

1 Check electrical appliances, cords, plugs and sockets regularly for damage, brittle cord insulations, frayed cords, melted parts and any burnt smell. Discontinue using an appliance immediately if you identify any damage, even if it still works.

2 Be extremely careful when using electrical appliances in the bathroom. Keep all appliances away from water, especially if you are in the shower or bathtub. Many deaths have occurred due to hairdryers or electric razors sliding into the water from the edge of the bath.

3 Always switch off the power before replacing light bulbs or when cleaning electrical appliances!

4 Never try to patch up or repair electrical appliances – you should leave this to a qualified electrician.

ALWAYS SWITCH OFF THE POWER BEFORE REPLACING LIGHT BULBS.

Health care for the family

Mishaps occur, regardless of how well a household is managed, and you'll be glad for a well-stocked medicine cabinet when they do. But it is also important to remember that prevention is better than cure when your family's health is at stake.

Practices for BEST HEALTH

You can never protect you and your family from all health risks, but one measure you can instill in them is to wash their hands. Always wash your hands after shopping – you never know when that cart was last cleaned – and if anybody in the family is ill, especially if they are suffering from a gastro-intestinal infection.

✴ Avoid furniture and plastics that have a strong odor; this indicates they are emitting chemical vapors that may be harmful.

✴ Plant-based fragrances can also be risky: "natural" doesn't necessarily equate to "safe." While essential oils can provide effective relief from colds, it's the dosage that makes them a poison, as there have been many cases of children suffering severe poisoning from essential oils. Always exercise great caution when using essential oils near children, and only use them as directed.

✴ Glass bowls and drinking glasses will inevitably drop and break every now and then. To prevent injuries, first gather any large shards, then cover the floor with damp newspaper or paper towel, which even the tiniest splinters will stick to. Finally, gather the paper up carefully.

Insider's hack Before buying paints or adhesives, check for any health risks. Pay close attention to any warnings on the packaging.

A well-stocked MEDICINE CABINET

Most of us have a small medicine cabinet somewhere, and more often than not it's a repository of ancient, leftover medication. This is not the way to do it! Your medicine cabinet should be stocked with supplies of current first-aid treatments and

ENSURE THAT YOUR MEDICINE CABINET IS WELL STOCKED.

medications. Above all, ensure that it contains the products you really need – and all well before their use-by date. It may be best to ask your pharmacist for advice.

✳ It's essential that your medicine cabinet can be locked and is childproof. Also keep it out of reach of small hands.

✳ Check regularly for products that are past their use-by date. If you can't get to a disposal site, mix intact pills with unpalatable substance such as dirt, cat litter, or used coffee grounds and discard in the trash. Never throw them down the toilet or sink! Dispose of opened bottles of liquids such as cough medicines or eye drops once you have used them.

✳ Replace bandages, dressings and disinfectants as soon as they run out so you do not get caught without in case of injury. It may be a good idea to keep an inventory list inside your medicine cabinet to make it easy to check its contents.

Insider's hack Always buy the smallest possible packets of any over-the-counter medicines. While

WHAT'S IN A MEDICINE CABINET

BANDAGES AND DRESSINGS	Gauze, elastic bandages, round-edged scissors, adhesive bandages of different sizes (including some for sensitive skin and waterproof dressings), disinfectant wipes (for small wounds)
IMPLEMENTS	Thermometer, disposable gloves, tongue depressors, tweezers, tick tweezers, hot/cold pack, small bright flashlight, nail clippers or scissors, eye cup
OVER-THE-COUNTER MEDICINES FOR	Pain, sore throats, heartburn, open wounds (antibacterial cream or liquid), digestive disorders (gas, diarrhea, etc.), allergies, insect bites, muscle pain, sprains, sunburn
FOR YOUNG CHILDREN	Liquid acetaminophen, diaper rash cream, teething gel, infant cough syrup, children's adhesive bandages, children's thermometer

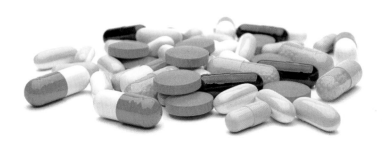

CHECK FOR PRODUCTS PAST THEIR USE-BY DATE AND DISCARD.

TAKE CARE

Avoid placing your medicine cabinet in the kitchen or bathroom, as the heat and humidity in these rooms can affect medicinal products. A place in the bedroom or hallway, away from direct sunlight, is a better option.

smaller packets may be relatively more expensive, you will not end up with leftovers that are no longer needed or past their use-by date.

Save money Alleviate the symptoms of colds with these home remedies. Gargle with saltwater to relieve a sour throat. Drink plenty of liquids. Use vapor rubs to soothe symptoms in children. Try black elderberry syrup to lesson the symptoms.

Kitchen cabinet HOME REMEDIES

We all value healthy nutrition for our families. In recent years, research has found that some popular foods can give a real boost to our health.

☀ Green tea has been a favorite in some families for generations. Research has discovered that it contains not only a number of vitamins and minerals, but also beneficial bitter compounds that are effective against a range of complaints.

☀ Green smoothies – made from fruit, green leafy vegetables and water (or coconut water) – are a relatively new trend, but there are plenty of recipes to try. Green smoothies are best prepared fresh; they provide all of the vitamins and fiber from the produce, plus a range of beneficial phytochemicals. You can prepare them in no time, and the blending process makes their healthy ingredients rapidly available to our bodies.

☀ A number of recent studies have shown just how effective plant substances can be: thylakoids from plant cell membranes, for example, suppress hunger, slow down digestion and therefore support weight loss, while some of the sulfurous substances in cruciferous vegetables are effective against germs. This is less surprising than it may sound, as plants produce these substances to protect themselves against micro-organisms.

Save money There is no need to rush to the nearest pharmacy to buy expensive remedies the next time you have a cold or flu. Homemade chicken soup made with carrots, onions, garlic, celery and a little parsley and salt is also effective, as these ingredients contain anti-inflammatory substances, and the liquid counteracts potential dehydration.

GREEN SMOOTHIES ARE BEST PREPARED FRESH; THEY PROVIDE VITAMINS AND PHYTOCHEMICALS.

Comfortable SICKROOMS

It often happens out of the blue: our nearest and dearest falls ill and is confined to bed for an extended period. While there is professional help available to assist the patient, the home, or at least the sickroom, needs to be catered to properly.

☀The room must be large enough for a bed that can be accessed from all sides, plus hold a bedside table or cabinet. The bathroom and toilet must be close by and accessible without negotiating stairs. You may need to install support handles and

BETTER HEALTH with vinegar

Dressing a salad with oil and vinegar is not only a good culinary choice, it's also a good health choice. The oil allows fat-soluble vitamins in the salad to be absorbed, and the vinegar acts as an antimicrobial agent, killing off about 80 percent of bacteria and fungi within minutes.

REMOVE GERMS FROM SALAD VEGETABLES

If you suspect that vegetables or lettuces have been contaminated or passed through unclean hands, place them in white vinegar for half an hour.

PANTRY DEODORIZER

Vinegar is a valuable basic to have in your pantry. An open bowl of vinegar effectively removes unpleasant odors, since it kills airborne germs as it evaporates. Never fear: the vinegar smell vanishes quickly after airing.

VINEGAR TO REDUCE FEVER

"Vinegar socks" can bring a patient's fever down. Soak cotton socks in diluted vinegar (1:5 ratio of vinegar to water), gently wring out the excess liquid and let the patient wear the socks for an hour at a time, with their feet wrapped in a towel. Repeat 2–3 times per day.

EASIER WEIGHT LOSS

If you are overweight and on a weight-loss diet, take a glass of lukewarm water with 2 teaspoons apple cider vinegar before each meal to reduce hunger pangs.

TAKE CARE WITH VINEGAR CONCENTRATE

Use vinegar with an acid content of about 6 percent, not vinegar concentrate. This is sometimes used for cleaning, such as to remove odors from the fridge, and is highly concentrated; use with care as the vapors can irritate the eyes and respiratory tract.

WHAT TO DO IN CASE OF POISONING

1 Nausea, vomiting, stomach cramps and diarrhea can be signs of food poisoning. If these symptoms don't improve after a few hours, or the patient develops impaired vision or even paralysis, call an ambulance.

2 Inexplicable changes in behavior such as sudden fatigue, agitation or trembling may be signs of poisoning in children, especially if a child also complains of nausea, headaches or dizziness. Find out what they've ingested – if it's cleaning agents, medicine, poisonous plants, pesticides or insecticides, call an ambulance!

3 Do not give patients anything to eat or drink while you wait, especially not milk! If they have ingested caustic substances, do not induce vomiting, but do give them plenty of water to drink to dilute the poison.

4 If possible, keep some of the product or food the patient has ingested for examination; this also applies to any vomit the patient may have brought up.

PROLONGED BED REST CAN BE BORING FOR PATIENTS, BUT BOOKS CAN HELP PASS THE TIME.

and air.

✳ Certain houseplants, such as spider plants and rubber trees, can be a welcome addition to the sick room, as these plants are proven to remove toxins such as formaldehyde from the atmosphere. But if your patient's immune system is compromised, you should remove potted plants altogether, as potting mix may contain germs.

✳ Prolonged bed rest can be rather boring for patients, but books and magazines can help to pass the time. Make sure the patient has a good reading light. Crosswords, television, films, music, and a computer or smartphone also provide distraction.

Easy fix Consider adding splashes of yellow or another cheery color to the room's decor to brighten the mood and prevent it from feeling like a hospital.

Insider's hack Make sure you vacuum or mop the floor daily to maintain optimum hygiene. Remove rugs from hard floors to make mopping easier and eliminate tripping hazards.

provide the bath or shower with a non-slip surface and a seat (see also pages 198–199, "Safety solutions for reduced mobility"). Keep in mind that patients should never shower or bathe alone and unassisted.

✳ Good lighting is essential for nursing purposes and medical examinations. Ideally, this can be controlled from the patient's bed. Finally, rooms, especially floors, should be easy to clean

Home pest control

Our homes are a veritable paradise for insects and spiders. They are warm and offer plenty of quiet, pleasantly dark and damp hiding places, and there is an abundance of food – from mold and mildew to dead skin cells and leftover meals – in our kitchens and pantries, bathrooms and bedrooms.

KEEP CALM if you spot pests

There is no need to panic if you spot the odd insect, as most are harmless. Don't rush to buy pesticides but look to exclusion and hygiene, and consider less-toxic controls such as baits and gels, first. Over-zealous pesticide use, not following the label and incorrect pest identification can raise unnecessary risks, especially to children and pets.

SPIDERS, unwelcome guests

Many people are afraid of spiders, but many kinds of spiders are harmless to us, and none actively attacks humans. Still, it is preferable not to have spider webs inside for the sake of aesthetics and cleanliness.
✳ To keep bugs away from your pets' dishes, place a border of baking soda around their food bowls to keep away six-legged intruders. And it won't harm your pet if he happens to lap up a little (though most pets aren't likely to savor soda's bitter taste.)

Insider's hack Trap and release harmless spiders. Put a glass or container over the spider, slide a piece of firm paper underneath, flip over and release the spider well outside your home.

Save money To keep insects outside, spray WD-40 on windowsills and frames, screens and door frames. Be careful not to inhale the fumes when you spray and don't do this at all if you have small children at home.

Not-so-harmless FLIES

A fly here and there is not a problem, but large numbers are annoying and should be controlled. Avoid fighting pest flies with chemical sprays and fogs that spread pesticide haphazardly, and try to exclude them or remove whatever attracts them. Flies carry nasty microbes from their last rotten meal and spread a wide range of diseases.
✳ Common houseflies are more than just a nuisance. As they walk over food they leave their feces, and potentially germs that can cause a range of diseases.

EXCLUDE FLIES FROM WHATEVER ATTRACTS THEM.

✳ During summer months, keep food covered and use a blue table cloth, flies avoid this color.

✳ The smell of basil, peppermint, lavender or tomato plants ward off flies – they don't like the fragrances of these plants.

Easy fix The best solution for dealing with flies is to install screens on your windows and doors.

TAKE CARE

Don't leave out excess pet food because flies will soon lay eggs in it. The same applies to your food and container recycling bins, keep them closed.

Water-loving MOSQUITOES

Mosquitoes will breed in just about any still, fresh water. Maintain swimming pools (use a skimmer) to prevent their floating eggs from hatching, and stock garden ponds with fish or creatures that will eat the larvae. Trash and blocked gutters and drains should be cleaned out or fixed. Treat puddles with anti-mosquito preparations containing the *Bacillus thuringiensis* varo *israelensis* (Bti) bacteria, which are harmless to humans.

✳ Keep the pests away from patios and balconies by hanging up a cloth sprayed with a few drops of clove or laurel oil. Alternatively, pour the oil into small bowls or an oil lamp. Another safe way to ward off mosquitoes is to pin or tie used dryer fabric softener sheets onto your clothing when you go outdoors. The scent of the sheets helps to repel the pests.

REPLACE A TORN SCREEN

Repairing a tear or hole in a screen is a quick and easy project. Here's what you need: straightedge, utility knife, piece of screen, wax paper, adhesive and craft stick.

1 Remove the screen and lay it flat on your workbench. Using a straightedge and sharp utility knife, cut a small square hole around the tear. Leave at least 1/4 in. of the old screen next to the metal frame.

2 Cut a patch of screening that will overlap each edge by 1/4 in. Lay wax paper under the screen to catch any adhesive drips. Center the patch over the hole, apply a bead of adhesive over the edges of the patch, and use a craft stick to spread through both patch and screen.

✳ Mosquitoes are attracted to your warmth and the carbon dioxide you breathe out. Netting will keep them out. Fans are helpful both indoors and out, as mosquitoes have trouble tracking you in a breeze. Sleep under a net or ceiling fan if you're troubled by buzzing in your ears.

Save money Avoid using electronic mosquito repellents. Choose a repellent with icaridin also known as picaridin as its active ingredient and if that doesn't work then try a botanical oil-based product or DEET.

ANTS commonly infest homes

Ants love accessible moist food, especially sweets and proteins. They usually invade homes from the outside; ant colonies send out food scouts first before dispatching large numbers of workers.

✳ Ants follow a scent trail, marching in a straight line one by one. Disrupt the trail by sprinkling dried mint leaves, crushed cloves or chili powder at the point where they enter the house. Once they lose the scent trail they can no longer find their way in. Or, draw a line with a piece of chalk or baby powder through the ants' route. The tiny gatecrashers won't be able to cross it.

✳ If fire ants plague your yard or patio and you're tired of getting stung by the tiny attackers, a flowerpot can help you quench the problem. Place a flowerpot upside down over the anthill. Pour boiling water through the drain holes and you'll be burning down their house.

Easy fix Wipe minor ant trails you find inside the home with diluted vinegar or lemon juice, or sprinkle with ammonium bicarbonate (also known as baker's yeast). Ants also dislike cinnamon. Next up, try baits from the super-market but the ones with borax don't usually kill the whole ant colony. Avoid DIY spray kits. If none of these work, or you are getting bitten, call in an exterminator.

WASPS ARE ATTRACTED TO SUGARY FOODS AND SWEET DRINKS.

BEES, HORNETS AND WASPS
have a nasty sting

Most wasps can be ignored, but some hornets and bees have a nasty sting. If you find one inside your home, it will usually leave again of its own accord through an open door or window. Avoid waving your arms in attempting to shoo these insects outside, as this may make them aggressive. Instead, make a trap by filling a narrow-neck bottle with diluted fruit juice and a little detergent and vinegar. They will fly in but won't be able to get out.

✳ Be careful not to swallow a wasp – they will sting if swallowed, and the resulting swelling in the throat can be life-threatening. If you are allergic to wasp stings you should always carry an Epipen.

✳ Don't let yellow-jackets and other wasps ruin your spring and summer fun. Their favorite place to build nests is under eaves. In the spring, mist some WD-40 under all the eaves of your house to block them from building nests there.

Tiny, irritating FRUIT FLIES

These little insects are attracted to overripe or rotting fruit, where they lay their eggs and reproduce very quickly. Once the fruit in your bowl is ripe, it's best to store it in sealed containers. Avoid leaving leftover fruit out in the open, not even in a trash bag. Consider buying a fruit-fly trap if you have an infestation, as they can be tricky to eliminate.

✳ The tiny flies you sometimes see rising from potted plants are not fruit flies but fungus gnats, which cannot be trapped in fruit-fly traps. Covering the soil with about 1/4 in. of dry sand and watering plants from the bottom can be helpful.

Easy fix Fill a small bowl with a little apple juice and vinegar, some water and a dash of dishwashing liquid. This mixture will attract fruit flies and cause

FRUIT FLIES LOVE OVERRIPE AND ROTTING FRUIT.

them to drown. Yellow or pale green bowls work best as these resemble old fruit and sick plants.

SILVERFISH in bathrooms and kitchens

These long-lived, slender, silvery insects with three tails live inside small crevices in moist areas and usually come out at night. Mostly, you will only see them as they scurry away when you switch on a light. Inside, they mainly feed on surface mold and skin flakes. Silverfish do not transmit disease, but an infestation may indicate a dampness problem, especially if you find them eating paper.

✳ When you find them, seal the cracks where they hide, and vacuum frequently to control silverfish in the long term. If you have big numbers or infestations coming from the roof, call an exterminator.

Save time Silverfish can't abide Diatomaceous Earth (DE). It rips apart their delicate silvery skin.

MICE AND RATS, unwanted visitors

Mice can be caught quite easily with mousetraps; you can opt for animal-friendly tilt traps if you'd prefer to trap and release. Tie mousetraps down with wire, as trapped mice may run with them for quite some distance.

✳ Mice are grain feeders. Peanut butter is the best bait. Do not use bacon or cheese; these foods spoil quickly and become smelly. Check your traps often.

✳ Rats are smarter and more cautious than mice. The main pest species are black rats and brown rats. Rats love to chew things and sometimes they start house fires by stripping the insulation from wires.

✳ Mice, rats, and even squirrels and bats are experts at finding every conceivable entry into the house. When you discover one of their entry points, stuff it full of steel wool. It is much more effective than foam or newspaper because even dedicated gnawers are unlikely to try to chew through such a sharp blockade.

✳ Don't let mice spend their winter vacation in your garage. To prevent this, place a few mothballs around the garage and the mice will seek other quarters. To keep mice out of your potting shed, put the mothballs around the base of wrapped or covered plants.

MICE CAN BE CAUGHT IN ANIMAL-FRIENDLY TILT TRAPS.

COCKROACHES leave a bad smell

Act right away if you see a cockroach in your home. They are unsanitary, produce an unpleasant smell and breed incredibly fast.

✳ You're most likely to find cockroaches in the kitchen by turning on a light at night. They will scurry back into hiding. You may also see empty egg cases or skins, a dust of droppings or brown smears where walls and floor meet. This is where cockroaches tend to run. Keep your food areas

TAKE CARE

Rats and mice love compost, and they in turn attract snakes that prey on them. Using a tumbling compost bin on a frame won't let them in.

scrupulously clean, empty the trash and don't leave pet dishes on the floor once the food has been eaten.

✳ Cockroaches prefer warm, damp weather so summer is peak season. You can detect many species from the little purses they build for their eggs.

COCKROACHES PREFER WARM, DAMP SPACES LIKE KITCHENS.

✳ To build nonpoisonous roach motels, wrap the outside of an empty jelly jar with masking tape, and rub the inside of the jar with petroleum jelly. Pour in an inch of beer and top it with a few small pieces of ripe fruit and 4–5 drops of almond extract. Place the unlidded jar under the sink or anywhere else cockroaches lurk. Roaches will be drawn to the appetizing aroma, climb into the jar (the tape gives them traction), and drop inside to feast—but thanks to the slippery walls, they'll be unable to escape. To dispose of the tipsy roaches, fill the jar with hot water and flush the contents down the toilet.

✳ Cockroaches like to hide. If you see one, there are probably many more. Big infestations call for professional help, but you can control low numbers with baits containing hormones or tiny doses of non-repellent insecticides. Household surface sprays will rarely result in complete control. Seal up all the places they hide and pull out the refrigerator, stove and dishwasher to clean thoroughly. Limit their food access with clean bins and sealed food containers. They adore most pet food. It takes very little food to raise a cockroach, so pay attention to detail.

Furniture and other BEETLES

Furniture beetle larvae feed within the wood and adults emerge from small round holes. A gritty dust falls from the holes (even years after the beetles have gone). They prefer old pine and unfinished wood,

FURNITURE BEETLES DON'T LIKE HEATED ROOMS.

or furniture that's always a bit damp.

✳ Small wooden items may be heat treated or frozen. Valuable pieces can be fumigated. Sometimes it is best to replace affected woods. Framing and the underside of flooring may be treated with borax. Request professional advice for which method will work best in your case.

✳ Newer hardwood, parquet floors and even bamboos may be attacked by the starch-loving powder post beetles. They move in quickly and leave through little round holes. A fine powder falls from these holes for many decades after they've left, which can fool people into taking unnecessary action.

✳ Many other species of beetles can damage wood. Ask an expert if you're unsure of the guilty party.

Don't put up with DUST MITES

Nobody ever truly sleeps alone. Dust mites are all over our homes, wherever there is food and moisture. Their feces trigger allergic reactions like red watery eyes, a runny nose or even breathing difficulties. Some easy precautions will help to alleviate the problem. Regular vacuuming is your first defense.

✳ Dust mites love down comforters. If you have a dust-mite allergy, use comforters with a synthetic filling and wash regularly at 140°F. Mites also live inside mattresses, closets and crevices in the floor. Vacuum and wipe these thoroughly and frequently. If you consult a pest expert, ask about low-allergenic solutions, as some pesticides can be irritating.

Insider's hack Wall-to-wall carpets are not ideal if you have allergies. Replace with smooth floors and only have rugs that can be easily removed for cleaning. Be sure your vacuum cleaner has a HEPA filter so that you aren't blowing the mites and their feces around the rooms.

FLEAS leave itchy bites

Pest fleas are usually either dog or cat fleas, with very thin adults that are about 2 mm long. Eggs may

be dropped in bedding or just about anywhere and these and the hatchlings are easily vacuumed up. The larvae tend to feed on skin cells and fungi in bedding, carpets, floor gaps or soil.

✳ Flea bites are not entirely harmless: fleas spread disease and parasites, including tapeworms. To rid your home of them, put a few drops of dishwashing soap and some water on a plate. Place the plate on the floor next to a lamp. Fleas love light and will jump on the plate and drown. Wash any affected textiles in a hot wash (at least 140°F), hang in the sun to dry or store them in your freezer for several weeks.

Insider's hack Young fleas wait for a vibration signal and then jump, hoping to reach a passing host. If you find them in a room that's been vacant (such as a vacation rental), vacuum or spray for fleas before allowing in people and pets.

HEAD LICE are a headache

Most children are exposed to head lice at least once. They generally contract lice at school or pre-school. Head lice suck blood and their bites cause scalps to itch. They lay up to seven tiny white eggs (so-called nits) per day, which take about a week to hatch. The nits are glued to a hair strand, close to the skin.

✳ Pharmacies stock effective head lice treatments. Try and choose the least toxic option, avoiding those that may be absorbed by the skin. Sometimes soaking the hair in conditioner and carefully combing the nits off with a special narrow comb can provide good control. Be sure to crush any adults until they pop. Head lice prefer clean hair, so over-washing may make things worse. Some botanical products will be mildly repellent and reduce re-infestation rates.

✳ Wash combs, hairbrushes, hairclips and other accessories with warm soapy water. Wash towels and bed linens in a hot machine-wash (140°F). For delicate clothing, transfer to a sealed plastic bag and keep in the freezer for several days to kill lice.

COMFORTERS WITH A SYNTHETIC FILLING ARE BEST FOR PEOPLE WITH ALLERGIES.

Dealing with FERAL ANIMALS

Introduced animal species gone wild, or feral, can be a huge problem. From rabbits and deer to foxes and cats, these creatures are a major threat to biodiversity and can damage people's property, especially in rural areas.

✳ Check with your government authority how best to deal with the animal problems you have. Fencing is most likely the easiest and most effective way to keep feral animals out of your property. Other forms of control need to be left to the experts.

WILDLIFE is a special case

A noisy nocturnal visitor on your property is usually a raccoon, possum or other nighttime creature. They can get into the roof or attic keeping you up all night. You should call in animal expert who can block the entry, often with a temporary one-way door. Don't try to deal with them yourself.

✳Few things can be quite as startling as a raccoon leaping out of your garbage can just as you're about to make your nightly trash deposit. Keep away those masked scavengers and other strays by spraying the outside and lids of your garbage cans with half-strength ammonia or by spraying the bags inside.

Insider's hack Keep bats from taking up residence in your attic by sprinkling moth balls around the attic.

Keep cool, keep warm

Our homes should not merely be a safe space, but also one where we feel comfortable and at ease. A little thought and planning goes a long way toward making this happen.

LET THE SUN'S WARMTH IN ON SUNNY WINTER DAYS BY OPENING UP THE HOUSE TO THE SOUTH AND WEST.

Heating and cooling ESSENTIALS

Save on energy costs, create a healthy climate inside, reduce greenhouse gas emissions and banish mildew before it sets in, by managing your home's indoor climate. Heating and cooling are the biggest energy users in the home, but with a few simple strategies, you can keep your home cozy in winter and cool in summer without running up huge bills.

HEATING sensibly

✳ Check regularly that your heaters are working efficiently. If you're unsure, have them serviced once a year.

✳ Your home's forced-air heating or cooling system helps to control dust by filtering the air. A standard cheap fiberglass filter protects your furnace from large dust particles and provides maximum airflow, but it does little to reduce household dust. More expensive pleated filters usually provide a good balance between cost and filtration efficiency. These filters trap 80 to 95 percent of particles 5 microns and larger.

TAKE CARE

Our ever-increasing desire for air-conditioning in summer can result in a nasty shock to the hip pocket. To beat the heat cheaply, visit the library, the movies or a shopping center in the middle of the day to use their A/C instead.

✳ But if you have family members with allergies, consider spending more on high-efficiency filters, which capture 99 percent of airborne particles as small as 0.3 microns (bacteria and viruses, fumes and pollen).

✳ Turn the heat down when you leave home and before you go to bed. Or, install a programmable thermostat to adjust the temperature accordingly.

✳ Let the sun's warmth in on sunny winter days by opening up the house to the north and west.

✳ Keep cold drafts out by sealing gaps around doors and windows and installing heavy curtains. And then keep the warmth in and save energy by closing doors between heated and unheated areas.

Staying cool in SUMMER

✳ Cool south- and west-facing rooms by installing temporary shutters or awnings, which you can then remove in winter. Or train a deciduous climber over a pergola on a south- or west-facing wall – when it loses its leaves in winter, it will let the sun in.

✳ On hot days keep the heat out by closing windows, blinds and curtains. Then when the temperature drops at night, open doors and windows to let the cool air inside.

✳ To cool a hot interior quickly, open two windows that are opposite each other to create a cross breeze.

Save money Portable or ceiling fans are cheap to run and effective. They circulate air over your body, which evaporates moisture and helps cool you down.

The right VENTILATION

Too much moisture creates a breeding ground for mildew. Improper ventilation is usually the cause.

✳ Opt for short, periodic bursts of ventilation to best maintain air quality indoors. Open windows three times a day for up to 10 minutes in winter, and a little longer in warmer months, unless you suffer from hay fever.

✳ If the kitchen or bathroom steams up, air the room at once by opening a window or turning on a fan.

✳ Open the windows when drying laundry inside the house to allow damp air to escape.

Insider's hack If possible, leave a clearance of about 1/4-1/2 in. between armoires or bookcases and your home's outer walls. Mildew can easily develop behind tall furniture.

IF YOUR HOME GETS TOO HOT IN SUMMER

1 Prevent the sun from getting into your home. Lower blinds, close the shutters and extend any awnings.

2 Let fresh air into your home in the cooler hours of the morning and evening.

3 Use a fan, either a permanent ceiling fan or portable floor or desk fan. Modern bladeless fans are particularly effective.

4 Place your feet in a bucket of cold water, have a cool shower or run cold water over your arms. You may also find it easier to sleep if you have a cool shower before going to bed.

5 If you can't reduce the temperatures inside to a bearable level, you may need an air-conditioner. Try running the air-conditioner just in the morning, and keep the house closed and dark in the middle of the day to keep the cooler air inside.

Safety against fire and severe weather

There are around 358,000 home fires in the United States every year, with more than 2,500 fatalities. Most domestic fires are caused by cooking or heating equipment, and one in every three death occurred in homes with faulty smoke alarms.

Common FIRE HAZARDS

Smoke escaping from fires is usually more dangerous than the fire itself. More people die from smoke inhalation than the actual flames. Asphyxiation kills more people than burns do by a 3:1 ratio. Fires also produce poisonous gases that effect your ability to see and think clearly. These toxic gases can make you drowsy preventing you from escaping quickly. Smoke also reduces the visibility to next to nothing, sometimes within minutes.

✳ According to the National Fire Protection Association, from 2012 to 2017 cooking equipment was the leading cause of home fires and fire injuries

TAKE CARE

It's vital to know how to minimize the fire risks in your home. A good online resource for home fire safety tips is: https://www.ready.gov/home-fires

and the second leading cause of fire deaths. The second leading cause of home fires and injuries is heating equipment which is the major cause of fire deaths in one- or two-family homes.

✳ Be careful with wood-burning stoves. Only burn dry, resin-free wood (hardwoods such as oak, maple, ash, and hickory are preferable to softwoods such as pine), otherwise excessive soot will deposit in the chimney. This residue may ignite and cause a chimney fire.

Quick and easy PRECAUTIONS

Having working smoke detectors on every floor of your home will increase your chance of surviving a

ONLY BURN DRY, RESIN-FREE WOOD, SUCH AS OAK, MAPLE, ASH, AND HICKORY.

home fire. Smoke alarms emit a loud noise if they detect smoke and need to be inspected and tested regularly.

✳ Keep a fire blanket in the kitchen in case you need to extinguish flames quickly. Place it somewhere in sight, or within easy reach, so you always know where it is.

✳ You should keep a fire extinguisher on every floor in your home. Learn how to use it yourself and show each family member how to use it. It is important to have fire extinguishers inspected regularly.

✳ Switch off electrical devices such as TVs, kitchen appliances and electric blankets whenever not in use. Cooktops, ovens, toasters and coffeemakers need to be protected against overheating.

✳ If you lock the front door at night, leave the key inside the lock, if it has one, for a fast exit.

✳ Keep keys handy for any windows and sliding doors that you lock overnight near any potential escape routes, in case you need to access them quickly as part of a home escape plan.

Easy fix Store important documents outside the home, for example in a bank safe-deposit box. Some documents are difficult to have reissued.

Insider's hack Take photos of your interiors, including furniture and home entertainment devices (make sure you photograph the serial numbers). This will allow any issues with your insurance claim to be settled quickly. Photograph bookshelves in sections, ensuring that the book spines are legible. Store these photos outside the home, or in the cloud. Not only will you have clear evidence of what you owned to present to your insurance in the event of a fire, it will also make it easier for you to keep track of your possessions.

FIRE! What to do now

Call 911 immediately. Tell emergency services the nature of the emergency, your name, address (including the floor if in an apartment), the scope of

TAKE CARE

Never try to extinguish burning fats and oils with water, as the water would vaporize immediately, causing the flame to flash in a jet of burning fat. Instead, cover the burning pot or pan with a large lid, or use a fire blanket.

the fire, and provide any information on potentially injured or missing people. Direct the fire department, as you know your home best. Keep in mind the following rules:

✳ If an electrical appliance is burning, disconnect the power supply first before trying to extinguish the fire; otherwise there is a risk of electric shock.

✳ Clear the house as quickly as possible – notify everybody in your house as well as your neighbors.

✳ Do not waste time – no getting dressed, trying to pack anything or investigating how the fire started!

✳ If possible, close the door of the burning room to slow down the spread of the fire and smoke.

✳ Escape toward the lower floors in multi-story buildings, by using the fire escape. Don't take an elevator, as you could become trapped inside.

Insider's hack Decide on a fire escape plan with your household, including how to exit each room safely and where your meeting point will be.

KEEP A FIRE BLANKET IN THE KITCHEN IN CASE YOU NEED TO EXTINGUISH FLAMES.

Avoid a nasty surprise at CHRISTMAS

Christmas is a time when outdoor decorating is ever-present. It's easy to get carried away, making the house look "just right" and enjoying a little too much "Christmas cheer" on the day … but you may end up with a fire on your hands. Christmas trees and lights are both potential fire hazards, but if you follow some simple guidelines, you won't put yourself and your family at risk.

✳ Fresh pine Christmas trees impart a wonderful aroma to the living room, but remember that this smell comes partly from the resinous pinewood, which is also highly flammable. Avoid placing any open flames such as candles too close to the tree, including where the pine needles may fall.

IT'S EASY TO GET CARRIED AWAY, MAKING THE HOUSE LOOK "JUST RIGHT" AT CHRISTMAS-TIME.

TAKE CARE

In the event of a fire, call your pets, such as dogs and cats, to you as you leave the building but do not search for them; never go back inside for them.

✳ Artificial trees are also flammable as they can melt when sufficiently heated. Make sure yours has been labelled or certified by the manufacturer as being fire retardant.

✳ Check whether your Christmas tree is firmly supported and located sufficiently far away from walls and flammable objects. Keep your tree well away from high traffic areas, particularly if you have pets or small children.

✳ Never leave candles burning unattended, not even for "just a moment" It's difficult to imagine, but an entire room can be ablaze within a matter of minutes (see also page 114, "Handling candles with care").

✳ Christmas lights wrapped around the tree or in your windows look gorgeous but are the biggest cause of Christmas fires. Never use lights that have fraying cords or broken bulbs, and don't try to jazz up lights by covering the bulbs yourself.

✳ Avoid overloading your outlets with too many plugs, or stringing more than three sets of lights together. It's easy to go overboard, especially if there's a friendly competition on the street for who has the best decorations.

✳ Make sure you switch off any decorative lights before you go to bed at night.

✳ Keep indoor lights for indoor use, and outdoor lights for outdoor use. This includes any extension cords. Indoor lights and extension cords aren't designed to be out in the elements and could short.

Save money Cheap strings of Christmas lights are a false economy, as they probably haven't passed the required safety standards. Spend a little more now on safety-rated lights, and you won't need to spend a whole lot more on cleaning up after a fire.

Protect against storms and
THUNDERSTORMS

As a homeowner, you need to take precautions so that your home does not cause injury or damage, and of course you don't want your home to become damaged in severe weather. There are several effective measures you can take:

✳ Check for damaged roof shingles and inspect your attic and any skylights for signs of water damage. Regularly check that your window and door seals are in good condition.

✳ Clean your gutters once every year or have them cleaned. Check downspouts. Remove any branches or twigs that extend over the roof, as falling leaves could block the gutter.

✳ Check regularly (at least once a year) whether all external parts of the house such as shingles, flashings, siding, gutters and deck or balcony railings are soundly attached.

✳ Secure any unattached objects on your deck, balcony or patio (such as market umbrellas) and retract awnings if high winds are forecast.

✳ Disconnect sensitive electronic devices from the electricity if there is a thunderstorm looming.

✳ If you live in a tornado-prone area, check that your home is tornado-rated and follow the safety

DISCONNECT SENSITIVE ELECTRONICS FROM THE ELECTRICITY IF THERE IS A THUNDERSTORM LOOMING.

precautions recommended by your local authority or the national weather bureau.

✳ In the event of a tornado, check the radio, internet or television for information. Follow any directions given regarding safety procedures and evacuations. Carry a portable radio and flashlight with you in case of electrical failure.

Prevent LIGHTNING damage

If you live in an exposed area, a lightning rod may be something to consider, despite the cost. Just make sure that it's "grounded" or it could cause more damage.

✳ Surge protectors are another way to prevent lightning damage. These ensure that your electronic devices are protected against power surges if lightning strikes the power supply.

Insider's hack Keep some flashlights on hand as soon as you see the first signs of a thunderstorm in case the power fails.

Protect your property

Hardly any other event leaves you feeling such a loss of safety and security in your home as a break-in. Apart from the material loss, many people find it difficult to come to terms with the fact that a stranger has invaded their private space.

Thieves often STRIKE BY DAY

Unfortunately break-ins are not uncommon: in 2017, there were more than 1.4 million burglaries in the United States, costing victims an estimated $3.4 billion in loss. Although this number is decreasing, most (67 percent) break-ins occur in and around the home. Cash is the most commonly stolen item, followed by jewelry and electronic goods.

※ Contrary to public opinion, not all break-ins take place at night: more than a third of them occur in broad daylight, especially in cities, where people don't know their neighbors well and unusual activity is often unnoticed. Many thieves are also so skilled – and homes so poorly secured – that burglaries happen very quietly within a matter of seconds.

※ Break-ins may even happen when someone is home, as thieves can sneak through unlocked doors and windows. This is especially the case during the warmer months when you might spend time in the backyard with windows open to catch the breeze. Whether you're home or not, always secure your doors and windows.

※ Using social media platforms like Facebook and Twitter can represent a security risk. Incarcerated burglars who were surveyed admitted to using status updates such as "Bermuda, here we come!" as an impetus for targeting a property. And Google Street view is a useful way to scope out potential burglary sites.

Ask the police for expert advice on how to secure your home.

※ Ask the police for expert advice on how to secure your home. There may be information events on home security, where you can ask specialists about how best to address your personal circumstances.

YOUR JEWELRY IS A PRIME TARGET FOR THIEVES.

Some police groups also use social media to provide updates – check online for what's on in your area. ✳ Suppliers of security technology can provide expert advice, and many companies specialize in monitoring private homes. But there are plenty of measures you can take yourself to make break-in attempts more difficult or prevent them altogether.

NEVER LET STRANGERS come in

Con artists, who attempt to gain access to your home while you are there, practice a sophisticated form of break-in. Most of the time they will use a pretense to get you to let them inside. Be wary of strangers claiming that they need to read your water or electric meter. A similar pretext is a claim along the lines of: "Your phone line seems to be faulty. Can we just come in to check?"

CON ARTISTS PRACTICE A SOPHISTICATED FORM OF BREAK-IN.

✳ Thieves have a vast repertoire of tricks, and unfortunately some of them even use children to ring your doorbell. Always be cautious with strangers, especially when there are two people at the door. One of them can be going through your belongings while the other distracts you.

CHANGE THE LOCKS

There are various reasons why you would want to change the lock on your door: perhaps you've let somebody use your keys but you want to ensure they cannot use them anymore. You don't need a locksmith as this task is easily accomplished. All you need is a screwdriver that fits the screw underneath the catch.

1 Locks are screwed inside the door rebate. To replace the lock cylinder, insert the key in the lock and loosen the screw underneath the catch.

2 Turn the key a little to the side, and the cylinder should pull out easily from the lock.

3 Insert the new cylinder into the lock and fasten it with the screw supplied. Use the same method to install a tamper-proof cylinder.

✳ Install a peephole at eye level in your front door so you can see who is standing outside. Also install sensor lights at the front and rear of your property to alert you to people approaching your home.

✳ Intercom systems let you distinguish unwanted visitors from friends and relatives. Choose a system with a camera, if you can, to be extra safe and prevent unpleasant surprises.

Save money Safety catches or chains on your front door provide effective protection. They prevent doors from opening fully, but just wide enough for you to check ID cards or accept mail or papers.

TAKE CARE
Never leave ladders, or other objects that can be climbed upon, lying in your yard. These include trash cans, strong trellises and outdoor furniture.

WINDOWS, SLIDING DOORS AND BACK DOORS MUST BE LOCKABLE.

Keep things safe IN YOUR ABSENCE

Most thieves enter apartments through the front door; while in single family homes, townhomes and semi-detached houses, they usually gain access through a back door or window that is hidden from neighbors or the street.

✳ Dead bolts make a break-in more difficult, and most thieves won't bother with a home that will take too long to break into. Opportunist thieves don't want to waste time, as their risk of discovery increases with every minute – most only give themselves about five minutes. Professional thieves are even quicker – for them, five minutes is a long time.

✳ Valuable objects (jewelry, money and portable electronic devices such as laptop computers) are best stored inside a safe embedded in a brick wall, or in a steel cabinet with a safety lock.

✳ Windows, sliding doors and back doors must be secure and lockable; replace them if necessary. Ensure window frames and doorframes are protected against being drilled or jacked open.

✳ Reinforced glass, which you can retrofit with an adhesive film, is a good option for doors and poorly visible access points.

✳ Never leave windows open or half-open, even if you are only away for a little while, and always lock your outside doors.

✳ Garden sheds should be firmly fixed to the ground to prevent lifting up. Also keep tools locked away in the shed, and never leave ladders lying around.

Easy fix Always turn the keys to outside doors twice to deadbolt them. That is much easier than having to argue with an insurance company that refuses to pay because your door wasn't deadbolted.

Insider's hack Simply leaving a couple of pairs of shoes by the front door and the radio on can be effective deterrents for opportunists.

Vacation PRECAUTIONS

Thieves seek out homes that are obviously vacant. A simple precaution is therefore to try to hide the fact that you are away.

✳ Don't announce your vacation plans and schedules publicly, especially not on online social networks.

✳ Ask a neighbor to put out and bring in your trash cans. Let a neighbor or friend park a car in your driveway to make it look like someone is home.

✳ Ask neighbors to take in your mail every day. Where this is not possible, request that your mail be held at the post office or forwarded. Suspend any newspaper deliveries so they're not left out side or in the mailbox all day. Avoid any online shopping that will deliver while you are away.

✳ Tell a trusted neighbor or friend who lives close by that you'll be away and ask them to keep an eye on the house. Tell them if you're expecting anyone to be in your home so they know to call the police if there is any suspicious activity.

Make sure your morning paper is not left outside all day.

CHECK YOUR FRONT DOOR

1 Most thieves gain entry through the front door, which is why it needs to be particularly strong. If the door sounds hollow when you knock against it, replace it with a burglar-resistant door. If you rent, you will obviously need your landlord's approval, but perhaps they will assume some or all of the cost.

2 Front doors should have a solid core and be installed in a sturdy frame that is firmly anchored into the wall, which will withstand even heavy kicking or beating.

3 Security reinforcement guard plates and lock cylinders must be protected against being drilled open, and you need to ensure the strike plate is firmly anchored in the wall. The lock cylinder should have at least six pins.

4 A door or jamb reinforcement plate prevents potential thieves from kicking in the door.

ENSURE THAT A MAILBOX STUFFED FULL OF FLYERS DOES NOT BROADCAST YOUR ABSENCE.

SECURE INWARD-OPENING WINDOWS BY SIMPLY PLACING POTTED PLANTS ON THE WINDOWSILLS.

＊ Install motion-activated floodlights that will stay on at night can also be a deterrent to thieves. As soon as they walk onto your property at night, they will be flooded in light and choose to run away.

＊ Install timers to switch lights on and off, turn a radio on and off, and move electric blinds up and down while you are away. There are special devices that mimic the flickering of TV sets, and smart light bulbs that can be controlled by a smartphone app.

＊ Alternatively, ask a friend or neighbor to do this for you, perhaps while they also water your plants and generally keep an eye on things. If possible, ask them to come at irregular times – there is always a chance that thieves may be observing your home for an opportunity.

TAKE CARE

Don't lower all your blinds. They provide little protection against break-ins, and are usually a certain sign that nobody is home!

＊ Mow the lawn just before you leave – a neglected yard can indicate that there is nobody home.

Easy fix Secure your inward-opening windows by simply placing potted plants on the windowsills. Thieves want to avoid the noise of falling pots.

Insider's hack Rather than using voice mail, divert calls to your cell phone. This lets you accept any calls, regardless of where you are.

BURGLAR ALARMS,
expensive but useful

Electronic alarm systems offer additional protection against break-ins, but come at a price. These systems consist of a central control unit and various sensors installed around the home. When armed, the unit triggers an alarm (such as a siren), activates cameras and transmits the alarm.

＊ Burglar alarms require sensors to be installed all over the home. These can include magnetic sensors on doors and windows, vibration detectors, glass breakage detectors, light barriers and movement detectors. The alarm is usually switched on and off via a keypad and PIN. Always post a sign in your yard that you have an alarm system, this alone will deter some thieves.

＊ These alarm systems cannot replace mechanical security measures, however, as alarms by nature only sound once a thief has successfully broken into the home or is at least about to. You will also need to clarify where any alarm should be transmitted to and in what form. If you have alarms transmitted to a private security service, they will usually attempt to contact you or send the police if you are not reachable. One note, there are often charges for the police to come to your home for a false alarm.

＊ As private security companies are a relatively expensive option, most people who install alarm systems trust that the noise and lights (a siren and/or blue blinking light on the home) will frighten thieves away and alert neighbors. Keep in mind, though, that this will only work if you avoid false alarms. These can easily happen when household members forget to switch off the alarm as they get back home.

✳ Installing sophisticated cameras is another good solution. These transmit images or videos online to your current location and can even send you an email with images if any irregular movement is detected. However, again these cameras will only trigger an alarm if somebody has already managed to enter your home. You will then have to call your 911 immediately.

Insider's hack If you decide on an alarm system, always have it professionally installed and steer clear of cheap products. Ideally, opt for a system that features additional sensors for fire, water, gas, excessive power consumption (such as when a cooktop is left on) or the failure of your refrigerator or freezer.

ALWAYS HAVE ALARM SYSTEMS PROFESSIONALLY INSTALLED.

JUST IN CASE

CHECK YOUR INSURANCE COVERAGE	Break-ins are traumatic enough already, but the problems can become enormous if you do not have adequate insurance coverage. Check your policy!
SECURE DATA	Keep copies of important documents and store invoices and appraisals of valuable jewelry, works of art and carpets securely. Back up important data, including photos of your home interiors, to DVD or external hard drive.
LABEL YOUR PROPERTY	Write down ID numbers or features that will allow you to identify your property, or attach such labels yourself, for example, using UV markers that can only be read in ultraviolet light. These are ideal for valuable carpets.
TAKE PRECAUTIONS	All of these measures support the work of police after a break-in and will improve your chances of getting your property back. They will also make any dealings with your insurance company a lot easier.
SMARTPHONE APP	Look for a smartphone app that connects you to emergency services staff and may provides your GPS coordinates when you use it.

Home Appliances

Handy household helpers

Our kitchens are equipped with a range of appliances that help make those domestic tasks easier. For the most part, they work tirelessly and unobtrusively, but to get the best results and longest life out of your appliances, it pays to look after them properly and use them only as they were intended.

SMALL APPLIANCES that can do (almost) anything

Food processors and stand mixers come with attachments and accessories that let you stir, grate, mix, shred, grind, puree and knead. Some models even have attachments for juicing citrus fruit or for making pasta. They often have a powerful electric motor to get the job done quickly and easily.

STAND MIXERS MAKE BEATING, MIXING AND WHIPPING A BREEZE.

✳ Many food processors, especially older models, are big and heavy so they tend to be left on the kitchen counter. Although bulky, they are relatively sturdy and stable. In recent years, smaller models have come on the market; assess how sturdy they are carefully before you buy one. It is also worth double-checking that all the machine's attachments and accessories are dishwasher-safe.

✳ Stand mixers make beating, mixing or whipping ingredients a breeze. Bowl size and basic attachments, such as whisk, "S" hook and paddle, vary from model to model, so determine your needs before purchasing. A variety of add-on attachments for making pasta, sausage or spiralizing may also be available but be sure the mixer you purchase offers an attachment port for these additions.

✳ An immersion blender, also called hand blender, makes it easy to blend soups, sauces, smoothies and pestos with the push of a button. This hand-held tool has a removable blending shaft for easy clean up.

TAKE CARE

Don't let a food processor work for too long with a heavy load. Taking a break when running for long periods will prevent the motor from overheating and ultimately extend the life of your machine.

Insider's hack Most food processors don't beat egg whites very well. A better technique is to use a standing mixer with its whisk attachments.

End dish drudgery with a DISHWASHER

Any household with more than one person will be well served by a dishwasher, and its capacity to wash big loads of dirty dishes day after day. A dishwasher does the job from start to finish: spraying the dishes with a constant stream of water at the pre-selected temperature, releasing detergent at the appropriate moment, rinsing with clean water and, finally, drying the dishes with a heating element.

✳ Modern dishwashers are more economical than doing the dishes by hand, especially those that let you select different programs according to washing intensity and load size.

✳ Only use detergents specifically intended for dishwashers. Never use the dishwashing liquid you use for handwashing, as it will foam up and spill out through the dishwasher's seals.

✳ Only place dishwasher-safe items in the machine. Take care with hand-painted or decoratively glazed china. If in doubt, it's safer to wash by hand.

✳ Rinse off food scraps before putting things in the dishwasher – do this right after use. Dishes with dried-on or cooked-on food should be pre-soaked in hot water and a little dishwashing liquid.

✳ Use a reputable brand of detergent, either an all-in-one tablet or a separate detergent and rinse aid. If your dishwasher has a reservoir for a water-softening agent, top it off with the recommended water-softening salt as needed. This is especially important in hard-water areas.

✳ Clean the filter and spray arms regularly. On newer dishwashers, these components are easy to remove and put back again.

STACK YOUR DISHWASHER CORRECTLY

Make sure the items won't prevent the spray arms from moving freely or obstruct tubes, sprayers or the soap dispenser, and that breakables don't risk touching if they vibrate during the cycle.

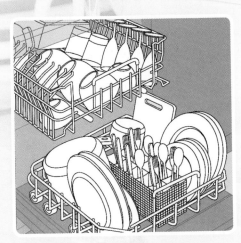

For maximum efficiency it pays to run your dishwasher fully and properly loaded.

Plates Insert in slots in the lower section, facing toward the center.

Cups, glasses and bowls Place in the top section. Stack bowls on an incline. Put glasses upside down between, not over, prongs.

Plastic items Place on top rack away from the heating element in the lower section that can cause melting.

Pots and pans Place upside down in the lower section.

Cutlery Place fork and spoon handles downwards into utensil baskets, and knive handles upward. Mix up the cutlery items so they don't "nest" into one another. Lay larger utensils horizontally across the top section.

Cutting boards and baking trays Place on the outermost edges of the bottom section.

✳ Don't leave dirty dishes in the machine for too long – it will only take a day or two to start to smell bad. If it ever gets to this point, run the machine on a hot water setting (at least 140°F) to kill off bacteria.

✳ If your dishes are not clean: check that water is flowing into the machine and heating up properly; make sure you are using enough detergent; and check that the dishes were stacked correctly.

✳ When buying a dishwasher, look for one that has an automatic shut-off valve to prevent flooding in the event of a burst inlet hose. These valves can also be retrofitted to your existing connection.

TAKE CARE

If you want to wash a stainless steel grease filter in the dishwasher, don't put it in with other dirty dishes as this can lead to food scraps getting caught in the filter.

Save time If your dishwasher is still full of water at the end of its cycle, don't call a repair service immediately. Check the filter at the bottom of the machine first. It might be blocked, preventing the machine from draining.

Easy fix If you are not using your dishwasher for a period, such as while away on vacation, sprinkle a few tablespoons of baking soda in the bottom to absorb bad smells. It will simply rinse away the first time you use your machine again.

Save money As an alternative to rinse aid, try using vinegar or a solution of 1 teaspoon of lemon juice in ½ cup of hot water.

RANGE HOODS control cooking fumes

To keep cooking smells from spreading through the kitchen and the rest of the house, a range hood is the modern equivalent of a chimney, sucking up fumes and venting them outside or trapping them in an active charcoal filter. All range hoods pass the air they take in through a grease filter to help prevent greasy fumes from dirtying our kitchens.

✳ Clean your range hood's grease filter once every couple of weeks, especially if you often cook with fat or oil. A filter clogged with grease is a fire hazard and will not work effectively.

✳ You should clean or replace active charcoal filters at the recommended intervals.

✳ Always turn your range hood on when cooking to prevent steam from condensing and pooling inside.

✳ If your range hood vents to the outside, open a window before turning it on to allow fresh air to

ALWAYS TURN ON YOUR RANGE HOOD WHEN COOKING TO PREVENT STEAM FROM CONDENSING AND POOLING INSIDE.

enter the room. This is especially important if you have a fireplace in your home, as the range hood can suck exhaust gases and even smoke into your home.

Insider's hack According to consumer surveys, it's worth paying a little bit more for a range hood. The more expensive models look better, do a more thorough job and are quieter to run.

MICROWAVE OVENS
for food in a flash

Gone are the days when people believed microwave ovens made their food radioactive. Many models now include grill and convection functions, and can completely replace a conventional oven in a small kitchen. When used correctly, a microwave will prove its worth as a practical, value-for-money kitchen appliance.

MICROWAVE OVENS COOK FOOD QUICKLY AND USUALLY REMAIN FAIRLY CLEAN INSIDE.

~~~~~~~~~~~~~~~~~~~~~~~~~~~~~~~~

To achieve even cooking results, stir food halfway through the cooking time.

~~~~~~~~~~~~~~~~~~~~~~~~~~~~~~~~

✳ A microwave's inner workings are complex. A microwave generates high-energy, high-frequency electromagnetic waves, which are beamed through an antenna into the interior of the oven. The waves cause the water molecules in our food to vibrate, producing heat. In effect, heat is generated from inside the food rather than being applied from outside as with conventional cooking. Microwaves don't have any heating effect on objects that don't contain water, such as plates and bowls. These only get hot as a result of contact with the food they contain, but that can be enough to make them very hot and care should be taken when removing any dish from the microwave.

✳ Microwaves cook food quickly and they usually remain fairly clean inside, unless you use the grill function. The downside of microwave energy is that it cooks food without browning it. For a perfect pizza or roast, you'll need to use your microwave's grill function if your model has one.

✳ To achieve even cooking results, stir food halfway through the cooking time. If your microwave has a rotating turntable, stirring may not be necessary.

✳ Food should always be fully cooked in the microwave because any bacteria present will not be destroyed if it is not heated to the recommended temperature. If you microwave a food prior to finishing it off in the oven or grill (usually to brown the food), always transfer it immediately to the other heat source. Use a cooking thermometer to assure foods have reached the proper temperature.

✳ Gold-rimmed dishware should not be placed in the microwave as the gold can melt and evaporate. The gold rims on your dishes can also cause sparks to fly inside the microwave.

TAKE CARE

Never put a glass jar with the lid screwed on in a microwave oven. The rapid heating will produce excessive steam pressure inside the jar and can cause it to explode.

Save time Microwaves are good for defrosting frozen food in a fraction of the time it normally takes. It's essential to use a low power setting because ice molecules don't absorb microwave energy well and thawed areas can therefore easily overheat.

Insider's hack Instead of using a cleaning spray, add vinegar, a few slices of lemon or dishwashing liquid to a bowl of water and microwave the mixture for 5–10 minutes. Leave for a few minutes more to allow the steam to work, then wipe out the inside of the microwave with a cloth.

Save money About half of a microwave oven's power consumption gets lost in the process of producing microwave energy, which means that your regular stove is a more economical option for heating large volumes of liquid. If you just want to boil water, an electric kettle is the most efficient way to do it.

A WALL OVEN INSTALLED AT A CONVENIENT HEIGHT WILL SAVE YOU FROM BENDING DOWN.

THE OVEN, heart of the kitchen

A typical all-in-one range has the oven located underneath the cooktop. This configuration is found in many kitchens but one drawback is that you can only cook at one temperature at one time. But some manufacturers have come up with duel-door ovens that split the oven space allowing you to cook at two different temperatures at the same time. A second drawback is that the oven area in these ranges is quite low, and you practically have to squat to put things in or take them out of the oven.

✳ Another way to do your baking is to have a wall oven installed at a height that provides easy access from a standing position. The cooktop is then installed as a separate unit in the kitchen counter.

✳ Gas ovens are a favorite to some, but only available to about half the homes in North America. Electric ovens let you choose heat types, such as convection or fan-forced where a fan circulates heat around the oven, or radiant heating where elements at the top and bottom heat the oven. If you often have several baking trays in the oven at once, choose convection heating.

✳ Those baked-on splatters and dribbles in your oven don't come off easily. Making ovens easier to clean is a challenge that manufacturers have been working on for many years. Improvements in enamel coatings have helped somewhat and there are a few gentle oven-cleaning methods worth trying (see page 175, "How to clean the oven"). The best method is the self-cleaning feature in your oven. This technology is time-consuming taking up to 4 hours but effective: the oven heats up to an extremely high temperature (900°F), turning greasy build-up into ash that can then be wiped away easily. The oven door remains locked until the oven cools down.

Save money Self-cleaning uses a lot of power to achieve the extremely high temperatures necessary for the process. If you wipe your oven out as best you can right after using it, you won't need to use this function as often.

Many options for COOKTOPS

If you're installing a new kitchen, you'll find plenty of options when it comes to cooktops. The first decision is whether to go gas or electric. If you opt for electric, you then have to decide on traditional coil burners or step up to a glass-ceramic cooktop that works with infrared radiation. Higher again in price, induction stoves use electromagnetic radiation to heat the bottom of compatible cookware while the cooktop itself remains cool – this safety aspect can be appealing for older people or families with young children. Infrared cooktops with pot sensors are also quite safe – the sensors turn the burner off when cookware is removed.

On an induction stove, only the pans get hot; the cooktop itself remains cool.

✳ The advantage of a gas cooktop is that you have instantaneous control over the heat source, whereas electric cooktops are slow to react and retain heat after they are turned down or off. Professional cooks prefer gas, but working with an open flame at home is not for everyone.

✳ Use an appropriate-sized burner for your pot. If the pot is too small for the burner, you will lose a lot of heat at the sides. Some cooktops have sensors that recognize the size of the pot and adjust accordingly.

✳ Take apart and clean gas burners regularly. Take care that the jets don't get blocked with cleaning product. An uneven, yellow-colored flame (rather than a bright blue flame) is a sign of a blocked jet.

✳ At all costs, avoid dropping sugary food or anything plastic onto a hot ceramic cooktop – an accident that can happen easily when making jams or preserves. Sugar or plastic will burn onto the surface and is almost impossible to remove without damaging the glass. Induction cooktops don't have this problem because they don't get hot.

✳ Never use abrasive cleaning products on a ceramic cooktop. If a pot boils over and leaves a cooked-on mess, cover the area with water for a few minutes to soften it up. A special glass scraper, available from appliance stores, can also be useful.

USE AN APPROPRIATE-SIZED BURNER FOR THE SIZE OF YOUR POT; OTHERWISE YOU WILL WASTE A LOT OF HEAT.

TAKE CARE

Don't keep using a ceramic cooktop with cracked glass. Liquid can seep through the crack, which creates a safety hazard.

✳ Dry coil burners thoroughly after cleaning to prevent them from rusting.

Insider's hack If you are heating water or soup on the stove, put a lid on the pot. Without a lid, it will take much longer to heat up and you will use more energy as the escaping steam takes a significant amount of heat with it. Turn the stove off at the right moment, too, to make the most of the residual heat instead of just letting it escape into the kitchen.

Save money If you've just bought an induction stove, don't assume you need to buy new pots and pans. Use a magnet to test the cookware you already have. If it sticks to the base, it will work fine.

FRIDGE and freezer

Being able to conserve food through refrigeration is pretty much taken for granted today (see page 154, "Use your refrigerator effectively"). The basic technology that makes a fridge work is relatively simple. First, a chemical refrigerant is compressed. As it compresses, the refrigerant briefly heats up but this heat is quickly dissipated through the condenser coils at the back of the fridge. The compressed refrigerant then flows through pipework in the walls of the fridge into the interior, where it is able to expand again. As it expands it draws in heat from its surroundings, thereby cooling the space inside the fridge. Finally, the refrigerant flows back out to the compressor, completing a cycle that continuously transfers heat from the inside of the refrigerator to the air outside.

✳ Leave space between your fridge and the wall to enable the condenser coils at the back to dissipate heat effectively. If your fridge is to be built in to your kitchen cabinetry, ensure there are ventilation holes in the toe kick panel.

✳ Don't leave the fridge door open for too long, as moisture in the air contributes to the build-up of ice inside the cabinet.

✳ Clean the inside of your refrigerator regularly with vinegar and water, or wipe it down with a solution of baking soda and water.

✳ If you don't have a frost-free freezer, prevent rapid ice buildup in your freezer by wiping down the inner freezer walls after you defrost with cooking oil or glycerine. When you defrost next time, the ice will come away form the walls easily.

✳ Thaw frozen food in the refrigerator. As it thaws it will act like an ice pack in the fridge, taking some of the load off the compressor and saving electricity.

DON'T LEAVE THE FRIDGE DOOR OPEN FOR TOO LONG, AS ICE WILL BUILD UP INSIDE THE CABINET.

* When all its contents are properly frozen, a fully loaded freezer uses about the same amount of energy as it would when half-empty. There is no good reason to follow the advice sometimes given to fill your freezer with half-filled bottles of water just for the sake of filling it to capacity.

* If you find water pooling in the bottom of your fridge or even leaking out onto the floor, the most likely cause is a blocked drainage hole. Normally, excess water drains out of the fridge and is collected in a small container near the condenser coils where it evaporates away. Poke a chopstick or knitting needle into the hole to clear it out.

Save time Drippy bottles and containers with leaks can create a big mess on your refrigerator shelves. Create coasters from plastic lids to place under food containers to stop any potential leaks. If they get dirty, throw the lids in the dishwasher, while your fridge shelves stay free of a sticky mess.

Save money Choosing the coolest possible place for your fridge can save you a lot of electricity. If you can avoid it, don't put your fridge next to the oven, even if it is well insulated.

ONCE A LUXURY, SPECIALTY COFFEE IS NOW COMMONPLACE.

COFFEEMAKERS and espresso machines

Alongside percolators, drip filters, pod coffee machines, French presses and stovetop espresso makers, modern coffee machines make it easy to prepare specialty coffee at home. Filter coffee machines (or drip machines) use either pre-ground coffee or freshly grind the beans for each cup. Filter coffee tends to be quite high in caffeine and melanoidins, substances formed during roasting that can irritate people with sensitive stomachs. If this affects you, you'll be better off switching to espresso.

* In an espresso machine, hot water is pressurized and forced through finely ground coffee. As it passes through, the water picks up the flavor and caffeine but not melanoidins, which means espresso coffee is easier on the stomach and often tastes better. Models range in how much work you need to do to prepare your cup, from café-style machines where you measure the amount of coffee and froth the

---

Expert advice

An energy-saving fridge light

Modern refrigerators are already fitted with LED lighting but you can install an energy-saving bulb in an older fridge, too. Clear out the shelf around the light and carefully remove the bulb cover (use a cloth if it's hot). Look for an LED bulb of the appropriate size in an appliance or hardware store – take the old bulb with you to check the wattage and size. Fit the new bulb carefully in place and replace the cover.

milk yourself, to fully automatic machines that use pre-measured capsules of ground coffee, which are removed and discarded after each cup. The higher the water pressure, the better the coffee. A good indicator of a well-made espresso is the crema, the light colored foam that forms on top.

✳ Rinse your drip coffee pot out with fresh water at the end of the day to prevent brown-colored stains that will ruin the flavor.

✳ If your machine has a water tank, empty it at the end of each day and fill it up with fresh water in the morning. Empty and clean the drip tray periodically as leftover coffee is an excellent nutrient solution for mold to grow in.

✳ Have your espresso machine serviced at the manufacturer's recommended service intervals to ensure it continues to produce high steam pressure.

Insider's hack   Coffee makers with pods produce a lot of waste in the form of used pods. Look for ones that can be recycled to ensure the plastic used to make them doesn't go to waste.

Save money   Coffee machine manufacturers usually recommend expensive products for descaling their machines. A cheaper option is to dissolve a tablespoon of citric acid or baking soda and a squirt of dishwashing liquid in hot water. Run the solution through the machine twice, then rinse by running the same amount of clean water through twice.

VACUUM CLEANERS,
a household essential

At the heart of a vacuum cleaner is an electric fan that creates negative pressure to suck in air. The air flows in through the nozzle, along the hose and into a bag, taking dust and dirt particles with it, which get trapped in the bag. The air continues through a filter and out the back of the machine. As the bag fills up, the strength of the suction declines and eventually the bag needs to be emptied or replaced. Bagless vacuum cleaners use centrifugal force (cyclonic separation) to collect the dirt in a container that needs to be emptied from time to time. These

ROBOTIC VACUUM CLEANERS MOVE AUTONOMOUSLY AROUND THE ROOM SUCKING UP DIRT.

Expert advice

Take care of small appliances

Small appliances are worth looking after properly even if the cost of replacing them won't necessarily burn a hole in your pocket. Empty the crumbs out of your toaster regularly to prevent the risk of fire. Empty your kettle completely after each use to limit the build-up of scale. A toaster oven is a very handy appliance for making more than just toast. Often food drippings make their way onto the rack, tray or crumb tray. Regularly remove them and wash in dishwashing soap. You should only ever give any appliance a wipe-down with a damp cloth; never immerse it in water.

machines maintain full suction at all times and save you the cost of replacement bags. They are, however, significantly noisier than regular vacuum cleaners with bags.

✳ The next decision to be made when purchasing a vacuum is whether to go with a canister or upright. Upright vacuums have traditionally been a favorite and are a top contender for homes with wall-to-wall carpeting. However, versatile canisters may be more useful in homes with tile and wood floors. Canisters have many attachments include a bare-floor brush to prevent damaging the carpet brush. They are also a good choice for homes with several flights of stairs for its ability to easily get between the railing.

✳ Rechargeable handheld vacuum cleaners are quick and easy to use, especially for tasks such as vacuuming out the car. Make sure you get one with enough suction to pick up crumbs and grains of sand with ease.

✳ At the upper end of the price range, cordless robotic vacuum cleaners are designed to move autonomously around the room sucking up dirt. Sensors and on-board microprocessors guide the machine around the room, preventing it from running into walls or falling down stairs, and returning it to its charging station when the job is done. On some models, the vacuum will transfer the dust it has collected to the charging station.

✳ Check your vacuum cleaner's powerhead and hose for obstructions periodically or any time you notice a decline in suction. A blocked filter can also cause poor suction. Some machines have filters that can be washed; otherwise, they'll need to be replaced.

Insider's hack Always extend your vacuum cleaner's power cord fully to prevent overheating. This is especially important for machines with high-powered motors.

Save money Instead of buying expensive scented tablets for your vacuum, simply put a few drops of perfume onto a folded-up square of toilet paper and place it in the vacuum cleaner bag.

TAKE CARE
Never suck up liquids with a regular vacuum cleaner. Instead, use a wet/dry vacuum specifically designed for the job. Or just mop up the spill first.

Make laundry day easier

The kitchen is not the only place where home appliances make our lives easier. They are also a big help when it comes to cleaning and caring for our clothing and household fabrics.

WASHING DAY is no longer hard work

Household chores can be wearisome. In days gone by, women with families (or the domestic servants of those lucky few) spent many hours a day doing the laundry. The washing machine marked a new era in managing the day-to-day demands of the household. Modern washing machines have a rotating drum driven by an electric motor, and include valves to control the intake of cold water, a heating element and a discharge pump to remove the dirty water. An electronic control system in the machine enables it to carry out a range of different wash programs.

✳ A huge amount of research and testing has gone into the various ingredients of laundry detergents. In addition to surfactants that keep the dirt suspended in the wash water, detergents contain water softeners to prevent scale deposits, anti-sudsing agents to prevent excessive foaming during washing, enzymes to break down stains and a fragrance. Detergents for whites often contain optical brighteners, too. These substances absorb invisible ultraviolet light and re-emit it as visible blue light, which combines with any residual yellowing in the fabric to look white. The overall effect is that whites appear "whiter than white," even though the fabric may not be entirely free of dirt and germs.

✳ Take care when washing heavily soiled items such as work clothes or cleaning cloths. Make sure there are

THE WASHING MACHINE MARKED A NEW ERA IN MANAGING THE DEMANDS OF THE HOUSEHOLD.

HIGH-EFFICIENCY WASHERS USE 25 PERCENT LESS ENERGY AND 40 PERCENT LESS WATER THAN TRADITIONAL ONES.

no hard objects lurking in your laundry, such as forgotten tools or shards of metal, as these will destroy your machine's rubber seals.

⁕ Don't overfill the machine. An overloaded washer will give poor results. At the other extreme, running the machine to wash a single shirt is a waste of energy.

⁕ Don't blame the little green sock monster for a missing sock. If it's not trapped inside a duvet cover, it might have found its way through the gap between the door seal and the drum and been pumped away with the wash water. Use a washing bag to prevent this from happening.

Insider's hack Always wash socks and knee-high stockings in pairs as they may change color when washed. Washing them together ensures they will be affected equally and will still match.

PROTECT the environment and save

High-efficiency washing machines are quite popular because they allow you to get your laundry beautifully clean in an environmentally friendly way. These washers use 25 percent less energy and 40 percent water than traditional machines.

⁕ Don't add too much detergent and never use more than the manufacturer recommends, as this will result in a soap overflow. And, take water hardness into account – the softer the water, the less detergent you will need.

⁕ Choose the appropriate washing program so the water level matches the laundry load. This protects the machine, especially during the spin cycle and saves energy.

⁕ Avoid the prewash cycle, which is unnecessary for most laundry and uses more water and electricity than needed.

TROUBLESHOOTING your machine

⁕ If your machine vibrates excessively or starts to move out of position during the spin cycle, it's likely the drum is out of balance, usually due to a particularly large or heavy item. Stop the machine immediately and remove the item in question. Spin it separately at a reduced speed – you might not get as much water out but you will reduce the risk of damaging your machine.

⁕ If your washing machine's door won't open, first make sure that the current wash cycle has finished. Next, check that the machine is plugged in, as some machines won't open without power. If there is water in the drum and you think something has gone wrong, try switching the machine to the drain part of the cycle. If still nothing happens, consult the troubleshooting section of the user manual or call customer service. Never attempt to force the door open!

⁕ Flooding caused by a burst washing machine hose can create a real mess. An automatic shut-off system can prevent many catastrophes. There are various designs, including double-walled hoses with a solenoid valve that will cut off the water the moment the slightest leak gets through the inner wall of the hose. Many new machines come with water shut-off systems already built in and there are various options to retrofit them to older machines.

✳ Bra underwires are one of the most common causes of service calls for washing machines. The underwires can easily find their way out of the drum and often end up getting stuck in the machine's heating element. In cases like this, the repair job involves taking the drum out of the machine, which is definitely not something you should attempt to do yourself. Place your bras in a delicates bag with a zip closure, or if possible, remove the wires from bras before washing them.

Insider's hack Don't wash in cold water all the time. Run your machine on a hot water cycle every now and then: otherwise a bacterial film will build up and the machine will start to smell.

Run your machine on a hot water cycle every now and then to prevent a film of bacteria from building up inside.

Save money Try using a laundry ball. There are various kinds on the market, including ones that contain mineral pellets that can clean a full load of wash without detergent. These products also have a water softening effect and last for hundreds of loads. Available through online retailers.

TAKE CARE

Using liquid laundry detergents exclusively can cause a sticky residue to build up over time. If you mainly use liquid detergent, switch to laundry powder every now and then.

DRYER BALLS ARE INEXPENSIVE AND LOOK LIKE A CURLED-UP PORCUPINE.

CLOTHES DRYERS are a big help

If you don't have a backyard where you are able to hang your washing out to dry, a clothes dryer can come in handy despite its high running cost. A dryer consists of a rotating drum driven by an electric motor, a heating mechanism to blow hot air through the drum (or warm air for delicate items) and a lint filter to screen the outgoing air. Moisture extracted from the clothing either leaves the machine with the outgoing air or is condensed with cold water and directed towards a drain. Most dryers allow you to select different temperatures and/or cycle lengths depending on whether you want your clothes to be completely dry or left slightly damp for easier ironing. Heat pump dryers are the most economical to run as they reuse some of the heat they produce rather than letting it go to waste. Heat pump dryers are more expensive to buy but the energy savings soon make up for the higher initial outlay.

✳ Laundry generally comes out of a dryer in better condition than clothes left hanging out in the wind. Towels come out soft and fluffy, delicates remain wrinkle-free and many items such as T-shirts need no ironing at all.

✳ Clothes dryers give such good results that they eliminate the need for you to use fabric softener in the washing machine.

✳ You can pretty much avoid ironing, too, if you take your clothes out of the dryer as soon as the cycle ends and hang them up or fold them right away.

✳ Spinning your washing thoroughly will make a significant difference to the amount of electricity your dryer needs to use. Water removed by spinning takes scale and detergent residue with it.

✳ Ensure you clean your dryer's lint filter after every cycle. Keeping the filter clean, improves your dryers efficiency, using less energy for each load.

Save time Spinning your washing at 1400 rpm, rather than 1000 rpm, can reduce clothes-drying time by 30 minutes.

Insider's hack Any delicate items you put in a washing bag for the washing machine should be left in the bag when you put them in dryer.

Save money You can throw a dryer sheet in the drum to make your laundry soft and fresh-smelling but a less costly alternative is to use a dryer ball (which looks like a curled-up porcupine) or a white tennis ball (don't use a yellow one as the color may bleed).

Dry or steam IRONS

Steam irons give better results than dry irons but their greater weight puts more strain on the wrist and they are also susceptible to scale build-up in hard-water areas.

✳ More elaborate steam-ironing systems, which come in various designs, get around these problems. Some models consist of an iron with a separate water tank and may include a scale filter and an accessory for steaming hanging garments; others require a fair amount of space and include a steam generator, an iron and an ironing board equipped with blowers to smooth out wrinkles in your clothing as you iron.

✳ Always check that the soleplate of your iron is free of residue before you start ironing.

✳ When ironing delicate items, apply the iron to the reverse side of the fabric only.

Save time When ironing, start with delicates first, then move on to the regular items. It's quicker for an iron to heat up than to cool down.

Easy fix If your iron doesn't have a scale filter and you want to save yourself the trouble of descaling it, use distilled water (available from hardware stores and supermarkets).

Insider's hack Do you have clothes that need starching? Instead of adding starch to the whole washing-machine load, just use spray starch on the specific garments while ironing.

TAKE YOUR CLOTHES OUT OF THE DRYER AS SOON AS THE CYCLE FINISHES AND YOU CAN PRETTY MUCH AVOID IRONING.

Personal care

There is a wide range of appliances designed to assist with personal hygiene and grooming, which are essential for our good health and well-being. Their proper use is essential to get the best results.

Make the most of MODERN TECHNOLOGY

Of course you can still shave with shaving cream and a razor, brush your teeth with an ordinary toothbrush, or use a hot-water bottle rather than a heating pad. But in most cases, a modern appliance will do as good a job (if not better) than its traditional counterpart.

ELECTRIC TOOTHBRUSHES
give a better clean

Although it will cost you more than an ordinary toothbrush, an electric toothbrush will leave your teeth significantly cleaner. Ideally, an electric toothbrush should have a small head to reach into every corner of your mouth. Especially effective at removing harmful plaque from your teeth, sonic and ultrasonic toothbrushes oscillate several hundred or several thousand times per second, generating pressure waves that dislodge bacteria from the teeth. While the tickling sensation of an electric toothbrush can take some getting used to, these cordless devices are completely safe to use as they draw their power from a small battery, which recharges when the brush is put back on its stand. Some also operate with regular disposable batteries. Electric toothbrushes are also practical for when you're travelling.

✳ Don't press too hard or scrub when using an electric toothbrush. Let the movement of the brush do the work.

✳ Clean your teeth every morning and evening – three times a day is even better. Spend two minutes at each cleaning and always work from the gum to the tooth. Don't forget to clean the spaces between your teeth with dental floss or interdental brushes – these areas are notorious breeding grounds for bacteria and gingivitis.

✳ Don't forget to replace the brush head on your electric toothbrush at regular intervals – be guided by the user manual as to how often this should be. If you have a mouth or throat infection, replace the brush head as soon as you have recovered.

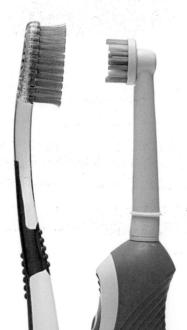

AN ELECTRIC TOOTHBRUSH SHOULD HAVE A SMALL HEAD TO GET INTO EVERY CORNER OF YOUR MOUTH.

HAIRDRYERS are an absolute must

A hairdryer works on one very simple principle – hot air can dry moisture a lot faster than cold air. The design of a hairdryer is equally simple – an electric motor drives a propeller, sucking air in at the back and blowing it out through a nozzle at the front. The air is heated by an electric element as it passes through.

✳ To avoid damaging your hair, don't use your hairdryer on its highest heat or speed settings, and hold it at a distance of least 8 in. from your hair.

✳ Keep the dryer moving back and forth over your head to prevent overheating any one area.

✳ To create more volume, blow air through your hair from underneath. On the other hand, if you want your hair to be as smooth and silky as possible,

FOR MORE VOLUME, BLOW THE AIR FROM UNDERNEATH YOUR HAIR.

Expert advice

How to use a dental water flosser

Many people swear by dental water jets. They love the clean feeling they get from the needle-like jet of water. The best models allow you to regulate the intensity of the water jet and are easy to keep clean.

★ A dental water flosser is not meant to replace a toothbrush and is not effective at removing plaque build-up from the surface of the teeth. Water jets are designed to clear away remnant debris after brushing, especially from tight corners where an electric toothbrush can't reach.

★ Move the tip at a 90° angle slowly along the gumline, cleaning around each tooth.

★ Try adding a little anti-bacterial mouthwash to the water in the machine.

★ Clean the entire machine regularly, including the water tank, tubing and jet tip. Don't leave water standing in the machine after use.

★ If you have gingival or periodontal pockets, seek your dentist's advice first. There is a risk that the water jet will push debris from between the teeth into the pockets, which can then lead to infection.

work from the roots to the tips of your hair. For most of us, the surface of each individual strand of our hair (known as the cuticle) is scaly rather than being smooth like a piece of thread. Blow-drying from the roots to the tips encourages these cuticle scales to lie down flat against each other. Hold your hair taut over a hairbrush as you blow-dry, which will help to achieve a flat, smooth result.

✳ If you want to clean your hairdryer's air intake, unplug it first. Then blow the dust out, using a vacuum cleaner if necessary.

Save money Don't blow-dry your hair right after washing it. Wrap your hair in a towel first and wait for 15 minutes. This will reduce the time it takes to blow-dry, saving a significant amount of power.

ELECTRIC BLANKETS
and heating pads

Heat can provide relief from all kinds of ailments: it promotes circulation, calms the nerves and relaxes the muscles. A heating pad or electric blanket also provides cozy warmth in bed – perfect for people who suffer from cold feet or winter chills. Heating pads and electric blankets contain filaments that are made warm by an electric current. A synthetic cover protects the heating components from moisture (such as sweat), and a shut-off switch protects against overheating to eliminate the risk of fire.

TAKE CARE
Never stick a sharp object into a heating pad. You may damage the heating filaments and risk an electric shock.

✳ Heating pads and electric blankets usually have a few different heat settings to choose from, as well as an automatic shut-off that turns the heat off after 1½ to 2 hours.

✳ Always keep electric blankets and pads flat, not folded, when in use.

✳ Clean a heating pad with a damp cloth and an all-purpose cleaner. Allow it to dry thoroughly. Fabric covers can be removed and washed. Ensure they are completely dry before using again.

✳ Check electric blankets and heating pads for any signs of wear or fraying around the cords before folding them away at the end of the season. If there's damage, throw them away.

Soothing and therapeutic
INFRARED LAMPS

Traditional incandescent light bulbs give off heat as a by-product of producing light. With infrared lamps, it's the other way around. Creating only small amounts of visible light, an infrared lamp's main function is to emit infrared radiation, which we feel as heat when it reaches our skin. This infrared radiation is converted into heat in the layers of the skin that lie a few millimeters below the surface.

Infrared lamps stimulate the circulation and various metabolic processes, and are used

CHECK ELECTRIC BLANKETS FOR WEAR BEFORE FOLDING THEM AWAY AT THE END OF THE SEASON.

clinically to treat muscular tension, arthritis, middle ear infections and sinus conditions.

✳ If you are applying an infrared lamp to your face, it is essential that you wear protective eyewear. Your eyes are unable to dissipate heat through the bloodstream, meaning they are susceptible to overheating with very serious consequences.

ELECTRIC SHAVERS
beat old-fashioned blades

Although some men continue to prefer wet shaving with a razor because they find it leaves their face feeling fresher, don't underestimate the advantages of dry shaving with an electric shaver. With an electric shaver there is virtually no risk of cutting yourself, you don't have to mess around with shaving cream, and it's easier to use when travelling.

✳ An electric shaver houses a small but powerful electric motor, which is powered from either electricity or a battery. The motor sets in motion numerous tiny blades within the shaver head. These blades oscillate back and forth or rotate behind a foil screen. Most shavers also have a beard trimmer with a larger blade that moves back and forth horizontally.

✳ Good-quality shavers have flexible, movable screens that follow the contours of your face. Premium models have adjustable settings to deal with different lengths of hair (such as three-day growth) as well as attachments for removing hair from the nose and ears.

Insider's hack While many men use aftershave, few bother with a pre-shave product. But there is a lot to be said for these products, which help the hairs to stand up for an especially close shave.

AN ADVANTAGE OF DRY SHAVING IS THAT THERE IS VIRTUALLY NO RISK OF CUTTING YOURSELF.

LOOK AFTER YOUR ELECTRIC SHAVER

DAILY	Use the small brush that came with your shaver to clear stubble out of the shaver head. If stubble is left in there too long, it will become a breeding ground for bacteria. You can rinse the shaver head and foil on many modern shavers under the faucet.
ONCE A MONTH	Use a special solution to clean the shaver head and foil hygienically. It's best to use the product recommended by the manufacturer in the user manual.
ONCE EVERY TWO YEARS	Replace the shaver head and foil. If the foil is ever damaged, replace it immediately to avoid the risk of injury.

Home entertainment systems

Almost every household has electronic devices with capabilities most of us couldn't have imagined 30 years ago. By far the most common among them is the television and its various home theater add-ons.

HOME ELECTRONICS should be treated well

As the value of our TV, DVD player, audio system, CD and DVD collections can add up to several thousand dollars, it's worth treating them well and using them to their full capacity.

TELEVISION, a mainstream medium

The TV has been center stage in our living rooms for several decades and, in some homes, the TV set is on several hours a day. Old sets with hefty cathode ray tubes have given way to flat screens, which deliver a sharper and far superior image while taking up a lot less space. Instead of an electron beam striking a fluorescent screen, the latest LED TVs produce images using millions of tiny light-emitting diodes controlled by just as many millions

OLD TV SETS HAVE GIVEN WAY TO FLAT SCREENS, WHICH DELIVER A FAR SUPERIOR IMAGE.

of tiny transistors. With standard flat screens only on the market for a few years, there is already a growing trend to replace them with high-definition (HD) models, which produce even sharper pictures because of the much higher number of pixels in their screens.

✳ Ultra-high definition (UHD or 4K) and LED TVs are the latest innovation and are capable of producing picture sharpness four times greater than your HD television set. Also on the market are 3D TVs, which are capable of producing images that appear to be three-dimensional when viewed with 3D glasses, but content is mostly limited to films and the effect isn't quite as satisfying as in the cinema, where the screen occupies most of your field of vision. TVs with curved screens, said to offer a more immersive viewing experience, are another

SOME DOGS GET SO EXCITED BY THE TV THAT THEY WILL JUMP UP AT IT AND MAY SCRATCH THE SCREEN.

Expert advice

Care for your flat-screen TV

The surface of a flat-screen TV is made of a delicate plastic and should be cleaned using only a slightly dampened microfiber cloth. If the screen is really dirty, put a tiny drop of dishwashing liquid onto the cloth (not onto the screen directly!) and wipe carefully.

Follow these other dos and don'ts when cleaning your TV:

★ DO turn the TV off first – so you don't interfere with the pixels and so that you can see the dirt more clearly.

★ DO use a soft cotton or microfiber cloth.

★ DON'T press hard: you can damage the screen.

★ DON'T use paper towel or rags: they are abrasive.

★ DON'T use window-cleaning fluid or any other chemical cleanser.

innovation.

✳ At the same time, the technologies through which images reach our TV screens have also proliferated. They now include transmission via satellite, antenna and cable, as well as online streaming and digital content accessed directly from our computers, DVD players and digital cameras.

✳ If you don't want pay TV or don't have access to it (either via cable or satellite), you can still watch free-to-air digital TV. All that's required is a digital receiver (built in to new TVs or available as a set-top box for older ones) and an antenna.

✳ Make no mistake: a large flat-screen TV weighs a considerable amount. If you want to mount yours on a wall, you will need to use a sturdy wall mount.

There are plenty of heavy-duty models on the market.

✳ Electronic devices will last longer if they are properly ventilated. Even though flat-screen TVs produce less heat than old cathode ray sets, they should not be squeezed into a tight cabinet.

✳ If your dog likes to watch TV with you, keep a close watch. Some dogs get so excited by the TV they will jump up at the images they see. The result can be claw marks on the delicate plastic surface of your TV screen.

Electronic devices will last longer if they are properly ventilated.

✳ If you want to watch TV without disturbing the rest of the house, use a pair of wireless headphones. They come with a stand that connects to your TV and transmits the sound to the headphones using an invisible infrared beam. When not in use, the headphones are returned to the stand, which also serves to recharge the batteries.

✳ For an even wider range of programs to choose from, a smart TV (or internet-enabled TV) will give you access to programming transmitted online and allow you to surf the web from your armchair.

✳ Unplug all your electronic devices whenever an electrical storm threatens, especially if you live in the country. Lightning does not have to hit your home directly to destroy your equipment. An overload caused by a strike hitting the grid some distance away is all it takes to do serious damage.

✳ If you have bought a big plasma screen TV, be very careful when moving it. Plasma screens must not be transported flat or on an angle as there is a risk the glass screen will crack under its own weight. Keep the screen vertical at all times.

Easy fix Many households have several devices they want to connect to the TV, such as a DVD player and perhaps a digital camera. If this applies to you, it's worth investing in an AV switcher. Essentially, this is a box with multiple inputs for your devices, one output to your TV and buttons that allow you to switch between the various inputs.

Insider's hack Costly, but well worth the effort if you are an audiophile, connect quality loudspeakers to your TV – or better yet, a surround sound system consisting of a receiver unit and five or up to seven speakers – to bring cinema sound into your home. Make sure you check the connectivity capabilities of your TV before you buy.

Save money If the sound or color on your TV suddenly becomes distorted, don't schedule an expensive service call right away as it's quite possible a cable has simply come loose at the back. Making sure all the connections are firmly pushed in will often solve the problem. Sometimes turning the TV off and back on again will also help.

IF YOU HAVE MULTIPLE REMOTES, STICK LABELS ON THE BACK SO YOU KNOW WHICH ONE'S WHICH.

Reach for the REMOTE CONTROL

By letting us send commands to our TVs with a beam of invisible infrared light, the remote control put an end to the days of getting up off the couch every time we wanted to change the channel or adjust the volume. On many of the latest TVs, the remote control is essential to access the full range of features. Remote controls need to be handled carefully to avoid damage.

✳ Be gentle when cleaning a remote control. It's best to use a dry cloth only. Moisture must not be allowed to get inside.

✳ If your remote control doesn't work as well as it used to, try using it directly in front of the TV. If this works, it's likely that the remote's batteries are running low and need to be replaced.

✳ If your remote control stops working completely, there are two options. You can get a new remote to suit your TV, or check if there is an app available for your smartphone or tablet that will work with your TV. Manufacturers of internet-enabled (smart) TVs often develop apps that allow you to connect to your TV via your home WiFi network.

THERE ARE SPECIAL CABINETS FOR HOME ENTERTAINMENT SYSTEMS, BUT SHELVING WILL DO JUST AS GOOD A JOB.

✳ If you have multiple remotes, stick labels on the back so you know which one's which. Universal remotes don't live up to their promise.

Easy fix Is your remote control constantly falling on the floor? Try putting a rubber band around each end to stop it from slipping off the coffee table.

The home MEDIA CENTER

While there are dozens of TV channels available, we are by no means limited to what's being shown on TV at any given time when it comes to choosing a movie or program to watch.

✳ For years, we used VCRs to record and replay TV broadcasts. VCRs encoded and recorded audio and video signals on magnetic tape contained within a cassette. They have largely gone out of use.

※ DVDs have sufficient storage capacity for a feature-length film plus a few extra features when recorded at standard resolution. DVD technology works by digitally encoding the video and audio data and recording it in the form of pits in the surface of the disc. A DVD player reads the information with a focused red laser beam.

※ Blu-ray discs are similar in appearance to CDs and DVDs but can hold more data – generally enough to hold a feature film and special features recorded in high-definition (HD) format. A Blu-ray player uses a "blue" laser to play these discs. Your TV and the connecting cable must also be capable of supporting the HD format in order to reproduce the higher resolution image properly.

※ It's easy enough to purchase feature films on DVD or Blu-ray, but if you like to make your own recordings of TV programs, a digital video recorder (DVR) is the way to go. These devices contain a hard drive much like that of a computer, and can record and replay vast amounts of digital content equivalent to hundreds of hours of TV programs. DVRs are operated via menus displayed on your TV screen, allowing you to schedule recordings, and to find, replay and delete the programs you have recorded.

※ The two main advantages of DVRs are that they let you skip through commercials quickly and time shift your viewing, meaning you can watch what you want when you want. Once a DVR's storage capacity is full, however, you will need to delete old programs or transfer them to DVD if you want to keep them long-term. This is not necessarily a straightforward process on all DVRs.

※ Some people still have a collection of movies on video cassette. It's worth repurchasing your favorite movies on DVD as the quality will be far superior to your old videos. You can transfer old TV programs or home movies recorded on tape to your computer hard drive using a special device to connect your VCR to your computer. Once on the computer, you can then burn the recordings onto DVDs. Another way to do this is with a machine that combines a video cassette player and DVD recorder in one. Or you can look for a video transfer service in the phone book or online.

※ A warning: don't leave it too long to transfer video to digital. Even if you don't watch them very often, recordings on videotape will lose quality over time as the strength of the magnetic signal fades and the plastic tape deteriorates.

Easy fix If you buy a Blu-ray player, you won't need to keep your existing CD or DVD player as – for the time being at least – Blu-ray players are able to read these earlier formats. Having just one machine saves shelf space.

Save money There are special cabinets designed for home entertainment systems but a basic, average-priced shelving unit of an adequate depth will do just as good a job. All you need to do is cut holes in the back of the unit for the cables to go through. A flat-screen TV can be placed on top or mounted on the wall above.

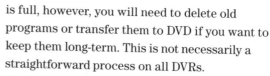

IF YOU STILL HAVE MOVIES ON VIDEOTAPE, YOU SHOULD TRANSFER THEM TO DVD OR HAVE SOMEONE DO IT FOR YOU.

Radios, cameras and telephones

Homes are equipped with all kinds of high-tech gadgets to serve our entertainment, information and communication needs. Sounds and images reach us through our radios, MP3 players, cameras and telephones.

NEWS AND MUSIC anywhere, anytime

There was a time when all music was live music, and when news travelled slowly by way of letters or telegrams. Now we can contact people by phone virtually anywhere on the planet at any time, and we can listen to news and music on the go, using devices that hold our entire collection of music and audio books in our pockets.

RADIO has a long history

Radio has come a long way since the earliest Morse code receivers were being used more than 100 years ago. But the digital age is changing radio more than anything ever has before; while no dates have been confirmed, it is expected that conventional radio will be shut down in a few years' time.

✳ Conventional radio technology is analogue – to transmit a sound wave with a frequency of 1000 oscillations per second, some property of the carrier radio wave (such as amplitude or frequency) is modulated to mimic the sound wave. With digital radio, on the other hand, the sound is converted into a numerical code and transmitted in encoded form. The receiver decodes the signal to reproduce the sound. Digital radio has many advantages – less interference, better sound quality and more efficient

use of available bandwidth. Pay TV providers often include digital radio stations in their packages, letting you listen through your television – radio stations operated by public broadcasters are a typical inclusion. Conventional radios are unable to tune in to digital broadcasts.

✳ Radio programs are also streamed over the internet. In addition to mainstream radio stations that stream their regular broadcasts online, there are thousands of small online-only stations operating all over the world. Among them are stations that

IN A FEW YEARS, CONVENTIONAL RADIO WILL HAVE BEEN COMPLETELY REPLACED BY DIGITAL.

specialize in specific genres, playing just one type of music around the clock. You can listen to online radio through your computer or smartphone, and there are also portable internet radios on the market.

CD AND MP3 players

Sound recording was revolutionized when CDs and MP3s took over from vinyl records, just as vinyl had turned shellac records into museum pieces 60 years prior. Both CDs and MP3s are less common than in the past due to streaming music and smartphones, however, they can still be useful for some people.
※ On a CD, digital information is stored in the form of tiny pits in the surface of the disc and read with an infrared laser beam. Unlike cassettes, CDs are not sensitive to magnetism. You can record information onto CDs in different formats – in addition to audio CDs for music, data CDs hold various other kinds of information. Using readily available blank CDs and a personal computer with an optical drive, you can read and write data CDs, and create audio CDs that will play in a conventional CD player. CDs offer very

TAKE CARE

Don't delete music or any other data from your computer after transferring it to your MP3 player. If you ever lose or need to replace it, you'll still have a backup copy of your music on your computer.

high sound quality no matter how many times they're played. Hissing and crackling are a thing of the past.
※ CDs have a limited storage capacity and some of this is spent on frequencies that are not within the range of human hearing. Compression technologies have been developed to store only those parts of the audio signal that we can actually hear. MP3 is the best known and most widely used of these. MP3 compression can increase audio storage capacity several times over. The great advantage of MP3 is that it enables portable players to hold the equivalent of thousands of CDs. Use your MP3 player with headphones – ideal when you want to go for a run or walk – or connect it directly to your home music system. Be aware, however, that your music's sound quality declines the more the signal is compressed.

Easy fix If you want to play your collection of CDs on your MP3 player or smartphone, freely available computer software will convert your CDs into MP3 files that you can then transfer to your MP3 player.

Insider's hack Most MP3 players can play more formats than just MP3s. If sound quality is as important to you as portability, don't use MP3s but download the full-resolution version of your music, using formats such as WAV or AIFF. Sure you won't fit as many songs on your player but you'll certainly get the most out of those you do.

AN MP3 PLAYER CAN HOLD THE EQUIVALENT OF THOUSANDS OF SONGS.

A DIGITAL CAMERA SHOWS YOU THE IMAGE YOU HAVE CAPTURED IMMEDIATELY AND ALLOWS YOU TO DELETE BAD PHOTOS.

Save money For a relatively small price, you can download music and audio books from digital media stores and store them on your preferred device. With this option in mind, you may find it's no longer worth paying a premium for the recording on CD. On the other hand, it may be worth getting a CD if it comes with a high-quality set of liner notes that cannot be downloaded – as is often the case with classical CDs.

DIGITAL CAMERAS take
great photos

Cameras using traditional film have had their day; digital photography has now taken center stage. Along with their ever-improving image quality, digital cameras offer a number of other advantages over their predecessors.

✳ A digital camera shows you the image you have taken immediately, so it's easy to delete bad photos.

✳ It's easy to email digital photos to your friends. And using the camera in your smartphone means you can send pictures right from your phone.

✳ You can edit and enhance digital photos on a computer using a retouching application.

✳ If you want a hard copy of your photos, digital images can be printed out easily.

✳ Your computer hard drive can hold millions of images and you can sort and search for your photos on a computer in the blink of an eye.

✳ Many digital cameras can capture high resolution (HD) video as well as still images.

Easy fix Like most other small electronic devices these days, cameras come with a plug-in battery charger. Put a label on all your chargers and

Expert advice

Buying a digital camera

When you're in the market for a digital camera, start by reading product reviews to get an overview of what's on the market.

When you get to the store, pay attention to the following points:

★ Do the size and weight of the camera feel comfortable in your hands?

★ Does it have an optical zoom (not just a digital zoom)?

★ Does it have a large display?

★ Is the lens speed adequate? Any camera can take a decent picture when there is plenty of light but this last point will determine how well a camera performs in low light conditions. In low light, a fast lens and powerful flash will prove their worth. On its own, the number of megapixels does not give much of an indication of image quality.

adapters as soon as you buy them so you'll always know which device they go with. Using the wrong charger can seriously damage your device.

Insider's hack If you want to sell something online, you'll improve your chances by adding a few photos taken with a digital camera. Include full shots of the item and close-ups of specific features.

TAKE PICTURES with your phone

Being able to take pictures with your cell phone is not only fun, it can be very useful. You don't have to have the latest smartphone to take pictures as even basic cell phones often include a camera.

✳ If you come to a trail map when going for a hike, take a quick photo and you'll have the map in your pocket.

✳ When something catches your eye in a bookstore but you don't have time or can't make up your mind if you want to buy it, taking a picture of the cover is a quick way to record the details if you decide you want to buy it later.

SELFIE STICKS ALLOW YOU TO TAKE GROUP PORTRAITS AT MORE THAN ARM'S LENGTH.

✳ In the event of a traffic accident, a phone camera will enable you to make a record of the scene.

✳ If you're driving in an unfamiliar city, take a photo of the street sign where you park your car. You'll always be able to find someone who can give you directions. You can even translate some foreign-language signs by taking a photo and loading it into a translation app.

✳ If you're finding your way around an unfamiliar city on public transportation, take a shot of the relevant section of a schedule to help you find your way back to where you started.

✳ If your partner impulsively tries on a funny-looking hat, or stands in front of a hilarious street sign, pull out your camera phone and capture the moment, then share it on social media.

✳ If you come across an interesting article or recipe in a magazine in the doctor's waiting room but can't concentrate on reading it, take a photo and you can look at it again later.

✳ Photograph your children or pets in spontaneous moments. In a year or two's time, you will be glad to have the memories to look back on.

Easy fix Once upon a time, you needed a camera with a self-timer to take photos of yourself. Selfie sticks allow you to take pictures of yourself – or group portraits with friends – at more than arm's length. The phone's camera can be operated in various ways such as voice command, Bluetooth, or a wired connection to one of the phone's ports.

Save money Use your smartphone as a scanner with an app that converts your photo into PDF or JPEG format. Some even transcribe the words into editable PDF text.

LAND-LINE PHONES are still with us

The phone has been connecting homes, businesses and public institutions for nearly 150 years. It has saved countless lives and made many aspects of our lives easier, notwithstanding the inconvenience of the occasional nuisance phone call.

✳ Early telephones converted sound waves into electrical impulses, which were transmitted along wires or by radio relays, amplified at various points along the way, and finally converted back into sound in the earpiece of the receiving party's telephone. Today, the world's telephone network operates on digital technology. Computers respond to dialling signals to connect callers in a fraction of a second, and speech is encoded and transmitted digitally.

✳ Cordless telephones use small transmitters and receivers to relay voice signals between the handset and base station using low-energy radio waves. These radio waves are much lower in intensity than all the other electromagnetic radiation that passes through our homes, so there should be no cause for

concern about using a cordless telephone. Make the most of the benefits of having a cordless phone and keep the handset close by. A cordless phone is not only convenient, it could also save your life, especially if you live alone.

The radio waves emitted by a cordless telephone are much lower in intensity than the other electromagnetic radiation that passes through our homes.

Easy fix The advice to avoid using the telephone during an electrical storm is only relevant in areas where telephone signals are transmitted through overhead wiring. In rare instances, lightning can strike telephone wires and an electrical surge can be transmitted all the way to a telephone handset. This risk does not apply to cordless telephones.

A CORDLESS PHONE IS NOT ONLY CONVENIENT, IT COULD SAVE YOUR LIFE IF YOU LIVE ALONE.

Computers and the internet

No piece of technology has brought about more change in our everyday lives, and in the business world, than the personal computer. Computers are pervasive in our homes and their impact has been all the more extensive for their ability to connect us to the world with a single click through the internet.

TABLETS AND SMARTPHONES ARE A COMPLEMENT TO CONVENTIONAL DESKTOP OR LAPTOP COMPUTERS.

TAKE ADVANTAGE of the benefits

Few people are able to, or indeed want to, avoid computers these days. The opportunities offered by computers and the internet are simply too great to miss out on. While the constant developments and emerging technologies can seem overwhelming, with a little help you really can stay on top of the information revolution.

The multi-purpose
PERSONAL COMPUTER

A computer is a true multi-purpose machine. Given the appropriate software program or application, a computer can do virtually anything. And yet, in broad terms, the inner workings of a computer are not all that complicated. At the heart of the machine lie one or more microprocessors – chips containing billions of tiny electronic components whose job it is to store and process information.

✳ The computer's monitor lets you follow what you are entering with the keyboard or mouse, see the results of the computer's work, and print what you see. All kinds of information can be entered: text, numbers, music, images, videos and much more.

Given the appropriate program, a computer can do virtually anything.

✳ The computer's basic functions are handled by its operating system – Microsoft Windows or Apple OS to name two common examples. Additional software applications can be installed to enable you to do a wide range of tasks, including word processing, data backups, numerical calculations, video editing, and so on. An application known as a browser lets you connect to the internet.

✳ Tablets and smartphones are a complement to – and to some extent a replacement for – conventional desktop or laptop computers. Highly portable, they operate without a mouse or keyboard. Tablets were mainly developed for browsing the internet, but they are also excellent for viewing photos and videos, reading e-books, listening to music, playing games and much more, especially when travelling.

✳ Smartphones are cell phones with an inbuilt chip that lets them perform an almost inexhaustible variety of additional functions. Extend your tablet or smartphone's functionality by installing small programs known as apps.

If your computer freezes and stops responding to commands, don't panic.

✳ Tablets and smartphones are operated via a touchscreen rather than a keyboard or mouse. Back at your desktop PC, keyboard and mouse technology has continued to develop with the advent of wireless models that work with Bluetooth technology.

Easy fix If your computer freezes and stops responding to commands, don't panic. You don't need to call in a technician right away. It might simply be a case of the signal between the computer and the mouse or keyboard getting stuck. Check that the USB connectors are firmly plugged in or, if you are using wireless devices, try replacing the batteries. If that doesn't solve the problem, turn the computer off (by unplugging it if necessary), wait a minute or two, then start it up again. This will often resolve the problem.

Insider's hack When buying a tablet, make sure you get one with enough storage capacity. As a tablet can be used for so many different things, people often find they end up needing more storage than they originally anticipated.

You can't have too much STORAGE CAPACITY

In addition to the working memory that it uses to carry out commands, a computer also has a permanent memory, where you can instruct it to store information that you want kept after the machine is turned off. It's important that your computer has adequate storage capacity, especially if you want to keep a lot of data. Storage capacity is generally measured in gigabytes or terabytes (1 terabyte = 1024 gigabytes).

✳ The most common form of permanent memory in a desktop computer is a hard disk. A hard disk contains a number of rapidly rotating magnetic platters. The computer writes information onto the surface of these platters in the form of a magnetic signal and can retrieve it when needed. The hard disk in a modern personal computer can hold several terabytes of data.

WHEN PURCHASING A COMPUTER, MAKE SURE IT HAS A LARGE-ENOUGH HARD DRIVE AND WORKING MEMORY.

✳ Solid-state drives (SSDs) enable data to be written and read faster than is possible with a hard disk. These memory chips have no moving parts. Thanks to falling costs, more and more computers are being fitted with SSDs. And installing one in an existing computer can improve performance.

✳ If you want to secure important data somewhere outside your computer or move it from one place to another, an external hard drive or solid-state drive will do the job. Another option is to copy your data to a reliable external server (known as "cloud computing"). Flash drives are another extremely convenient way to store data. Just a few inches long and a less than an inch thick, these mini memory devices will connect to any computer's USB port. Flash drives are inexpensive, range in capacity from 2 Gb to over 64 Gb, and slip easily into your pocket.

Easy fix USB ports are often inconveniently located at the back of the computer. If you use them all the time, or if you want to connect more devices to your computer than you have ports, pick up a USB hub, which is essentially a multi-socket adapter for your USB port. Connect it to a free USB port with a cable and put it in an easily accessible position.

THE INTERNET, an everyday essential

In the last 20 years, the internet has grown rapidly to become one of the most important sources of information and means of communication in the world today. Surfing the internet is a quick and easy way to find all kinds of everyday things such as schedules, places to shop, opening hours, special offers, the latest news, and so on. The internet's use as a communication tool (for example, email and video calls) is growing steadily, too.

✳ To connect to the internet you need an account with an internet service provider (ISP). Most major cable broadband or satellite connections and phone companies offer this service but there are many other ISPs out there as well. For a monthly fee, your ISP will provide you with access to the internet. Most of the data on the internet flows through the world's existing telephone or cable wires. Additionally, internet access is available through mobile broadband via cell phones and other mobile devices. Keep an eye on mobile broadband such as 5G offerings as they may become more popular in years to come.

✳ To surf the internet, you will also need a piece of software known as a browser. Common examples include Internet Explorer, Safari and Google Chrome. A web browser will generally already be installed with your computer's operating system. You don't have to stick with the pre-installed option, but can download one of the others from the internet (you should always use the official website to do this). You should also download updates when they become available (again from the official website) since an outdated browser will not perform as well.

PICK UP A USB HUB — ESSENTIALLY A MULTI-SOCKET ADAPTER FOR YOUR USB PORT.

＊ You will also need a device called a router. This is a box that manages the connection between your computer and the internet, and is either supplied by your ISP, the company that provides you with internet access or available in electronic stores. The router plugs into your phone or cable outlet, so you may also need a device called an ADSL filter in order that your phone line can continue to handle telephone calls as well as internet traffic. There are also ADSL routers that handle both internet and phone.

＊ Ideally, you should use a WiFi (or wireless) router. This will provide a wireless network within your home, allowing your computer and any other internet-enabled devices (other computers, tablets, smartphones, smart TVs) to use the same internet connection without having cables running all over the house.

＊ If you find the instructions for setting up all this equipment are not clear enough to manage it on your own, or you have specific needs, call in a technician to help. You will probably only need someone to come once and it will be worth it to get everything up and running properly.

＊ From time to time, you may come across the term "WLAN." "WLAN" and "WiFi" are used interchangeably to refer to wireless internet access, although they are not strictly the same thing. "WLAN" (which stands for "wireless local area network") is a generic term that refers to any wireless computer network, while WiFi (a play on words with "hi-fi") is a proprietary name that refers to a particular networking technology used by most WLANs.

SETTING UP A WIFI (WIRELESS) NETWORK IN YOUR HOME WILL ELIMINATE MUCH OF THE NEED FOR CABLES.

You can order a router, which lets you connect to the internet, directly from your ISP when you open an account.

＊ Protect your wireless network by selecting the WPA2 security option and a password that is not easy to guess, made up of lower-case and upper-case letters, numbers and punctuation marks. Write your password down then enter it into your wireless router (or ask a technician to do it for you). You will need this password to connect any other computer (or smartphone) to your wireless network. Write your password down and keep it in a safe place.

An INTERCONNECTED WORLD
of information

There is an astronomical amount of information on the one billion websites that make up the internet. A search engine, such as Google, Bing or Yahoo, will help you find what you are looking for. Simply enter one or more keywords, or a string of text, and in a fraction of a second the search engine will present you with a list of websites on which your search terms appear.

＊ Websites in other languages can be translated using services such as Google Translate, which can handle dozens of languages in either direction. Google Maps provides detailed maps, directions and satellite images. The world's largest encyclopedia, Wikipedia, contains articles that are constantly

ONLINE COMMUNICATIONS HAVE GIVEN RISE TO ALL KINDS OF NEW SYMBOLS, SUCH AS THE "LIKE" BUTTON.

being updated by its users, and anyone can edit an article. Articles typically include images and links to related articles or websites.

✳ Social media sites, such as Facebook, enable you to send news and photos to your friends and family. Twitter is a better option if you want to send shorter messages to a wider public. Smartphone apps such as WhatsApp allow you to send various kinds of messages to your contacts, including images, audio, video and details of your current location.

✳ Skype is an online telecommunications tool that allows you to make regular and video calls anywhere in the world. Video calls are only possible between registered Skype users, but it's free to register and free to use. If you open a paid account with Skype with your credit card, you can also use the service to call standard landlines and cell phones anywhere in the world at virtually the rate of a local call.

✳ Online communications have given rise to all kinds of new abbreviations and symbols, such as

the ubiquitous "like" button, used to express one's approval to the online community at large. Others are called "emojis," which convey a broader range of emoticon expressions than the original smileys :) or :(as well as characters and words.

Save time If you like to keep up with current events, the internet is a great place to find news and information. Most major newspapers and magazines have websites that are constantly updated. For many readers, online news (which may be free or involve a reasonably priced subscription) has replaced the daily newspaper.

Save money If you use the internet a lot on your smartphone, you should sign up for an unlimited data plan. This way you can surf the net for as long as you like at any time of day. Without an unlimited plan, your bill may hold a nasty surprise in the form of excess download fees, which may occur if you download movies online, listen to internet radio or make a lot of video calls. Unlimited data plans can often be bundled together with good deals on a home phone line and/or a cell phone plan with mobile data for your smartphone.

Set up your EMAIL ADDRESS

Once you get online, you'll want to be able to send and receive email messages. Your internet service provider usually provides you with a free email account with an address that will look something like this: *yourname@providername.com.* Your ISP should also provide you with the details you need to access your account through an email application (usually included with most operating systems). These details will include your email address, the server addresses for incoming and outgoing mail, your username and password (which you should change right away).

✳ When you are online, any incoming emails are downloaded to your computer and any messages that you have written are sent out.

✳ Here is how to set up your email account: Open your computer's email application. Go to "Settings" and select "New account." Enter your account details into the pop-up window. Choose the account type "IMAP" rather than "POP." Give your account a name (such as "My account"). Enter your email address and name. Enter the address of the server from which to retrieve your mail – it may begin with "mail" or "imap." Then enter your username and password.

When you are online, incoming emails are downloaded to your computer and outgoing messages are sent out.

✳ Next, enter the address of the outgoing mail server – it may begin with "smtp" or be identical to the incoming mail server. You may need to re-enter your username and password. If you have the option to use an encrypted connection (SSL), activate it to ensure your messages will be transmitted in an encrypted form. Specify how often you want the email program to check for new messages (such as every minute, once every 10 minutes, and so on). Then, save your settings and close the window.

✳ If you encounter problems setting up your email account, look at the "Support" pages relating to email on your internet service provider's website, or call your ISP's technical support line. They will usually be able to solve the problem.

✳ There are numerous web-based email providers, such as Gmail and Outlook, which you can access from any computer. These are a good option if you travel or change ISPs regularly.

WHEN USING A CREDIT CARD TO MAKE PURCHASES ONLINE, MAKE SURE THE WEBSITE IS ENCRYPTED.

COMPUTER SECURITY

1 Install anti-virus software on your computer and keep it up to date. Viruses are often hidden in email attachments. Don't open attachments if you are at all unsure about where a message has come from.

2 Never give your banking details over the internet. No bank will ever ask you to provide account details online. When using a credit card to make purchases online, make sure the website is encrypted. This will be indicated by the presence of a padlock symbol and "https" in the address bar.

3 Many online stores ask you to register with your email address and a password. Use a different password for each site and keep a separate list of your passwords in a safe place.

4 A safer alternative to using your credit card online is to use a secure online payment service such as PayPal.

PRINTERS and SCANNERS

You can connect printers and scanners to your computer via a USB cable or WiFi. Inkjet printers are the most common and least expensive printers. They produce decent-quality text and images by spraying tiny droplets of colored ink onto the page. By comparison, laser printers are more expensive to buy but are cheaper to operate, especially if you do a lot of printing. Unlike inkjet, laser printouts are water resistant. Less expensive laser printers only print in black and white; color laser printers cost a lot of money. If you send a lot of letters and want easy-to-read mailing labels, you may want to buy a separate label printer that can print self-adhesive labels of various sizes.

✳ A scanner uses light to capture printed text or images, which you can then save to your computer. Inexpensive flatbed scanners are the most common variety; these are suitable for photos, too. When buying a scanner, pay attention to the maximum resolution and scanning speed. If you have a lot of documents to scan, look for a scanner with an automatic document feeder. You can save scanned texts as either images or PDF files. You can then use a text recognition (OCR) program to convert the text into an editable format, which you work on in your word processor. If you have a lot of old slides or negatives to scan and archive, a high-resolution film scanner will give the best results.

✳ You can also buy an "all-in-one" printer, which combines print, scan and fax facilities in one device. They are quite small and inexpensive, and so a good option for a home office.

Save money Buy a printer that has a separate ink cartridge for each color so you will only have to replace one color at a time when they run out. A printer may be inexpensive to buy, but the cost of replacement ink cartridges can really add up. Also look for alternatives to buying brand-new cartridges made by the printer manufacturer. In many areas, there are cartridge-refilling services, and you can also find generic cartridges online for just about any printer that cost less and are not necessarily any lower in quality than the manufacturer's brand.

Keep your COMPUTER CLEAN

It doesn't take long for a computer keyboard to get pretty dirty. First disconnect the keyboard from the computer, turn it upside down and give it a shake. Suck up any remaining dirt with a vacuum or blow it away with a hairdryer. To clean the keys, rub with a moist cotton swab dipped in baking soda.

✳ If your computer monitor is dusty, wipe it off with a clean, soft, slightly moistened cloth.

TAKE CARE

Don't clean keyboards or computer monitors with water. If the smallest drop gets inside, it can destroy your equipment.

The SMARTPHONE runs the smart home

Intelligent homes are the way of the future, equipped with networked appliances that can be monitored and controlled with a smartphone or tablet, even from the other side of the world. Believe it or not, you can even use smartphones to make phone calls!

BETTER THAN A REMOTE

There is a growing trend to replace conventional remote controls with smartphones, using specific apps developed to control various appliances. Programming your DVR to record a TV show with your smartphone when you're out of the house is just one example.

HOME SURVEILLANCE AND SECURITY

In the event of a break-in, intelligent alarm systems with sensors and cameras in and around the house can alert your smartphone and send images of the scene (and possibly footage of the intruders). Similar technology allows a smartphone to function as a baby monitor, picking up sounds and images from the child's room.

ANSWERING THE DOOR

Smart intercom systems let you answer the door with your smartphone, speak to your visitors via video-link, and then open the door remotely. Smartphone encryption technology means your phone can serve as a virtual key for electronic locks.

KEEP AN EYE ON IT ALL

With smart home technology, you can use your smartphone to monitor and adjust just about anything in the home that has smart (internet-enabled) technology, including lighting, window coverings, heating and cooling systems, and so on. No matter where you are, you can check the current temperature inside and outside the house, in your refrigerator or freezer, or even in your aquarium. Smartphones can alleviate worries about household mishaps large and small, with monitors to alert you if the water level in your basement starts to rise or your potted plants start to dry out. And rest assured: your robot lawnmower will let you know immediately if it ever gets involved in an accident.

Around the house

A home has long been more than just four walls and a roof. Utilities including running water, heating and electricity for lighting, and appliances are all essential parts of what makes a house a home. It becomes especially clear just how important these basic services are any time one of them happens to fail.

CEILING FANS USE A LOT LESS ENERGY THAN AIR-CONDITIONERS, AND OFTEN PROVIDE ENOUGH COOLING.

AIR-CONDITIONED comfort

Air-conditioners are part of life today with three-quarters of all the homes in the United states using them. They cool the home with a cold indoor coil called an evaporator. A condenser is a coil that releases collected heat out into the environment. The compressor or pump moves a heat transfer fluid or refrigerant from the evaporator to the condenser.

＊ Packaged central air-conditioning systems have the evaporator, condenser, and compressor all located in one cabinet which is placed either on the roof or a slab outside the home. The air comes into the home through an exterior wall or the roof to circulate through the homes air supply and return ducts and are connected to the home's heat furnace.

＊ Split or ductless systems are an economical choice when adding air-conditioning to an older home that doesn't have A/C. In these systems, the outdoor cabinet contains the condenser and compressor and the indoor cabinet contain the evaporator.

＊ You can fit a window or wall unit to an individual room such as an office or bedroom. They come in a variety of sizes to suit different room dimensions.

＊ Other than dusting and cleaning air-conditioner ducts, there is not much you can do to keep the system running efficiently. Modern systems usually provide years of trouble-free service. Call in the professionals if you notice any problems or there is a decline in performance.

Expert advice

The cost of air-conditioning

Three-quarters of American households run some sort of cooler. Air-conditioners might be very effective coolers but they are also the most expensive cooling systems to buy and run. They are a major culprit with home energy consumption in summer. Electric fans, however, use only a fraction of an air-conditioner's energy, costing just a few cents an hour to run.

★ Try using your air-conditioner in short bursts together with a fan – the cool air will move around more efficiently.

★ If you don't have a fan, turn up the thermostat on the air-conditioner. Every 2°F warmer will save 10 percent on your cooling costs.

★ On extremely hot days, turn on the air-conditioner early in the morning to prevent it from having to work too hard to remove heat later in the day.

Save money Ceiling fans use a lot less energy than air-conditioners, and often provide enough cooling for much of the time you would otherwise be using your air-conditioner. Make sure you choose a fan with a reverse switch – the fan can be reversed in winter and used together with the heating system to force heated air, which has risen to the ceiling, down again, reducing the demand on the heating system and therefore its energy consumption.

ELECTRIC HEATERS ARE USEFUL ON THEIR OWN OR IN COMBINATION WITH OTHER METHODS.

Cozy up to an
ELECTRIC HEATER

For quick and efficient heat, electric fan or radiant heaters are useful on their own or in combination with central heating. They require little maintenance other than keeping them free of dust, but always follow any safety guidelines for their use.

✳ Dust and debris can hinder an electrical unit's heating speed and output, so give electric heaters an annual spring cleaning before the weather gets chilly. With the heater switched off and completely cool, carefully vacuum the heating element, housing and any internal parts with a brush attachment. When they're not in use, store portable heaters in their original boxes or in trash bags that you've tied shut to prevent dust from collecting.

✳ If the fan in a fan heater stops spinning, turn it off and unplug the heater, allow it to cool and then investigate. If the blades seem to be jammed, remove the heater cover and clear away any debris. Give the fan a spin by hand to see if bent components are the problem, and try straightening them out, if possible, with pliers. If the fan seems to be loose, tighten the set screw at the fan's hub. If none of this does the trick, the fan motor may be defective.

Easy fix   If you have gas heat in your home, regular servicing of your furnace is suggested. Manufacturers recommend bi-annual servicing for the first 10 years with annual servicing thereafter. Check your furnace filter monthly and change it when it's dirty to assure better heating and cooling throughout the year.

Let there BE LIGHT!

Although we now take it for granted, electric light at the flick of a switch is a breakthrough that has only been around for a hundred years or so. In earlier times, there was little escape from the inevitable: it was light in the morning and dark at night. The only way to have light at night was with an open flame from a piece of kindling, a candle, a gas light or something similar – a solution that often resulted in the house catching fire, if not the entire city.

✳ There are various ways to produce electric light. Incandescent bulbs (now phased out in many parts of the world) use electric current to heat a metal filament until it glows. Besides light, incandescent bulbs emit a lot of heat and the inherent waste of energy is the reason why many countries have banned the sale of these bulbs.

✳ In a fluorescent tube or compact fluorescent bulb (CFL), the electric current excites mercury vapor in an evacuated glass tube, causing it to emit ultraviolet light, which in turn causes a phosphorous coating on the inside of the tube to emit visible light. The mercury content in CFLs can pose an environmental hazard so it's worth checking if facilities for recycling used bulbs are available in your area.

✳ Modern LED bulbs contain specially treated crystals that emit light (and only a small amount of heat) when a current is applied. There are two kinds of LED bulbs – those that produce all three primary colors (red, green and blue), which combine to form white light, and those that produce ultraviolet light and make use of a phosphorous coating to convert the UV into visible white light.

✳ LED bulbs have many advantages. They last up to a hundred times longer than other bulbs; they use

WE NOW TAKE IT FOR GRANTED, BUT ELECTRIC LIGHT HAS ONLY BEEN AROUND FOR A HUNDRED YEARS OR SO.

Expert advice

Ending wattage confusion

When purchasing CFLs or LED bulbs, the wattage shown on the pack gives you only an approximate idea of the bulb's brightness. The true measure of brightness is a unit known as the "lumen", so look out for brands that specify brightness in lumens.

Most of us still have a rough idea of the brightness of incandescent bulbs of various wattages.

The following guide will help you choose a CFL or LED bulb equivalent in brightness to various incandescent bulbs (CFLs are roughly one-quarter the wattage and LEDs are even less).

LUMENS	INCANDESCENT	CFL	LED
220–250	25 watts	2–8 watts	2–3 watts
450	40 watts	8–12 watts	4–5 watts
750–900	60 watts	13–18 watts	6–8 watts
1100–1300	75 watts	19–22 watts	9–13 watts
1600–1800	100 watts	23–30 watts	16–20 watts
2600–2800	150 watts	31–55 watts	25–28 watts

90 percent less energy than incandescent globes; they don't contain any toxic substances such as mercury; they give their maximum light output the moment they are switched on; they are available in a range of socket and bulb sizes to suit just about any light fixture; and, they are available in a range of light output ratings and color temperatures from warm white to neutral white to daylight white.

Save money Although lighting constitutes only a small proportion of your household electricity consumption, you can still save money by installing LED bulbs in as many of your light fixtures as possible, especially the ones you tend to leave switched on for long periods.

Insider's hack Because LEDs emit essentially no heat and are low voltage, they are a child-safe option.

ELECTRICITY

From the power lines in the street, electricity reaches your home through the meter box, which usually also houses a number of fuses or circuit breakers. Electricity meters are secured with lead seals and may only be opened by qualified personnel. Wiring runs from the meter box to carry electricity to all parts of the house, with each circuit typically protected by its own circuit breaker. Overhead lighting and outlets are

WHEN THE POWER FAILS, VERIFY WHICH CIRCUIT BREAKER HAS TRIPPED.

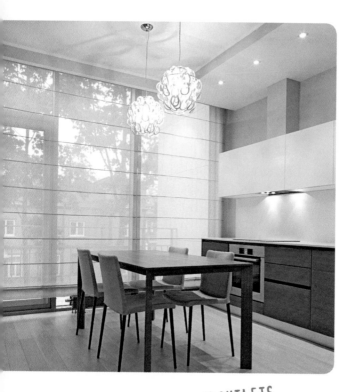

OVERHEAD LIGHTING AND OUTLETS
ARE NORMALLY INSTALLED
ON SEPARATE CIRCUITS.

normally installed on separate circuits and employ different gauge wiring. Wiring for the light circuit is of a smaller gauge because the energy demand is less than that of the power circuit. Most dwellings have multiple power (and sometimes light) circuits. Your stove, oven, hot-water system or any other appliance that draws a lot of power will usually be on a separate circuit protected by its own circuit breaker.

✳ Circuit breakers are now more common than fuses. A circuit breaker has a switch that allows you to turn the circuit on or off manually. Your circuit box may also contain a ground fault circuit interrupter (GCFI, also known as a safety switch), which will greatly improve electrical safety in your home. If a residual-current device is not present, you should have one retrofitted.

✳ If the installing electrician neglected to do so,

label each circuit breaker with the area of the house it supplies power to. This will make it easier to turn the power off in the right area when there is a fault or work needs to be done on the wiring.

✳ If an electrical appliance or a light source stops working, try to localize the problem. Verify whether it's the ground fault circuit interrupter or a specific circuit breaker that has tripped.

✳ Unplug any defective appliances immediately. If a switch or outlet has been damaged, have it replaced as soon as possible.

Save money Surge protectors with a switch for each outlet can save a lot of electricity, as many appliances continue to draw power when in standby mode. A switched surge protector will let you turn off all but the appliances you are actually using.

WATER and plumbing

Water supply lines enters the home below the floor, passing first through a supply valve and then the water meter. There is often another valve installed just after the meter, which can turn off the water supply or stop water draining out of the household plumbing if the meter ever needs to be replaced. Once past the meter, the pipework divides into branch lines that supply various areas of the home. In some cases, each branch line will be fitted with its own valve to allow the water supply to be shut off independently.

✳ Sewage pipes that take wastewater away from the home are usually made of PVC (or terracotta

TAKE CARE

If you live in a hard-water area, don't waste your money on "magnetic" or "high-frequency" descaling devices that are designed to be installed around the outside of water pipes. These devices are completely ineffective.

in older services) and are much larger in diameter than the incoming water supply pipes. The largest in diameter are those that receive wastewater from the toilet. The sewage pipework comes together into a single pipe that leads out into the underground sewer and on to a wastewater treatment facility.

✳ Domestic hot-water heaters function in a variety of ways. Storage water heaters consist of a large tank heated by gas or electricity. Although the tanks are well insulated, hot-water storage systems use energy around the clock to keep the water hot. More economical, continuous-flow systems known as tankless hot-water heaters, use gas or electricity to heat water only as it flows through. Tankless heaters are more expensive to purchase and install however they conserve approximately 30 to 50 percent more energy, take up less space, and last longer than storage heaters.

✳ Regardless of whether you heat water with gas or electricity, showers are more economical than baths.

✳ Become familiar with the location of your water supply valves and water meter. Make sure they remain easily accessible at all times and the valve turns easily. The main valve will allow you shut off the water to your entire home in the event of a leak or when plumbing work needs to be done.

Insider's hack If your home's outgoing sewer pipe does not have a backflow valve, you should have one installed. If the sewer ever gets backed up, which can happen in the event of heavy rain or flooding, the valve will prevent sewage from flowing back up through the plumbing and out of your household drains.

Save money If you're going away for any length of time, turn your hot-water system off.

SHOWERS ARE MORE ECONOMICAL THAN BATHS.

Expert advice

Deal with water damage

Whether it's a burst pipe, rising damp or a leaking roof, water damage requires quick action.

★ Turn off the water supply as quickly as you can. You may be able to turn off just the affected branch line, but if you're in any doubt, turn off the water to the entire house.

★ If there is a water leak near an electrical box, turn off power to the affected area at the main main circuit panel.

★ Call a plumber – or an emergency plumbing service if necessary. If there is a genuine risk of the leak causing an electrical fire, also call the fire department.

★ If the water is coming from an apartment above you, alert the occupants or, if you can't reach them, the building manager.

★ Once the leak has been dealt with, pull up or remove wet carpets and other affected objects, and open the windows to allow the room to dry out. In severe cases, you may need to hire a water damage restoration service.

chapter 8

Minor Household Repairs

Tools no home should be without

Knowing how to do a few simple repair jobs yourself can save you a lot of money. A set of good-quality tools is an essential starting point.

BASIC EQUIPMENT
for home handiwork

With a few good tools, you will be surprised by how many jobs around the house you can accomplish yourself. Hardware for specific jobs – such as nuts and bolts, screws, nails or wall plugs – can be purchased as needed.

❋ You can buy all the elements of a basic toolkit separately but you'll probably get a better deal if you buy them together as a kit. The main thing is to get good-quality tools. Cheap tools made of inferior materials will soon let you down. Here is a list of a few essentials:

❋ Mid-weight claw hammer

❋ Set of screwdrivers of various sizes, including both flathead and Phillips-head tips. For certain jobs you might also need special-purpose screwdrivers for other types of screw, such as torx screws, which have a six-pointed star head.

YOU CAN BUY THE ELEMENTS OF A BASIC TOOLKIT SEPARATELY BUT YOU'LL PROBABLY GET A BETTER DEAL IF YOU BUY THEM TOGETHER AS A KIT.

❋ Cordless electric screwdriver – if you do a lot of jobs that require a screwdriver, this will come in handy. Most cordless models are also fine for small drilling jobs and some feature a magnetic tip to hold on to screws and a light on the end to illuminate the work area.

❋ Set of socket wrenches with a ratchet handle and extension pieces

❋ Pair of needle-nosed pliers for pulling small objects out of tight spaces

❋ Pair of combination pliers – useful for a wide range of tasks

* Pair of pincer pliers for pulling out nails
* Pair of tongue and groove pliers for pipes
* Set of files and rasps
* Small handsaw
* Selection of sandpaper in various grades
* Tape measure
* Level
* Screw clamps or clutch clamps
* Utility knife
* Double-sided adhesive tape
* Stud finder – choose one that can wood and metal studs and electric wiring as well
* Mixing bucket
* Small putty knife
* Safety glasses with side protection
* Painting gear: brushes in a range of sizes, rollers, a paint tray, masking tape, drop cloths, paint- stirring sticks, paint scrapers. Beware of buying the cheapest brushes in the store – you'll end up picking bristles off your freshly painted walls.
* For plumbing jobs: selection of faucet washers, thread seal tape, plumber's putty, plumbing lubricant for faucet threads and hose clamps.

It's not worth buying a tool you don't need very often, especially if it's something you can borrow or rent.

Easy fix   When you buy screws, nails or anchors, get a few more than you need for the job at hand. Over time, you will build up a stock of various supplies and you won't have to go to the hardware store every time you need a nail.

Save money   It's not worth buying a tool you don't need very often, such as a hammer drill or an electric sander. There are places that rent tools at reasonable prices and they usually offer free advice on how to use them. They will also deliver larger items that may not fit in your vehicle.

USING TOOLS SAFELY

1 Always wear safety glasses to protect your eyes from flying fragments and liquid splashes. Wear a dust mask when sanding and don't hesitate to put on a pair of earmuffs when working with loud power tools. A sturdy pair of work gloves will protect your hands from cuts and splinters, while disposable gloves will keep paint and varnish off your skin.

2 If you are moving heavy objects around, wear steel-capped boots to protect your feet (especially your toes). If you need to work up high, use a strong, steady ladder. Don't climb up on a chair!

3 Ensure your work area is well lit. If you can't see what you're doing, you run the risk of an accident and you won't do a good job. When using any tool with moving parts (such as a drill), it's essential to tie back long hair and secure loose clothing.

ELECTRIC DRILLS do more than drill holes

An electric drill is the centerpiece of any toolkit. Don't skimp when buying a drill, as you will find it's a versatile tool with a range of attachments so it can be used on all kinds of jobs. Buy a reputable brand with a variable speed setting. You can buy attachments for specific purposes as and when you need them. There are two kinds of chuck (which holds the drill bit) to choose from – keyed chucks, or the more convenient keyless chucks (these allow you to change bits with a twist of the wrist).

✳ Since we commonly use drills to drill holes into masonry walls to attach things using wall plugs, it's worth buying a hammer drill that can do this job easily. The hammer action can be switched off when drilling wood or metal. If you do a lot of jobs that involve drilling into concrete, a powerful rotary hammer drill is an even better option.

> ## Since we commonly use drills to drill holes into masonry walls, it's worth buying a hammer drill.

✳ For drilling small holes in wood or metal, you'll need a set of HSS drill bits in a range of sizes up to 1/6 in. HSS stands for high-speed steel, referring to the material the bits are made of. For larger holes in wood – between 1/16 in. and 1/2 in. in diameter – Forstner bits are ideal. To make much larger holes in wood or sheet metal – a hole in the back of a cabinet to pass cords through, for instance – a holesaw is

the way to go. Brick or stone walls require masonry bits – 5/32, 3/16 and 1/4 in. bits are three good sizes to start with. Use your drill's hammer action when drilling into these materials.

✳ Drilling holes is by no means the only thing you can do with a drill. You can choose from a wide range of attachments designed to fit into a drill chuck that will enable you to take on all kinds of jobs, including grinding discs, polishing wheels, wire brushes and even mixer attachments for stirring paint.

Insider's hack If you have a drilling job that requires a good deal of precision, don't attempt to do it with a handheld drill. Buy a drill stand to hold your power drill steady and clamp the workpiece into position.

TOOL CARE and storage

Make the effort to store your tools appropriately – ideally in a large-enough toolbox to keep everything well organized. If you buy a set of tools in a ready-made kit, this may have a toolbox in which each item has its own place. Additional tools, especially larger items, can be kept outside the box on a set of shelves in your shed or workshop.

✳ Make a habit of cleaning your tools after each time you use them. Your tools will last longer and will always be ready to use the next time you need

THERE ARE TWO KINDS OF DRILL CHUCKS — KEYED AND KEYLESS (SHOWN).

them. To prevent rust, ensure tools are completely dry before putting them away.

✳ From time to time, apply a little spray oil to pliers and cutting tools such as scissors and pruning sheers and spread the oil over the tool with an old rag. Avoid getting oil on wooden parts!

✳ Clean paintbrushes immediately after use. Rinsing under running water is all that's needed for water-based paints. If you are taking a break from painting for an hour or two, you can simply place brushes in a plastic bag or wrap in plastic wrap without rinsing.

✳ If you've caught the DIY bug, why not make yourself a mini-workshop with a set of shelves and an old table for a workbench? Putting a pegboard up on the wall will give you a handy place to hang up most of your tool collection. Make sure the floor of your work area is easy to keep clean. Don't forget: where there's woodwork, there's sawdust.

✳ From there, it's only a small step up to a semi-professional workbench with drawers, compartments and a vise. The only limits are your budget and the amount of space you can spare.

Save time Before you get started on a job, gather together all the little bits and pieces you need (nails, screws, wall plugs) and put them in an old egg carton to keep them organized.

Easy fix Clear plastic organizers with lots of compartments are great for storing nuts, bolts, nails and screws in a way that lets you see what you have at glance. Organizers of this kind are available in various shapes and sizes from hardware stores, discount stores or dollar stores.

Save money Although it's best to use new nuts and bolts, you don't necessarily have to throw away fasteners that have gone a bit rusty. Try putting them in a glass of cola and leaving overnight. Cola drinks contain phosphoric acid, which reacts with iron oxide (rust) to form a stable protective barrier. It's a trick that can give new life to all kinds of rusty old hardware.

IF YOU'VE CAUGHT THE DIY BUG, WHY NOT MAKE YOURSELF A MINI-WORKSHOP?

TAKE CARE

Don't leave saws lying around unprotected as their sharp teeth can easily cause injury. Cut a piece of garden hose to fit your saw blade, slice the hose open lengthwise and put it over the blade to act as a protective cover.

Easy-to-master basic skills

It doesn't take too much skill to hammer a nail into a wall, drill a hole for a wall plug or cut a piece of wood with a saw. With a few simple tips, these are jobs that anyone can master.

NAILS ARE GOOD FOR THINGS THAT AREN'T TOO HEAVY, SUCH AS LIGHTWEIGHT PICTURES.

Nailing how TO HAMMER

Hammering in a nail to hang something on is one of those eternal household jobs – and it's not limited to hanging up (lightweight!) pictures, either. With a nail in the right spot, you can hang up a bunch of herbs to dry or instantly improve the look of a bare expanse of wall with a string of lights. Nails come in every size imaginable. Ordinary steel or galvanized nails are the most common. For specific jobs, you might also use U-shaped staple nails, hooks that can be hammered into the wall or upholstery tacks. Use steel nails to join two pieces of wood together or to attach something to a wooden surface; use galvanized nails to hang a lightweight picture on a wall, or for outside jobs.

✳ Hammering a nail is a quick skill to learn. Practice on an old piece of wood first. Hold the nail carefully between your thumb and index finger and gently tap the nailhead, keeping it as straight as possible to keep it from bending or breaking. When the nail has a firm hold in the surface, take your hand away and hammer it home.

TAKE CARE

Always hold the nail toward the top (or nailhead) when starting to nail, leaving a gap between your fingers and the surface to be nailed. This will reduce the pain if you miss the nail and hit your fingers accidentally.

Easy fix If there is nowhere to put loose nails down safely while you're doing a job, use a piece of double-sided adhesive tape to stick them somewhere within easy reach.

SCREWS of all shapes and sizes

Browsing through hardware stores, you'll find that there are several things to consider when deciding which type of screw to buy. Apart from the size (diameter and length) and the material (steel, brass, etc.), there is also a variety of different screw-head shapes to choose from – round, countersunk and domed to name just a few.

✳ Then there is the type of screwdriver a screw is made to be used with – flathead, Phillips head, hex head (or Allen wrench) – and the type of thread, ranging from threads that are designed to be used with a nut to threads for wood, sheet metal or particleboard that are designed to cut their way into the material.

✳ When it comes to nuts, the choice is simpler. Most importantly, the nut has to be the right size to fit the screw or bolt. In addition to ordinary nuts, there are lock nuts that resist coming loose (typically with an inner nylon sleeve), wing nuts that are easy to tighten and undo by hand, and dome nuts that cover the end of the bolt to keep things clean and prevent injury.

✳ Always choose the appropriate screw for the job and use a screwdriver that fits snugly to avoid damaging the screw head. If you wreck the screw head, it's very hard to get a grip with a screwdriver and the screw can be a real pain to remove.

It's very easy to wreck the screw head if you use a screwdriver that doesn't fit snugly. Once the damage is done, the screw can be a real pain to remove.

✳ A multi-bit screwdriver is an especially useful tool. It comes with a set of interchangeable tips designed to fit a variety of screw heads. It gives you many screwdrivers in the one tool, reducing the chances of damaging a screw head with an ill-fitting screwdriver.

HAMMER A NAIL, NOT YOURSELF

Most of us have had the unpleasant experience of missing the nail and hitting our finger instead. It can be enough to turn you off ever picking up a hammer again. But here's a simple trick to take the pain out of hammering in a nail.

1 Take a piece of stiff cardboard and cut a strip about 4 in. x 1 in. in size.

2 Cut a slit in one end of the cardboard strip and insert a nail through the slit.

3 Use the strip to hold the nail in position and hammer it in – gentle taps to begin, then firmer strokes to drive the nail home.

✳ Get a screw started by turning it by hand, then use an appropriate screwdriver. Give screws a quick rub with a bar of soap before using to reduce the amount of force needed to screw them in.

✳ If you are fastening something with a number of screws, put each screw in and tighten gently. Once all the screws are in place, tighten them all firmly. Doing it this way makes it easier to get all the screws lined up with their screw holes and allows you to make last-minute adjustments.

Expert advice

Remove seized screws

It's a real annoyance when a screw won't budge. Here are a few things you can try, depending on what's causing the problem:

★ If the screw is rusty, a squirt of penetrating oil such as WD-40 will often help. Give the oil a few minutes to work.

★ If a screw head has been damaged, try turning the screw with a pair of combination pliers. Take care as the pliers can easily slip or, if the screw is fixed in tight, the head may break off completely.

★ If the head of a Phillips or hex screw has worn to the point where you can't get a grip with a screwdriver, try grinding a slot across the screw head that will then allow you to use a flathead screwdriver instead.

★ If all else fails, the screw can be drilled out.

WITH A MULTI-BIT SCREWDRIVER, YOU WILL ALWAYS HAVE THE RIGHT SIZE SCREWDRIVER ON HAND.

Easy fix Before undoing any screws that you are going to need again, have a container ready to put them in. If you just put them down anywhere, it's easy for one or two to get lost and you'll have a hard time finding them again.

Insider's hack To make wood screws hold even more securely, dip them in wood adhesive before screwing them in.

Don't be afraid TO DRILL

If you take proper care, a power drill is not a difficult tool to use. Always make sure the drill bit is securely tightened in the chuck. Use general-purpose HSS drill bits to pre-drill holes for wood screws. If you need to make a larger hole (1/4 in. or more), it's a good idea to start with a smaller bit to drill a pilot hole, which will then serve as a guide for the larger drill bit. Starting with a smaller bit also makes it easier to correct any mistakes you might make.

✳ Another common use for a drill around the home is to drill holes in masonry walls to fasten things using anchors. For this, you will need to use a masonry bit and your drill's hammer action. Before you begin, use a stud finder to make absolutely sure that there are no pipes or electrical wiring where you intend to drill.

✳ The drill bit you use should match the size of the plug – use a 3/16 in. drill bit for a 3/16 in. plug. Choose screws to suit the length of the plug. The diameter of the screws should be such that you can easily screw them in by hand about a quarter of the way into the plug, but no further than that.

The drill bit you use should match the size of the plug – use a 3/16 in. drill bit for a 3/16 in. plug.

✳ Drilling creates a lot of dust. If you have carpet, cover the floor below where you intend to drill or, better yet, ask a helper to hold the vacuum cleaner nozzle underneath where you drill to catch most of the drill dust as it's being created.

✳ Use a pencil to clearly mark the spot where you want to drill. Make a cross rather than a small dot – that way you will still be able to see your mark even if the drill slips on initial contact.

✳ Always keep the drill perpendicular to the wall. Start on a low speed and then increase it. If you are pre-drilling with a smaller bit, take care when changing bits as they are likely to be quite hot immediately after use.

✳ Drill to a depth about 20 percent further than the length of the anchor to allow for any drill dust that may get pushed to the end of the hole. Take one of the screws you intend to use and insert it into the hole to check the depth. Don't use an anchor for this purpose – once an anchor is pushed into a hole, it's designed not to come back out again.

Easy fix You can remove old anchors with a pair of needle-nose pliers. Grip the plug with one point of the pliers inserted into the center and the other on its outer surface. Rotate the anchor as you pull it out.

KEEP AWAY FROM ELECTRICAL WIRING

1 When drilling into existing walls, you want be sure to avoid electrical wiring. Invest in a high-quality live wire detector. Good ones can be pricey but it's well worth the money as they are much more precise and are also able to detect plastic pipes and wood studs. Look for one at hardware and home improvement stores.

2 Place the stud finder with wire tracing mode onto the wall. Flip the switch on the stud finder to "AC" mode. Move the finder along the wall, with the front towards you and the flat side against the wall. Some will have a small meter that will begin to show voltage as the stud finder gets close, others will have several lights that begin to light up.

3 Move the stud finder over the electrical wires. On metered finders, when they are exactly over the wire, the meter will read 120 volts, or 220 if you are in the vicinity of appliance wires such as the stove. A stud finder that uses a light band will show all the lights becoming illuminated when the stud finder is directly over the wire. If you move slightly to the left or right of the wire, one of the lights will go out.

4 Mark the precise location of the found wire with a marker, then use that mark as a reference to avoid that area when drilling.

IF YOU NEED TO DRILL INTO A TILED WALL, IT'S PREFERABLE TO CHOOSE A POSITION THAT MEANS YOU DRILL THROUGH THE GROUT BETWEEN THE TILES.

＊ Stick a piece of masking tape over the spot where you intend to drill. You can mark the spot directly on the tape and it will prevent the drill bit from skidding around on the glazed surface of the tile.

＊ With a hammer and nail, make a small mark on the tile surface. Start drilling on low speed, then increase the speed as you go. Apply gentle pressure and don't use the hammer action on the drill.

＊ If you rent, you should check with your landlord before drilling holes in the wall. It goes without saying that you will be responsible for any damage you cause, such as broken tiles or punctured pipes.

Insider's hack If you're drilling a hole overhead, cut a tennis ball in half and place it over the drill bit to catch most of the drill dust. And don't forget to wear safety glasses!

Insider's hack If you don't have a helper on hand to catch drill dust with the vacuum cleaner, use adhesive tape to stick a coffee filter to the wall just below the spot where you are drilling.

Save money If you want to drill a hole to a precise depth, there's no need to buy a special accessory for your drill. Simply wrap a piece of masking tape around the drill bit to mark the desired length.

ANCHORS, toggle bolts and other hardware

Now that you have drilled the hole to the right depth, it's time to insert an anchor. The modern wall anchor is an ingenious invention. As a screw works its way into an anchor, it forces the anchor to spread apart. Toggle bolts come with the screw (or bolt)

DRILL THROUGH TILES successfully

If you need to drill into a tiled wall, it's preferable to choose a position that means you drill through the grout between the tiles. Provided that the grout channel is wider than the hole you want to drill, you will always be able to conceal the hole again with fresh grout.

＊ Sometimes you won't be able to avoid drilling through a tile. To minimize the risk of cracking, avoid drilling too close to the edge of the tile.

TAKE CARE

Don't attempt to drill into stoneware or natural stone tiles. They are simply too hard for an ordinary masonry bit.

already in place. Under normal loads, the anchor resists being pulled back out of the wall. As well as keeping a grip on the wall, it also holds the screw firmly in place, preventing it from being pulled loose. The screw can only be removed by unscrewing in a counter-clockwise direction.

✳ For brick, stone or concrete walls, use plastic anchors. If you can't push the anchor in with your thumb, give it a gentle tap with a hammer, using a piece of cardboard to prevent marks on the wall if necessary. Finally, fasten an appropriately sized screw. Tug on the screw to make sure it has a secure hold before you put a load on it.

✳ For drywall, there are special plugs and anchors to suit different situations. The right type of plug for the job will depend on the particular composition of your wall.

ADHESIVES are a good option

In some situations, an adhesive can be a better option than using screws. Generally speaking, it's harder to take things apart again once they have been joined together with adhesive, but there are some exceptions to this rule, for example reusable adhesive tapes and strips.

✳ The type of adhesive to use will depend on the materials being joined and the load to be supported.

For some jobs, such as gluing pieces of cardboard together, an all-purpose adhesive is fine. Simply apply a thin layer of adhesive to both surfaces, wait a minute or two, then press together.

✳ Use wood adhesive to join two pieces of wood together. Hold the pieces firmly together with a screw or clutch clamp until the adhesive has dried.

✳ In most cases, you'll want to use a special-purpose adhesive designed for the material you are working with. There are adhesives to suit hard plastics, metal, fabric, wallpaper, polystyrene, and so on. No matter what the material, make sure the surfaces to be bonded are clean, dry and free of grease or oil, and always follow the directions.

✳ Alongside conventional solvent-based adhesive, there are reactive adhesives, which develop their bond strength through a chemical reaction. Two-part epoxy adhesives, for example, consist of a resin and a hardener that need to be mixed together thoroughly before being applied.

✳ Superglue sets very quickly and has a high bond strength. Its adhesive properties arise through a

CHOOSE FROM A VARIETY OF PLUGS AND ANCHORS TO SUIT DIFFERENT SITUATIONS.

chemical reaction that occurs in the presence of moisture. Superglue works best when there is a reasonable amount of contact surface; it is less effective on smooth surfaces.

✳ Another way to achieve strong adhesive bonds is with a hot-glue gun, which works with adhesives that melt when heated. Glue guns are loaded with sticks of solid glue. They should only be used on materials that can withstand high temperatures.

Save time When using a two-part adhesive, applying a hairdryer to the bond can speed up the setting process. Ensure the two parts are perfectly aligned – there's no going back once the glue has set.

THE RIGHT SAW for every material

When you need to cut a piece of wood or pipe to length, reach for a saw. A small handsaw can cut wood, plastic and even lightweight pieces of metal.

✳ For heavier wood beams, use a larger handsaw or an electric circular saw (not recommended for beginners). Another option is to get the hardware store to cut your wood to size for you.

✳ For smaller woodwork jobs, a backsaw has a broad blade with fine teeth and a stiffening rib along the top, which helps to make a nice straight cut.

✳ To join two pieces of wood at a right angle, you need to cut them both at an angle of exactly 45°. A miter box, made of wood or plastic, has slots cut into its sides that provide a guide for a saw to cut a piece of wood at an angle of exactly 90° or 45° to the left, right or diagonal. To ensure a clean cut, clamp the wood firmly in place before you begin. The result will be a perfect miter joint with the two pieces fitting together smoothly.

✳ Use a hacksaw for cutting larger metal objects. It has a thin blade with finer teeth than a wood saw.

✳ An electric jigsaw with a set of blades for different materials is a handy tool for a range of cutting jobs. But it's only worth investing in one if you're going to use it frequently.

✳ A jigsaw is ideal to cut shapes out of plywood, particleboard or MDF. If you wish to cut a section or shape out of the middle of the sheet, start by drilling a hole large enough to accommodate the jigsaw blade, insert the blade and start your cut.

Insider's hack Always hold the object you are cutting securely in place with clamps or a vise. This is especially important if you are using power tools.

AN ELECTRIC JIGSAW WITH A SET OF BLADES FOR DIFFERENT MATERIALS IS A HANDY TOOL FOR A RANGE OF CUTTING JOBS.

The CORKSCREW is a great all-round tool

In the late 18th century, when it was becoming increasingly common to put wine in corked bottles rather than barrels, the Englishman Samuel Henshall invented the corkscrew. In its basic form, a corkscrew is a metal spiral that has a handle. Today, just about every home has one – and there's a lot more this simple device can do besides opening bottles of wine.

EASIER DRILLING

When attempting to drill into hard materials, power drills have a tendency to skitter around on the surface. To prevent this, use the point of a corkscrew to make a preliminary indentation on the surface that will help the tip of your drill get a better grip.

EXTRACTING WALL ANCHORS

Twist the corkscrew into the plug far enough to get a firm grip, then gently pull the anchor out of the wall.

TIME TO PULL THE PLUG

If a rubber plug gets stuck in the plughole of your bathtub or sink, boring through it with a corkscrew will get it out in no time.

UNTYING KNOTS

The sharp point of a corkscrew can be very handy when untying stubborn knots in a piece of string or a shoelace.

BLOCKED NOZZLES

It's common for the nozzle of a tube of caulk to get blocked when the caulk dries and hardens on contact with the air. A corkscrew is a quick and easy way to clear the blockage.

Fix problems with your plumbing

Running water is a modern convenience that cannot be valued highly enough. It's important to know what to do when the water in your home stops flowing the way it should, keeps running when it shouldn't, or fails to drain away properly.

Solve problems with FAUCETS

As mysterious as the miracle of running water may seem, the pipework that brings water to our faucets is usually not all that complicated. Any time you intend to do a job involving the pipes that bring water into your home, remember to turn off the supply to the area you are working on. Anticipate that some water will run out of the pipes and have cloths ready to soak it up.

Change a FAUCET WASHER

A dripping faucet is annoying. It wastes water and (if it's a hot-water faucet) also energy. In traditional faucets, a faulty washer is the most common cause.

WHEN A FAUCET IS DRIPPING, IT'S USUALLY ONLY A FAULTY WASHER.

✳ First, turn off the water valve or, if there is one, the valve for the branch pipe you are going to be working on. Remove the faucet handle, then use a wrench to undo the top part of the faucet, also known as the spindle. The washer, which consists of a rubber seal fixed onto a brass stem, is located at the bottom of the spindle. In some cases, the washer will be held onto the spindle with a retaining screw. With the spindle removed, wipe out the faucet seat to ensure it is free of dirt and minerals. If necessary, use a descaling product to remove minerals build-up from the faucet.

✳ Insert a new washer into the spindle (take the old washer with you to the hardware store to ensure your new one is the right size). Then put the faucet back together, applying a little plumbing lubricant (also available from hardware stores) to the threads to keep them from seizing up.

Easy fix Save yourself the effort of repairing old faucets. With age, the inner workings of a faucet can become brittle and encrusted with scale. Once it gets to this stage, it's better to replace the faucet completely.

Save money If a faucet is jammed shut, try pouring club soda over it. It contains small quantities of carbonic acid to help to loosen up rust and other forms of corrosion. Leave for 10 minutes, then gently tap the handle of the faucet with a rubber mallet to get it moving again.

A SHOWERHEAD WITH A HEAVY BUILD-UP OF SCALE SHOULD BE CLEANED OR, BETTER YET, REPLACED.

TOILET TANK problems

There are a few things that can go wrong with your toilet tank:

✳ If water keeps running from the tank into the bowl, it's possible that the sealing washer on the outlet valve of the tank needs to be replaced. Remove the outlet valve, check the black rubber washer on the bottom, and replace if necessary.

✳ If you have an older-style tank with a float ball, the ball may have developed a leak. It may then fill with water and no longer be able to rise to cut off the inlet valve, resulting in a continual flow of water from the tank into the bowl. A temporary solution is to remove the float ball, empty the water inside, dry it off and repair the leak with packing tape.

✳ If the toilet won't flush even though the tank is full, the flush lever may have become disconnected or broken off completely. Remove the lid to see what's going on. If the lever has come loose, simply reconnect it; if it has broken, it's probably better to replace it than try to repair it.

Change a SHOWERHEAD

If you live in a hard-water area, you will need to descale your showerhead or hand shower from time to time. If there is a heavy build-up of scale, it may be better to replace the showerhead completely – a lot of scale is a sign your showerhead has done quite a few years of service and the cost of a replacement is not astronomical. Most hardware stores have a range of decent-looking models to choose from.

✳ Turn off the shower faucets and loosen the showerhead using an open-ended spanner or a pair of tongue and groove pliers with a cloth to prevent

Expert advice

Patch a burst pipe while waiting for the plumber

If a water pipe starts leaking, you need to act quickly (see also page 271, "Deal with water damage"). The first thing you need to do is turn off the water supply as soon as you possibly can. But if you need water before the plumber arrives, here is how to patch

up a pipe temporarily. A piece of garden hose or bicycle inner tube cut open lengthwise can do the job. Wrap it around the broken pipe several times and secure it with hose clamps – you should always keep a few of these around the house. If you're desperate, several layers of packing tape can also work as a temporary fix.

IF YOU CAN'T LOOSEN THE NUTS ON THE SINK TRAP BY HAND, USE A PAIR OF TONGUE AND GROOVE PLIERS.

scratching the chrome finish. You may have to apply a fair amount of force to get it loose, especially if the thread is encrusted with scale. Unscrew the showerhead all the way (taking care not to drop it). Wipe the thread clean, wrap with plumber's sealing tape and screw on the new showerhead firmly.

✳ If you would rather keep your old showerhead and want to descale it, see page 44, "Descale a showerhead or faucet aerator."

Clear a BLOCKED DRAIN

You've pulled the plug out and checked that the sink strainer is free of debris, but still the water won't go down. The first thing to try is a plunger. Place the rubber bell over the plughole and pump the handle up and down. Often this is enough to clear the blockage. If you succeed in getting the sink to drain again, allow the faucet to run for a while to give the pipes a good flush through.

✳ If a plunger doesn't do the job, put a bucket under the drain and loosen the two large slip nuts on the U-shaped odor trap. If you are not able to loosen the nuts by hand, use a pair of tongue and groove pliers, opening the jaws wide and applying the gentlest possible pressure. Be cautious, as water may gush out into the bucket. If the trap is clogged, use a bottle brush to clean it out, give it a good rinse then screw it back into place.

✳ If it's not the sink strainer or the odor trap that's causing the problem, the blockage is somewhere further along the drain pipe. With the trap removed, try feeding a drain-cleaning snake into the pipe to clear the blockage. If this doesn't work, it's time to call a plumber.

Easy fix A piece of coat-hanger wire can be very handy for cleaning out a blocked drain. If you bend the end of the wire into a small hook, you can use it to fish things out of the drain. Wrap a few layers of double-sided adhesive tape around the end and you can use the wire to pick up dirt or retrieve a small object such as a hairpin or a dropped screw.

BLOCKED TOILET emergency!

If water won't go down the toilet, first try using a toilet plunger to solve the problem. Place the plunger over the drain hole and pump the handle up and down vigorously. In most cases, the water will drain away in a rush. Flush the toilet two or three times. If the water level only goes down slightly, try using the plunger again.

✳ If this doesn't solve the problem, you can try using a drain-cleaning snake, available from hardware stores. Before you begin, you need to bail all the water out of the toilet bowl. Put on a pair of long rubber gloves before tackling this task. Slide the drain snake in with a rotating motion until you encounter resistance. Continue pushing and rotating until the snake works its way through the blockage and the water drains away. If you are not able to solve the problem with this technique, you will need to call in a plumber as the problem is likely to be more serious.

Damage to floors and walls

Dirty marks on walls and damage to wood or carpet floors are common household mishaps. But fixing minor problems like these can be just as easy a job as stopping a door hinge from squeaking.

Patch up a WOOD FLOOR

Scratches and dents in wood or laminate floors can be patched up with wood filler in an appropriate color. Available from hardware stores, this typically comes in a tub often with a small tool for applying it. There are also more elaborate wax repair kits that come with several colors of wax, a device to melt the wax and a tool to smooth down the excess.

⁎ Ensure the damaged area is clean and dry, then fill it with your chosen filler material. Lay a piece of plastic wrap over the top to protect your fingers and press down firmly on the filler to ensure it gets a good hold on the rough surface of the damaged area. Use a plastic tool to smooth down the surface.

⁎ Allow the product time to set as specified in the directions, then sand if necessary. Some floor surfaces will need to be finished with a clear sealant such as polyurethane – if possible, be guided by the manufacturer's advice here. If you want to apply a sealant, look out for touch-up pens that allow you to apply a small amount conveniently.

Repair a CONCRETE STEP

It's not uncommon for small pieces to chip off the edges of concrete steps. If your steps are very old, larger chips can occur, especially if you live in a frost-prone area where water can seep in through cracks then freeze and shatter the concrete. Wear work gloves and safety glasses when working with concrete. Put a barricade across the stairs to eliminate the risk of people accidentally tripping over the form or stepping on wet concrete.

⁎ If the broken surface is smooth, rough it up with a hammer and a cold chisel, making grooves to allow the repair material to get a good grip. Clear away any loose pieces of concrete and dust. Apply a concrete-priming product designed to promote adhesion and allow it to soak in to the surface.

⁎ Build up your form with boards. A single board pressed against the vertical face of the step and fastened temporarily in place will usually do the job. If you are repairing the corner of a step, you will need to use two boards fastened together at a right

TO PATCH UP A WOOD FLOOR, ALL YOU NEED IS A TUB OF WOOD FILLER AND A SUITABLE TOOL.

DON'T SETTLE FOR A REPLACEMENT TILE THAT'S ONLY AN APPROXIMATE MATCH TO YOUR EXISTING TILES.

Replace a CRACKED TILE

A cracked wall or floor tile is unsightly. Any time you lay new tiles, it pays to keep aside a few spare tiles to allow for future repairs. For this job you will need: a hammer, chisel, scraper, square-notch adhesive spreader, tile adhesive, grout in a color to match the existing grout, grout squeegee and sponge.

✳ Use a hammer and chisel to remove the damaged tile, taking care not to damage any of the adjacent tiles. Always work from the center of the tile toward the edges. Remove all the remnant tile

angle. Reinforce the area to be repaired by driving two screws into the step before applying fresh concrete over the top.

✳ Fill the damaged area with patching concrete or a concrete mix using 2 parts portland cement: 8 parts fine aggregate: 1 part water. Press in firmly with a trowel and smooth down the surface. Allow plenty of curing time before removing the form.

REPAIR CARPET

Damage to a carpeted floor need not be a total disaster if you have a spare piece for a patch. Patching is not recommended for older carpets as the new piece will stand out too much. For a professional-looking result, you will need: a carpet knife, carpet adhesive, seaming tape and a hammer.

1 Cut out a square of carpet around the damaged area and cut a patch of new carpet to match the size. Apply a small amount of carpet adhesive around the edge of the cut-out area.

2 Stick carpet seaming tape around the edges of the cut-out square. Peel the backing off the tape to expose the adhesive surface.

3 Align the patch of new carpet with the cut-out square, press it down onto the seaming tape and tap around the edges with a hammer to secure it into position.

adhesive and grout surrounding the tile you have removed. Use a scraper tool to ensure the prepared surface is smooth and clean, then use a vacuum cleaner to get rid of any dust.

✳ Apply tile adhesive to the surface with a square-notch adhesive spreader and put the new tile in place, ensuring it is aligned perfectly with the surrounding tiles both horizontally and vertically, and that the gaps are even on all sides. Press firmly on the tile to ensure the adhesive gets a good grip. Leave overnight for the adhesive to set.

✳ The next day, mix up the grout according to the package directions and use a squeegee to push it into the gaps around the new tile – diagonal strokes are best. Once the grout starts to set, clean off the surface of the tiles with a damp sponge.

Easy fix If your tiles were laid a long time ago and you don't have any spares, look online for dealers that specialize in old or discontinued stock. Don't give up! There may be a match for your classic 1960s tiles out there somewhere.

Insider's hack Don't settle for a replacement tile that is only an approximate match to your existing ones; for example, an ivory-colored tile when what you really need is beige. A better solution is to create an accent by adding a patch of mosaic tiles in a contrasting color. In fact, why not turn adversity into opportunity by taking out an entire row of tiles and replacing it with a decorative mosaic border?

Invisible WALLPAPER REPAIRS

It may be possible to conceal minor damage to wallpaper with a touch of paint, but, if not, you will need to replace a section of the wallpaper. If you've kept a few spare pieces the last time you replaced the wallpaper, you're halfway home. Otherwise, you'll have to replace the wallpaper on at least that wall. Unlike tiles, it's virtually impossible to track down old or discontinued wallpaper. Although some brands of wallpaper may have styles that

IF YOU'VE KEPT A FEW SPARE PIECES WHEN YOU WALLPAPERED, YOU'RE HALFWAY HOME.

remain on the market for many years, it is likely there will be a noticeable color difference between a new roll and wallpaper that has been up on the wall for a while.

✳ Assuming you have a suitable leftover piece for the job, cut out a rectangular piece slightly larger than the section to be replaced, taking care to ensure that the pattern will line up with what's on the wall. Position the replacement piece over the damaged area and run a sharp utility knife around the edge to cut out an identical-sized piece of the underlying wallpaper. Dampen the damaged section, then carefully use a scraper to remove it, re-dampening as necessary.

✳ Use a broad, soft brush to apply wallpaper paste to the replacement piece and stick it over the hole. Use a small paint roller (available from hardware stores) to press the edges down firmly.

CAULK IS REMARKABLY RESILIENT, BUT OVER TIME IT CAN START TO LOOK WORSE FOR WEAR.

Insider's hack Work quickly as patching compound sets within about 5–10 minutes. Be sure to keep the compound sealed tightly, otherwise it will dry out and be useless for future projects.

REFRESH CAULK
in the bathroom

Caulk is a remarkably resilient material but, over time, caulk can start to look worse for wear (especially in areas prone to mold). You will need to remove and replace it.

✳ Start by removing the old caulk and any dirt adhering to it. It pays to be thorough because if any of the old caulk is left behind it will prevent the new bead from adhering properly. You can follow up with a chemical caulk remover, but ensure that the area is well ventilated. Give the entire area plenty of time to dry out completely.

✳ Apply masking tape along both sides of the gap to be sealed. Put down a sheet of plastic or some old newspaper to keep caulk from ending up where it's not wanted.

✳ Once you have applied the caulk, wait a few minutes for it to develop a firm skin, then carefully remove the masking tape. If there are any untidy edges, use your finger, dipped in soapy water, to smooth them down.

Insider's hack With a bit of practice, you can apply caulk freehand, smoothing down the caulk with a finishing tool after spraying with soapy water. The downside of masking tape is that pulling it off can create tiny gaps between the caulk and the underlying surface. These gaps provide a great environment for mold spores to grow in.

PATCH HOLES in the wall

Dents, dings and nail holes are part of owning a home. You can repair them with these easy tips. Put down a sheet of plastic or some old newspaper to protect the floor beneath the work area. Use prepared self-primed patching compound to fill holes. For small drill or nail holes, make dent over the holes by pressing and twisting the handle of a putty knife into the hole. For larger holes, look for a patching kit that includes stick-on mesh patches. Place the patch over the hole before applying the compound.

✳ Press the compound firmly into the hole and use the putty knife to smooth over the surface. Leave it for a few minutes then brush over the area with a wet brush. This ensures that the patch will be virtually invisible once it dries.

FRESH PAINT over
drywall or wallpaper

A fresh coat of paint, whether applied directly to drywall or over existing wallpaper, makes a room feel a lot cleaner and more inviting. Modern water-based latex paints make painting easier than ever and they are available in just about any color you can imagine.

✳ Before painting, check your walls for holes, cracks and peeling paint, and remedy any problems you find. Use painter's drop cloths to protect the floor. Many do-it-yourselfers use plastic sheets but these don't do nearly as a good a job. Proper drop cloths don't tear easily, they absorb splotches of paint, they are not slippery and they are not that expensive to buy.

✳ Apply painter's tape around the doors and windows and along the top of baseboards. Remove the plastic covers from light switches and electrical

TAKE CARE

Be careful when painting around outlets. With the plastic cover removed, it's easy for paint to get inside and compromise your safety.

outlets, and protect their inner parts with painter's tape. Use a sturdy ladder if you need to reach up high and wear appropriate clothing, including a solid pair of closed shoes.

✳ Start by painting the edges and corners of the room with a brush. Then switch to a roller and a paint tray. Apply just a small amount of paint to the roller each time, rolling it back and forth over the rippled section of the tray to ensure it's evenly loaded. Apply the paint to the wall, first with

APPLY CAULK

Before you begin, thoroughly clean the area to be caulked and leave it to dry. You will need: caulk tube and applicator gun, water sprayer filled with soapy water (use dishwashing liquid), craft stick, old towel and a utility knife.

1 Place the tube in the gun and cut off the tip to release a silicone bead about 3/16 in. in diameter. Apply the caulk in a continuous bead in about 3 ft. lengths to start.

2 Lightly spray the bead with soapy water, taking care not to wet any surfaces to which caulk is yet to be applied. Start at the bottom and work upwards if you are working on a vertical corner.

3 Smooth the bead with the curved edge of the craft stick held at almost a right angle to the surface. Wipe the caulk off the stick onto a piece of towel. Leave to cure for 72 hours.

horizontal strokes then straight, vertical ones. Finish one area before moving on to the next.

✳ If the color of the new paint makes it hard to tell which areas you have painted, adjust the lighting in the room to help you see the sheen of the wet paint, or if there is wallpaper on the surface, use the edges of each sheet to keep track of your progress. Avoid drips in the surface, which are usually caused by applying too much paint.

✳ If the new paint doesn't completely conceal the previous color with a single coat, wait a few hours then apply a second coat. In some cases, a third coat may be required, especially if the previous color was quite dark. When you are finished, ensure the paint can is properly closed and wash your brush and roller out thoroughly under running water.

WATER-BASED LATEX PAINTS ARE AVAILABLE IN JUST ABOUT ANY COLOR YOU CAN IMAGINE.

Save time The smell of fresh paint can hang around for quite some time. You can help get rid of the smell by placing two halves of a freshly cut onion in opposite corners of the room. Chemicals in the onion will help absorb the odor of latex paint and in one or two days it will be completely gone.

Easy fix If you want to come back to a painting job the next day, you can wrap your paint roller tightly in aluminium foil or plastic wrap overnight.

Insider's hack Mix paint by carefully turning over the can a few times and stirring with a wooden stirrer before each use, as the color pigments quickly settle to the bottom of the can.

Save money Large S-shaped hooks, available from hardware stores, are handy for hanging paint buckets on a ladder.

Fix a SCRAPING DOOR

Over the years, a door's hinges can wear or its wood can change shape to the point where the door starts to scrape on the floor. While this may seem minor, it's a problem that you need to address promptly to prevent serious damage to the floor.

✳ If the door is fitted with "slip joint" hinges you'll be able to fix this problem yourself. Estimate how many millimeters the door needs to be raised, keeping in mind the space between the top of the door and the doorframe. Take the door off its hinges and measure the diameter of the hinge pins (vertical metal shafts around which each hinge pivots).

TAKE CARE

Taking a door off its hinges is not a job to tackle on your own. Get someone to help you, especially when it comes to putting the door safely back in place.

* Buy spacer washers that fit perfectly over the hinge pins and that match the hinges in appearance. Place the spacers over the hinge pins and hang the door back on its hinges. Check to ensure the door swings freely without scraping.

* If the door is fitted with "butt" hinges, then repair is much more difficult and specialized, and is best left to a qualified carpenter.

Silence SQUEAKY HINGES

A squeaky, creaky hinge on that door or fence gate can really get on your nerves. With a spray of oil or a dab of grease, it's an easy problem to solve.

* Lubricate the hinges with Vaseline or grease, or spray them with penetrating oil such as WD-40, taking care to protect the adjacent wall and carpet. Swing the door back and forth a couple of times to spread the lubricant. The hinges should now open and close silently.

Save time When you don't have oil on hand, you can stop a door from squeaking in an instant by applying a squirt of shaving cream to the hinges.

Change a DOOR KNOB OR HANDLE

If a doorknob or handle is no longer doing its job properly, replacing it with a new one is not a difficult task. It's best to remove the old handles and take them with you to help choose a new set.

* If you choose hardware that are a different size or shape to your old doorknob set, bear in mind that you will need to drill holes in different positions and patch the existing holes with filler, and then repaint the area, before you start.

* If your old set had a one-piece faceplate (with the handle and keyhole on a single metal plate), it's easiest if you choose a new set that also has a one-piece plate, with the new plate slightly larger than the old one so that it completely covers the mark left on the door by the old hardware. The distance between the doorknob and keyhole on

YOUR NEW DOORKNOB OR HANDLE SET MAY HAVE SCREW HOLES IN DIFFERENT POSITIONS FROM YOUR OLD SET.

hardware of this type is standardized (although antique fixtures may vary from this standard).

* Choosing a set with separate plates for the handle and keyhole will involve more work as the entire door will need to be refinished to remove the marks left behind by the old one-piece faceplate.

* Once you have chosen your new doorknob set, you're ready to get started. Look for a small screw that keeps the handle on one side of the door in place – it will often be on the underside of the handle. Remove the screw and remove the screws that hold the faceplate onto the door. Now pull the handles away from the door – one will have a square shaft, the other a matching square slot with a screw hole for the screw that holds the handle onto the shaft.

* Assemble the new faceplates and knobs the correct way to suit your door, then install the handles by inserting the shaft through the door and into the handle on the other side. Ensure the faceplates are straight and fasten with wood screws to the door. Use a thin drill bit to pre-drill holes for the screws. Press the loose handle firmly against the door and secure it with its little screw or split.

Marks on furniture

Our valuable furniture often has to weather a lot of rough-and-tumble, especially when there are children or pets at home. The good news is that you can repair minor scuffs and scratches without too much trouble.

SCRATCHES AND CRACKS in wood

A scratch or stain on a polished wood surface is a real nuisance. But if the damage is not too deep, it's an easy problem to solve. Fine scratches on polished wood can usually be removed with a soft cloth and furniture polish in an appropriate color. To finish, polish with a dry cloth to restore an even shine to the surface.

✳ For slightly deeper scratches, you can use a plastic scouring pad. These are gentler than sandpaper, which can strip off a wood finish in seconds. Start by thoroughly cleaning the area with the scouring pad, always working in the direction of the grain. Apply furniture oil such as hardwax to an old piece of cotton such as a bed sheet and saturate the area by dabbing repeatedly. Allow the oil to soak in for a few minutes before wiping away the excess with paper towel or a soft cloth.

REMOVE FINE SCRATCHES ON POLISHED FURNITURE WITH A SOFT CLOTH.

SMALL DENTS IN WOOD FURNITURE CAN BE FILLED WITH CANDLE WAX.

✳ Even larger scratches and cracks still can be repaired with wax filler, using an applicator that comes with the product. Take care to choose a filler that matches the color of your furniture. It's also possible to knead different colored waxes together to create just the right color. The wax comes in sticks that you warm slightly with your hands before use. Use the applicator tool to take a small amount of wax and press it into the damaged area. Smooth down the surface and use a soft cloth to remove any excess right away. Clean the applicator while the wax is still soft.

Easy fix Small dents in inconspicuous locations can be filled with candle wax. Choose a candle to match the color of your furniture – but be aware that some colored candles are white in the middle. Light the candle and allow wax to drip into the dent. Beeswax, which can also be melted in a small pot, is good for light-colored wood. Give the wax a minute or two to cool down and begin to solidify, then press it in firmly with your finger and smooth down the surface.

Save money Conceal fine scratches in dark wood furniture by rubbing damp coffee grounds into the area.

Wax filler for repairing wood comes in a wide range of colors, which can be kneaded together to create just the right color.

Re-glue a CHAIR LEG

A wobbly chair leg is most likely caused by a loose joint between one of the legs and the frame that supports the seat of the chair. On older chairs, this joint is often made with a mortise and tenon, with one piece of wood slotting into the other; on newer chairs, legs are attached to the frame using wooden dowel pins inserted into holes and held firm with adhesive. A wobbly leg is a sign that fresh adhesive needs to be applied to the joint.

✳ Start by separating the two parts of the chair. If they don't come apart easily, use a hammer with a piece of scrap wood to protect the surface.

✳ Thoroughly clean all the contact surfaces of the joint (the mortise and tenon or the dowels and drill holes) by scratching or sanding off all the old adhesive. If possible, replace the old dowels, pulling them out with a pair of combination pliers and tapping in new ones with a hammer.

✳ Apply wood adhesive to the contact surfaces of both pieces and join them together. The grooved surface of the dowels will need a generous amount of glue. Once you have joined the two pieces together, use a damp cloth to immediately wipe away any adhesive that gets squeezed out.

✳ For the wood adhesive to make a secure bond, you need to clamp the pieces together while the adhesive is drying. Use a large clutch clamp to secure the chair and leave the clamp in place for several hours until the adhesive has dried. To prevent the clamp from leaving marks on the wood, place sturdy cardboard or thin wood scraps between the clamp and the chair.

✳ If it seems as though regular wood adhesive is not holding, or if you want the chair to be especially sturdy, use a polyurethane adhesive for additional bond strength.

Insider's hack If the glued joints of a chair have failed a number of times, this indicates there is a fundamental design problem. You can reinforce the critical areas using small angle brackets that you simply screw into place. Pre-drill holes with a small drill bit to prevent the wood from splitting.

REINFORCE CRITICAL AREAS OF YOUR CHAIR USING SMALL ANGLE BRACKETS THAT SCREW IN PLACE.

ONCE THE FILLER HAS SET, SAND IT DOWN, STARTING WITH COARSE SANDPAPER THEN SWITCHING TO FINE FOR A SMOOTH FINISH.

FILL AND SAND wood

With a suitable-colored wood filler, you can easily repair holes up to 1/4 in. in size in your wood doors, doorframes, window frames, windowsills, baseboards, and so on. The ideal time to do this is right before giving woodwork a fresh coat of oil, varnish, stain or paint.

⁕ Clean the area thoroughly, ensuring that all loose material is removed.

⁕ Fill the hole with wood filler. For larger holes, you may need to do the job in two stages. The best tools for the job are a narrow-bladed scraper and your fingers (wear disposable gloves). Use enough filler for it to protrude slightly from the surrounding wood surface.

⁕ Allow the filler to dry and set hard overnight. Sand it down the next day, starting with coarse sandpaper (60 grit), then moving up the grades to fine (180 grit) for a smooth finish. The patched area will now be barely noticeable. If you paint over it, it will be completely invisible.

Repair a SHELF SUPPORT

Many cabinets and shelving units have shelving supports that can be placed at different heights. This is an especially common feature in self-assembled furniture. If too much weight is put on a shelf or if a shelf is installed incorrectly, the shelf support can rip out of the vertical panel, often taking a chunk of particleboard with it. But don't panic: the damage can be repaired.

⁕ To complete this job you will need a two-part filler the same color as the shelf (typically white). Thoroughly mix together the required amount of resin and hardener, and fill the damaged area using a narrow-bladed scraper. Draw the scraper across the surface of the filler to level it off. Leave for one to two days to allow the filler to set completely (follow the package directions).

⁕ Drill a new hole to the right depth and in the exact position required, then insert the shelf support.

Insider's hack When you're putting together self-assembled furniture, follow the directions carefully. Make sure you have the necessary tools and lay out all the parts to make sure you know what goes where. This is especially important for all the screws and fastenings, as they often look alike. Count these small components to check that nothing is missing – sometimes a surplus amount will be provided.

Adjust CABINET HINGES

With screws here, there and everywhere, modern cabinet hinges look complicated at first glance. But, with a Phillips-head screwdriver in hand, it's actually quite easy to make adjustments to get your cabinet doors to hang just the way you want them to.

⁕ To adjust the vertical position of a door, loosen all the screws that hold the hinges onto the body of the cabinet (marked A in the image, opposite). The elongated screw holes in the hinges allow you to move the door up or down slightly. Once you're satisfied the door is in the right position, tighten those screws back up.

✳ To adjust the gap between the door and the body of the cabinet (in other words, the length of the hinge), first carefully loosen the screws located on the body side of the hinges closest to the back of the cupboard (B). This will allow you to slide the horizontal part of the hinge back and forth. Once you have the door in the right spot, tighten the screws back up.

✳ Some hinges have another screw on the body side of the hinge (C) that allows you to make both horizontal and vertical adjustments. On cabinets with two doors, this adjusting screw can be useful for minimizing the gap between the doors. Use trial and error, turning the screw clockwise or counterclockwise until you get the best result.

Easy fix When loosening or tightening door hinges, always work from top to bottom.

Insider's hack Work with care when adjusting cabinet hinges. A slight turn of a screw often makes a significant difference.

REPAIR A CABINET door hinge

If you accidentally bump into an open cabinet door, the cup hinge can rip right out of the door. The image, right, shows the area where a cup hinge attaches to a cabinet door. Although this kind of damage can look pretty bad at first, it is relatively easy to repair especially if, as is usually the case, the hinge itself remains unscathed.

✳ Use a flathead screwdriver to remove any loose wood particles.

✳ Fill the damaged area with a repair compound (such as epoxy putty, available from hardware stores) in a color to match the door. Use a narrow-bladed scraper to spread the compound and smooth the surface down.

Fill the damaged area with epoxy putty, available from hardware stores.

✳ Press the cup hinge into the large hole while the compound is still soft and then leave it to harden. The directions on the package will indicate the product's curing time.

✳ Carefully drill two small pilot holes for the fastening screws. The holes must be smaller than the screws to ensure the screws get a good grip. Gently tighten the screws with a hand screwdriver (don't use an electric screwdriver).

A SLIGHT TURN OF A SCREW OFTEN MAKES A SIGNIFICANT DIFFERENCE.

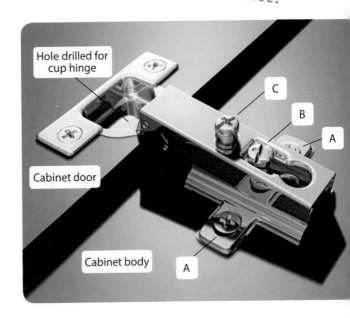

Hole drilled for cup hinge

Cabinet door

C

B

A

Cabinet body

A

Electrical safety

A few simple, regular checks and good habits to follow can help to keep you and your family safe from electrical problems and emergencies. Keep these tips in mind whenever you use an electrical appliance, and take particular care that whenever you do any DIY repairs or installations around the house, you always follow the golden rules of electrical safety.

DON'T DO IT yourself

The installation of electrical wiring and equipment is governed by local regulations and standards. It's best to hire a licensed electrician to install fixed wiring and associated lights, outlets and built-in appliances such as electric stoves. You can replace bulbs and fluorescent tubes, repair fuses, reset circuit breakers, check cords and plugs for damage, and install low-voltage recessed lights, provided you follow the instructions. You may also assist an electrician with unskilled tasks, such as digging ditches.

CHECK ELECTRICAL CORDS AND PLUGS FOR SIGNS OF DAMAGE.

Care and MAINTENANCE

Check electrical cords and plugs for signs of damage. Choose one room a month and examine all the electrical cords attached to appliances and lamps within it, looking out for cracked or worn insulation, exposed bare wires and black spots – a particularly alarming sign, as these are generally caused by sparks from the plug or appliance.

✳ Inspect the plugs, too, and ensure they're not cracked, that there are no bent or rusted prongs and that the cord and the internal wiring aren't loose – give the cord a gentle tug to make sure it's secure and open the plug to check the connections inside. If you spot any of these problems, replace the cord, plug or both – or replace the appliance altogether.

✳ Pull the plug, not the cord, from the socket. If you repeatedly tug on the cord to unplug an appliance from the outlet, you're bound to loosen some connections inside, which could cause a short in your system. Always grasp the plug firmly on both sides and pull it out straight from the socket. If a socket is stiff to use, it could be that the internal workings are worn and it needs to be replaced.

✳ Keep cords away from heat. Electrical cords often get tucked along baseboards, under heaters or around the back of the toaster because they look untidy. But a toaster can melt through a cord and constant proximity to a heater can cause the cord insulation to crack.

✳ Use childproof covers or plugs on unused outlets if you have small children or pets. Some electrical outlets have built-in safety features that prevent a child from getting an electric shock by inserting something into one of the outlet openings, but it's still wise to protect the outlets with covers to prevent their internal workings from being damaged.

✳ Spot the signs of a hidden fault. A hot plug or outlet could indicate a wiring fault. Other warning signs are flickering lamps, fuses blowing frequently or a circuit breaker in the main panel or box tripping repeatedly. Call an electrician to trace the problem.

What to do if the POWER FAILS

If you have no power, and neighboring houses are also without power, there's a power grid failure. Report it to your relevant electricity authority.

✳ If you have a ground fault circuit interrupter (GFCI), check whether it has tripped. Try to switch it on again if it has. If it won't switch on, the fault is still present in the system. Call an electrician to rectify it.

✳ If you don't have a GFCI, and your house is the only one without power, there may be a fault in your supply cable or your main supply fuse may have blown. Don't touch it. Report the failure as above.

TAKE CONTROL OF AN ELECTRICAL EMERGENCY

If you get a minor shock from an electrical appliance, a plug, outlet or other wiring accessory, stop using it immediately. Get a repair expert to check the appliance for grounding safety, and replace damaged parts as quickly as possible. If someone receives a major shock, DO NOT touch bare flesh. Follow these steps to deal safely and swiftly with an electrical emergency.

1 Immediately turn off the source of the current if you can. Switch off and unplug any appliance involved in the accident if it's safe to do so, or turn off the power completely at the main switch on the house's circuit-breaker or fuse panel or box.

2 If you are unable to do this, grab the person's clothing and drag them away from the source of the current, or stand on some insulating material such as a book and use a broom or a similar long wooden object to move the person or the source of the current.

3 Lay a conscious but visibly shocked person flat on their back with their legs raised slightly and cover them with a blanket. Call 911. Monitor their breathing until the ambulance arrives. Don't give them any food or drink. Cool visible burns with cold water, then cover them with a dry sterile dressing. Don't apply ointment.

IF THERE IS A POWER GRID FAILURE, REPORT IT TO YOUR RELEVANT UTILITY COMPANY.

Care and maintenance of
SWITCHES AND OUTLETS

Receptacle or outlet testers (available from hardware and home improvement stores) will alert you to a variety of faults in your electrical outlets. Following the instructions and guide directly on the tester, insert it into any outlet and based on the light combination, it will indicate whether no fault is indicated and the outlet is safe. It can also indicate a reversal of the active and the ground or if the polarities are reversed both are unsafe. The tester will also indicate if a ground is active or not connected which is unsafe. Finally, the tester will confirm that a GFCI is functioning properly.

✳ Test all ground fault circuit interrupters (GFCIs) every month to ensure that they are working. First, press the GFCI's Reset button to make sure the unit is on or check that the trip switch is in the On position.

Expert advice

Dos and don'ts of electrical safety

Always ...

★ Wear safety glasses when working around electricity.

★ Unplug a lamp or appliance before attempting to repair it.

★ Turn off power to a circuit at the main switch in the circuit-breaker or fuse panel before working on it.

★ Use a voltage tester to make sure a wire isn't live. Do this before you touch the wire!

★ Use plastic-handled tools for electrical work. Even better, do as electricians do and wear a rubber jacket as well.

★ Call in a qualified electrician as quickly as possible.

Never ...

★ Stand on a wet or damp floor when working with electricity. Put as much insulation as possible between you and the source of a shock. Wear rubber-soled shoes and stand on a rubber mat.

★ Touch metal plumbing or gas pipes or fixtures when working on electrical wiring or appliances.

★ Use two hands to open a breaker panel or box, pull out a fuse or test an outlet or switch. If a job can be done with one hand, just use one hand.

★ Use aluminium or wet wooden ladders if you're working near overhead power lines or a live circuit.

★ Attempt to clear a blockage in a toaster without first unplugging it from the wall socket.

Then plug in a radio at a nearby outlet and turn it on so that you can hear it from the outlet. While the radio is playing, press the Test button on the GFCI – the radio should go off. Press Reset again or flip the switch back to On – the radio should come back on. If the GFCI fails this test, have it checked by an electrician and replaced if necessary, as this is an indication that it would not trip and cut off the power if an electrical fault developed.

✳ Even if your household power circuits have built-in GFCI protection, it's good practice to always plug in outdoor electrical power tools, such as electric mowers, hedge trimmers and shredders, plus any power tools like drills being used outside, into a dedicated GFCI outlet or an GFCI adapter. Test it before each use and it will protect you from a potentially lethal electric shock if you should accidentally cut through a cord.

✳ Old metal switch and outlet wall plates may look attractive but they are often inadequately grounded, and old connections and terminals make them potential hazards – a metal plate that comes in contact with a live wire can deliver a shock if you touch it. Plastic is the safer bet for most domestic situations, or switch to modern metal switch plates with up-to-date safety features and grounded connections and plastic mounting blocks.

✳ Simply checking all the plugs on your appliances each year could save you a lot of money and untold distress in fixing heat damage or replacing damaged appliances. Open up each plug and check that the connections are all secure, there are no loose wires,

OLD METAL SWITCHES MAY LOOK ATTRACTIVE BUT THEY ARE OFTEN INADEQUATELY GROUNDED.

the cord is securely gripped by the plug, the pins aren't loose and that the plug itself isn't cracked. Do not, however, attempt to open plugs that are sealed in manufacture.

✳ When you check your plugs, check all the cords, too. The outer sheath must be intact, with no nicks, cuts or fraying. Any damage can expose the internal cord cores and you could get an electric shock from touching the cord. You can make a temporary repair by binding damaged cord with electrical tape, but always replace the whole cord as soon as possible.

Easy fixes for LIGHT FIXTURES

Broken or damaged ceiling fixtures are rare. These lights or fans are generally replaced for decorative reasons. Don't ignore them entirely, though: the plastic boxes can become brittle over time and crack, or pull-cord switches may break or fail. Whenever you replace a blown bulb, use an energy-

TAKE CARE
Voltage coming into your breaker box can deliver a fatal shock. Never attempt any electrical work unless you know exactly what you are doing. The power supply must always be disconnected before starting, and a licensed electrician must carry out any installations.

WHENEVER YOU REPLACE A BLOWN INCANDESCENT BULB, USE AN ENERGY-SAVING REPLACEMENT.

saving replacement, and whenever you replace a light fixture, make sure the new one is suitable for use with energy-saving bulbs.

✳ You should always unscrew a light canopy before you decorate – let it slide down the cord and protect the whole light fixture by wrapping it in a plastic bag. But if you or previous occupants haven't done this in the past, you may find that your canopy is stuck with paint around the edges when you go to remove it.

✳ Turn off the power to the lighting circuit in that room by switching off the relevant circuit-breaker in the panel, then run a sharp knife around the edge of the canopy to cut through the paint. If this doesn't free the canopy, you'll have to break it instead. Wearing safety goggles and work gloves, crack the canopy with a hammer. Remove the pieces then have the fixture replaced with a new one.

✳ Wiring in a new lighting circuit in a kitchen should be left to a professional electrician. But you can install task lights yourself that plug into outlets and attach to the wall or the underside of your cabinets to give you better working light on your countertops. You can fit a chain of lights around the kitchen, all plugged into one another, with just the first in the chain plugged into the outlet. These are usually LED types and sold in kit form, together with all the clips, screws, cable clips and connecting cords you'll need. Allow one light for every 1 1/2 ft. of counter space.

✳ Lay the fixture out before you start work, to make sure you're happy with the spacing. Ensure there's an outlet within easy reach of the master light. Screw the clips to the underside of the cabinets, plug in the cords that join the string of lights, then lift them into position and tuck any excess cord under the cabinets. Plug in, switch on and then test each light in turn.

✳ Halogen recessed lights in the ceiling give off a crisp, bright light and add a contemporary look to a room. But the lights themselves get very hot in use, and if they aren't properly protected they can cause a fire in the ceiling void above. When you next change a bulb in one of these lights, take out the surround, too, by releasing the clasps that hold it tight to the ceiling. Feel through the hole or shine a flashlight to see whether there is a solid or fire-retardant enclosure above the light. If there's no sign of a fire hood, ask a qualified electrician to assess its safety. You may need to replace it with a low-heat alternative such as a fluorescent or LED. These have the benefit of using less power, too.

When ELECTRONIC DEVICES crash

When your internet connection goes down, your smartphone decides the party's over, your computer freezes, or there's no picture on your TV screen, don't abandon all hope immediately. There is often a simple solution that will get your device up and running again.

✳ When a battery-powered device stops working, recharging or replacing the batteries is an obvious place to start. Connect the device to its charger or power adapter to see if this solves the problem. If it does, allow the batteries time to charge or replace them as needed. A dirty battery contact or one that has lost its springiness is also a common problem. If a contact is dirty, carefully scratch it clean.

✳ Loose cables are another common reason for devices to stop working properly. Check to see if any power cables or other connecting cables have come loose and push them back in securely.

✳ For any device with a microprocessor – and that includes smartphones, MP3 players, televisions and just about any electronic device you can think of – restarting will often help. If you are no longer able to restart or shut down a device in the usual way (in other words, if the device is completely frozen), cut the power by pulling the plug. While you will lose any unsaved data, the advantage of restarting is that the operating system of the device will also "forget" whatever task it was attempting to execute (including the task that caused the problem) and will return to its normal state when it restarts.

✳ Connecting a new peripheral device or installing a new piece of software can sometimes cause your computer to pack it in. Try restoring the computer to its previous state and then restarting.

✳ Some devices have self-test functions that they run through when you turn them on. Most also have a reset function that can be activated by pressing a particular combination of keys or a hidden reset button – check the user manual for details. Resetting will force the device to restart and, in some cases, restore the device to its factory default settings.

Easy fix A quick solution for a loose battery is to fold a piece of aluminium foil several times over and squeeze it in between the battery and the contact. This will ensure an uninterrupted flow of electricity from the battery to the device.

DON'T DESPAIR – OFTEN SOMETHING SIMPLE IS ALL IT TAKES TO GET YOUR DEVICE UP AND RUNNING AGAIN.

Expert advice

WiFi gone bye-bye?

If your home internet connection goes down, disconnect the power to all the devices that are involved in providing your connection (modem, router, etc.). Wait for 20 seconds and plug them back in again. In most cases, this will solve the problem.

★ If this doesn't work, check which lights are illuminated on your router and consult the user manual to see which ones should be on when the device is working properly. The lights will tell you whether the router is receiving power, whether it is able to establish a connection to the internet, and whether there are any computers connected to the router.

★ If your router appears to be working and your computer is able to locate and connect to your WiFi network but you still can't get online, the problem probably lies somewhere outside your home. If you suspect this to be the case, contact your internet service provider's technical support service.

Needle and thread

There's no need to take your clothes to a tailor for minor sewing jobs. There are a few things anyone can do, even if you are completely new to sewing. And it's always a pleasure to be able to say you did it yourself.

IF YOU SEW OFTEN, IT'S WORTH INVESTING IN A DECENT-SIZED SEWING BOX OR BASKET.

SEWING KIT essentials

It's well worth keeping a basic sewing kit around the house – essentially, this is a set of sewing supplies in a small box with various compartments. With a sewing kit at the ready, you will be able to deal with minor problems without having to first go out and get the supplies you need.

✳ It's inevitable that your collection of sewing materials will grow over time as you acquire things for specific jobs – different colored threads, buttons, darning wool, and so on. It's worth getting a decent-sized box to allow room for your sewing kit to grow. A beginner's sewing kit should include the following items:

✳ A small pair of pointed scissors

✳ Sewing thread (cotton) in several colors – black and white are essential along with whatever colors feature most prominently in your wardrobe
✳ Several needle threaders (they break easily)
✳ Two sets of sew-on snaps, silver and black
✳ Safety pins in various sizes
✳ Sewing needles in various sizes
✳ Dressmaking pins with colored heads
✳ Darning needles with a large eye and blunt point
✳ A darning egg or mushroom
✳ Soft elastic, 2 yd. long x 1/2 in. wide
✳ A thimble
✳ A tape measure

You can find sewing supplies at a fabric or craft store or online.

Save time Keep all the threads together in your sewing kit and have them sorted by color. When you need thread of a particular color, you will know at a glance whether or not you have some in your kit or not.

Easy fix Keep your needles in a pincushion, not a container. Weave them into the cushion horizontally rather than sticking them in vertically. That way you will be able to identify them more easily and there is less chance of them falling out.

Insider's hack Rather than keeping your safety pins loose in a little box or compartment, thread them all onto one large safety pin (such as a quilter's pin) to keep them all together securely.

Save money Instead of buying a large supply of buttons that you may or may not need, make a habit of keeping the replacement buttons that are either sewn onto a garment or provided in a little bag with just about every item of new clothing these days.

KEEP THE THREADS IN YOUR SEWING KIT SORTED BY COLOR SO YOU KNOW WHAT YOU HAVE AT A GLANCE.

Get the knack of THREADING A NEEDLE

If you have never picked up a sewing needle before, the crucial first step of passing a thread through the eye can be a real stumbling block. But there are a few tricks that can help you master this task.

✳ The first step is to choose an appropriate-sized needle. Use a thin needle for light fabrics, and a thicker one for heavier fabrics. Thin needles have a small eye, while thicker needles have a larger one. Cut a piece of thread 1 1/2–2 ft. long (about an arm's length) and pass it through the eye of the needle. If you can't get the thread to go through the eye, try moistening it between your lips or use a needle threader (see box, right).

✳ Tie a knot close to the other end of the thread or, better yet, several knots on top of one another. This will prevent the thread from pulling straight through the fabric when you start sewing.

Expert advice

Needle threaders

A needle threader comes in handy no matter how experienced a sewer you are. Insert the needle threader's wire loop through the eye of the needle – because the wire is stiff you'll find it's much easier to get through than a piece of thread. Then pass the thread through the wire loop and allow both ends to hang down. Pull the needle threader back through the needle's eye. It will pull the thread with it and the job is done!

★ Needle threaders are also useful for other jobs where you can't use a needle, such as restringing beads onto silk thread.

IT'S NO BIG DEAL IF AN ELASTIC WAISTBAND BREAKS – REPLACING IT IS NOT DIFFICULT.

※ Start by pulling out the old elastic. There will usually be a small hole in the waistband that allows you to do this. If not, cut the seam on the inside of the waistband to create a 1/2 in. opening to gain access to the elastic.

※ Cut a length of new elastic the same length as the old one. Poke a safety pin through one end of the elastic and close the pin. Now slide the safety pin into the waistband and, by manipulating the safety pin through the fabric, push it through the length of the waistband. Take care to keep the elastic from twisting along the way and make sure the tail end does not disappear into the waistband.

※ To finish, overlap the ends by 1/4 in. and sew them together with a few stitches. Leave the small hole in the waistband open. It's not visible and nothing is going to slip out.

Replacing an ELASTIC WAISTBAND

As annoying as it may be when your underwear or swimsuit keep falling down because the elastic waistband has broken, it's really not a big deal. Fixing the elastic is an easy job. It's best to replace the elastic completely – if it has broken in one spot, you'll usually find it has become brittle and crumbly along its entire length. For this job, you will need a piece of elastic the right width and a safety pin.

SEW A BUTTON on a shirt

This is one of the most common sewing jobs. Thread a needle with about 18 in. of thread in the right color and strength, then tie several knots in one end. Or, you can double up the thread and tie the two ends together. If you do it this way, you'll only need to make half as many stitches.

※ Ensure the button is free of any remnant pieces of thread, then hold it on the shirt in the correct position and push the needle from the back through the fabric and one of the button's holes. Pull the needle all the way through until you reach the knot at the end, then pass the needle through the other button hole and back through the fabric. Repeat a few times. For buttons with four holes, it's up to you whether you want to make the stitches parallel or crossing over each other diagonally.

TAKE CARE

It's a false economy to start a sewing job with a short piece of thread. A short thread has a greater chance of slipping out of the needle or leaving you without enough to tie off the job securely at the end.

＊ Once the button is securely attached, make a few horizontal stitches on the inner side of the shirt, then tie the thread off and cut off any excess.

Save time With each pass of the needle, make sure there are no loops of thread or knots forming. It's usually not possible to correct mistakes of this kind and you will have to cut the button off and start again.

Insider's hack If you don't have (or can't find) exactly the right color thread, choose something a shade darker than the material as it will be less noticeable than a lighter color. An exception to this rule: buttons on dress shirts are almost always sewn on with white thread.

BUTTONS ON DRESS SHIRTS ARE ALMOST ALWAYS SEWN ON WITH WHITE THREAD.

SEW ON A COAT BUTTON

When a button comes off a coat, it doesn't mean a trip to the tailor. But there is a certain technique with the heavier fabric to ensure you leave enough room for the material to sit easily beneath the button. You will need strong thread and a heavy-gauge needle with a large eye.

1 Tie a large knot in the end of the thread. Place the button in position with two crossed matches between the button and the material. Push the needle from the back through the material and one of the holes in the button.

2 Pass the needle through one of the other holes in the button and back through the material. Repeat several times, leaving the matches in position.

3 To finish, remove the matches and wrap the end of the thread around the bundle of threads between the button and the coat, which creates a stem. Secure the thread with a few more stitches on the inner side of the coat and tie off the ends.

DARN THE HOLE BY PASSING THE DARNING THREAD OVER ONE THREAD AND UNDER THE NEXT.

DARN HOLES in socks

Darning socks has gone out of fashion these days. But it's annoying to throw out a favorite pair of socks when one of them has a hole. Time to get out your trusty darning egg or mushroom!

✳ Slide your darning egg or mushroom in under the hole to make it easy to work on the problem area. Take a blunt-tipped darning needle with a large eye and thread it with wool to color-match the sock – if you knitted the socks yourself, you'll probably have leftover wool. Start a reasonable distance from the edge of the hole. Don't tie a knot in the end of the thread; simply leave about 4 in. hanging out.

✳ Sew a row of tightly spaced stitches back and forth across the hole so that you end up with a

SHORTEN A SKIRT HEM

First take down and iron flat an existing hem, then mark the new length with pins and turn the skirt inside out. You will need: a skirt, tape measure, dressmaking pins, needle, tacking thread (of contrasting color), chalk, scissors, sewing thread.

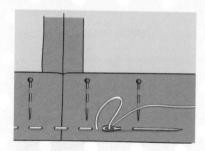

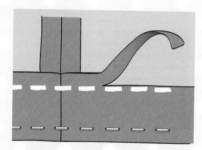

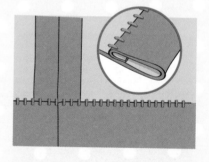

1 Lay the skirt flat, fold up and pin hem at right angles to the edge. Check skirt for length, then tack (weave the needle in and out of the fabric to create even running stitches about 1/4 in. long) close to the fold. Remove pins and press.

2 Measure and mark with chalk the hem allowance (how deep the hem is): 2 3/4 in. for a straight skirt, less for a flared one. Trim excess fabric at the chalk mark.

3 Turn the hem edge under 1/4 in., iron flat, then hemstitch in place. Bring the needle through the hem; opposite this point, catch a single thread of fabric. Direct the needle diagonally through the hem 1/4–1/2 in. to the left, and continue around the hem. Once the hem is complete, remove the tacking.

series of closely packed threads running parallel to each other across the hole. Don't allow the thread to draw the hole together.

✳ Turn the darning mushroom 90° in your hand. Now repeat the process by making another set of tightly spaced stitches back and forth across the hole, interweaving these stitches with the first set by passing the darning thread over one thread and under the next. To finish, sew a few stitches with each end of the thread to secure it on the inside of the sock and cut off any excess.

Insider's hack Little girls' winter tights often develop holes in the knees. Rather than darning them, buy crocheted patches or appliqués with kids' motifs and sew them on. Children will like these more than hand-darned patches.

Repair a BROKEN ZIPPER

Zippers are a wonderful invention – until they stop working. Every now and then, zippers get stuck or develop a habit of coming undone on their own. Here are a few tips that may help:

✳ If a zipper is hard to move, run a bar of soap or a candle along the teeth and open and close the zipper a few times to spread it out. Soap or candle wax will act as a lubricant.

✳ A broken or missing pull tab can be difficult to replace even if spare parts are available. The best solution may be to thread a small piece of leather cord through the slider. A paperclip can also serve as a temporary fix.

✳ If a zipper has worn and become loose, try pressing the two halves of the slider gently together with a pair of pliers.

RUN A BAR OF SOAP ALONG THE LENGTH OF A STUBBORN ZIPPER TO ACT AS A LUBRICANT.

Loops for HANGING TOWELS

If you prefer to hang your towels on hooks rather than towel racks, one way to prevent the towels from sliding off the hook is to add a loop to the towel. It's not that difficult to attach a loop and you'll be happy that towels won't end up on the floor.

✳ Buy some cord about 1/8 in. wide in an appropriate color. Use an awl or the point of a punch-style can opener to make a hole in the seam of the towel and pull a piece of cord through the hole. Make a second hole about 1–1 1/2 in. further along and pull the cord through from the same side of the towel. Tie a knot in each end of the cord to prevent it from pulling through and the job is done.

Save time A slightly rough-and-ready but no less effective method is to thread a stainless steel key ring through the towel close to the seam.

Easy fix You can get loops for towels that require no sewing. Made of plastic with a snap on either end, they come with a small plastic awl for making a hole through the towel. You then simply connect the two sides of the snap through the hole.

Index

Image credits